THE LOST THREAD OF GOD'S LOVE

Phyllis Gruesbeck

TEACH Services, Inc.
PUBLISHING
www.TEACHServices.com • (800) 367-1844

World rights reserved. This book or any portion thereof may not be copied or reproduced in any form or manner whatever, except as provided by law, without the written permission of the publisher, except by a reviewer who may quote brief passages in a review.

The author assumes full responsibility for the accuracy of all facts and quotations as cited in this book. The opinions expressed in this book are the author's personal views and interpretations, and do not necessarily reflect those of the publisher.

This book is provided with the understanding that the publisher is not engaged in giving spiritual, legal, medical, or other professional advice. If authoritative advice is needed, the reader should seek the counsel of a competent professional.

Copyright © 2021 Phyllis Gruesbeck
Copyright © 2021 TEACH Services, Inc.
ISBN-13: 978-1-4796-0950-5 (Paperback)
ISBN-13: 978-1-4796-0953-6 (ePub)
Library of Congress Control Number: 2021900658

All scripture quotations, unless otherwise indicated, are taken from the King James Version (KJV) Public Domain.

Scripture quotations marked NKJV are taken from the New King James Version®. Copyright © 1982 by Thomas Nelson. Used by permission. All rights reserved.

Scripture quotations marked NIV are taken from THE HOLY BIBLE, NEW INTERNATIONAL VERSION®, NIV® Copyright © 1973, 1978, 1984, 2011 by Biblica, Inc.® Used by permission. All rights reserved worldwide.

New International Version (NIV)

Published by

www.TEACHServices.com • (800) 367-1844

Table of Contents

1. God's Love is Constant 5
2. My Leap of Faith. 25
3. The Reason—God's Love Story. 41
4. God's Way is the Best Way. 45
5. A Gift from God for Our Day—John at Patmos. 56
6. The First Sabbath on Earth 70
7. God's Official Seal 82
8. No Other Gods 86
9. The Next Two Commands 100
10. Love Thy Neighbor As Thyself 104
11. A Lesson on Obedience (The background which led up to the giving of the manna) 111
12. The Sabbath in Nehemiah's Day 124
13. It's Everybody's Sabbath. 130

14. Change of the Julian Calendar 140

15. Jesus' Parents Taught Him to Keep the Seventh-day Sabbath Holy. 142

16. Jesus Even Kept it Holy in His Death 154

17. Your Debt of Sin—Nailed to the Cross. 164

18. Jesus Said He Would be Crucified 172

19. Jesus Walked with Them. 182

20. Jesus—Worship Him—He is God. 188

21. Jesus, Founder of the Christian Church 195

22. The New Baby Church. 207

23. The Original Antichrist in God's Own Church. 214

24. How Did Antichrist Get in God's New Baby Church 218

25. The New Baby Church in Deep Trouble 228

26. Last-Day Promises from God 232

27. The Test and Positive Proof to Tell Whether You Are Obeying God or Antichrist 250

28. Why Did God Make Sure The Whole Bible Is True? 253

In Memorial. 259

CHAPTER ONE

God's Love is Constant

———◆◆◆———

I have always loved Jesus. Yes, from the very first day I can remember! Both of my parents loved Him too! At first, God's love came to me through my mom's parents, and later, it came to me through my dad. I've learned that love has many facets. And that it is not always lollipops and ice cream cones. In fact, it has taken me my whole life to understand why God allows bad things to happen to good people. It seems as though a lot of us struggle with that. And when you're treated roughly, it becomes even more difficult to believe that God is a God of love.

More than once, I have angrily screamed at Him for not giving me the protection I felt I needed. But now I know why it has to be that way. There is someone else in the mix. I've written a book about him, too. It's called *The Devil Made Me Do It*. I hope my plight will help you understand why God allows bad things to happen to those who love Him. How grateful I am that God the Father allowed His Son Jesus to die to pay for the sins of everyone who will accept His payment on the cross for them.

At this time in my life, I can look back and realize how very blessed all of us are if we had parents who loved God and introduced us to Him while we were still very young. My family did this for me. In this life we need the love of God every single moment. We live in a rough world! Knowing God is what makes it possible for us to make sense of everything that happens to us. Thank You, Lord, for revealing these insights to me! Thank You for giving me very loving parents.

My mom died the day I was born. Dad didn't talk about her much. I think it was too painful for him. He was a beautiful Christian, and he became acquainted with Jesus through her. Then, they got married, and pretty soon, they had a baby boy—my brother. What delight he is to me to this very day. We are eight years apart. When he was born, the doctor told her she should never get pregnant again. He told her it would kill her if she did. Sometimes, in spite of our best efforts, things don't work out the way they should. Consequently, she did get pregnant, and I was the result.

As soon as I was born, she went into a coma and died. Dad lost his sweetheart and my brother, his mom. He has never even once said anything about losing his mama because of me. I love him dearly for that; he is so very special. I think his life has been much more difficult than mine, but he doesn't talk about it.

The few times Dad did talk about our mom, he told me how wonderful she was. My brother and I are looking forward to meeting her and Dad someday when Jesus comes and wakes them up to take them and us to heaven. It will be so exciting for us to see our parents again. Such experiences make us long for the soon return of Jesus. The signs Jesus gives us in Matthew 24 certainly point in that direction. What a glorious future we have access to—salvation that is. He will take all who love Him, and we will all spend eternity together.

My brother and I were both blessed through my mom's parents, and later through our dad. I don't even want to think about what my life would have been like if my grandma and grandpa on my mother's side of the family had not taken care of us. Unfortunately, for my brother, that time was limited—I think because of all the trauma of losing his mama. He went through too much trauma to really appreciate them. My emotions are very tender when I think about the love I have for him. I lived with my maternal grandparents from the day I was born until my dad remarried. I have many fond memories of them and am looking forward to the day when Jesus raises them from the grave.

My fondest memory is of the family worship my grandpa had before breakfast every morning. He never missed a day, and he always began it with prayer. And what prayers they were! Peaceful, humble words with God. Then he read passages from the Bible. He was a loving and gentle man who truly loved the Lord. A quiet peace enveloped us as he read. I felt like I was wrapped in God's love. Now, I know it was none other than the Holy Spirit lovingly placing His arms around our little family circle. To this day, I am very grateful for those special times with God. I know without a doubt that this love from my family and from my God is what has seen me through my whole life.

God provides as much protection as He can for each and every one of us. But Satan does not want us to trust God. All around us we can see there is a battle going on between good and evil—and between Christ and Satan. Jesus won that battle when He died on the cross for us and will come to our aid. Because we too face our own personal battle with Satan, each person's experience is unique. No matter how difficult this life is, God has put Himself at our call to help us and to draw us to Himself. Even if we don't realize it! All of us are on His minds. Look at this beautiful promise He gives us. "I will never leave thee, nor forsake thee" (Heb. 13:5, KJV). We are the ones who do the forsaking. He comes back even after we kick Him out of our life. He woos us to Himself through the Holy Spirit. But He won't just barge in and bully us as the devil does. We have to invite Him to come into our heart, or someone who loves Him has to intercede for us. He won't just barge in—uninvited.

God keeps track of every one of us. He does not forsake us just because we are rejecting Him. He speaks to us through the Holy Spirit and lets us know how much He loves us. All of us are on His mind. When we have a desire to know Him, He sends the Holy Spirit to impress us to read our Bible and pray. He does not push us. Instead, He pleads with us to accept Him into our life. Do you realize that the Bible is a record of the history of the human race? I had to listen very hard when I first started listening for the Spirit's voice. I could hardly hear it—it was fleeting and quiet. I begged Him to help me hear more of His promptings.

I have found that the more I obey Him, the more intense His voice becomes. He knows whether I love Him or not. David said, "If we have forgotten the name of our God, or stretched out our hands to a strange god; Shall not God search this out? for he knoweth the secrets of the heart" (Ps. 44:20–21). (Read Ps. 139:1–24.) I find that very comforting. He works for each one of us, whether we love Him or not because He knows our heart. It has never been God's will that anyone dies. He is the life-giver—not the destroyer of life. He protects our freedom of choice even though it grieves Him when we turn our backs on Him.

> *It has never been God's will that anyone dies. He is the life-giver—not the destroyer of life.*

Do you realize that Jesus—the One who died to pay for our sins, works with the Holy Spirit to intercede and protect our freedom to choose? Just look at this revelation! God will not save us against our will. But! Regardless of whether we come to Him or not—He works to win and soften our hearts. It is Paul, who is talking. He tells us that Jesus intercedes for us too. And he does it in such a way that we know he is talking about Jesus. He begins by saying, "this *man*."

Then he gives us identifiable marks, so we will know who he is talking about. He tells us this about the man. "But this man, because he continueth ever," Let's stop right there. Jesus is the only *man* who has ever lived forever. Yes! There are men who did not die and went to heaven. But they had not been in existence forever. And they were taken before their time to heaven. Then Paul goes on to tell us it is a man who "hath an unchangeable priesthood." Jesus is the only man who has a priesthood like that. But Paul doesn't even stop there. He goes on to say, "Wherefore he is able to save those to the uttermost that come unto God by him, seeing he ever liveth to make intercession for them" (Heb. 7:24–25). Jesus is the only man who can intercede for us.

But he doesn't even stop there. He gives us undeniable proof. He says, "For such an high priest became us, *who* is holy, harmless, undefiled, separate from sinners, and made higher than the heavens; Who needeth not daily, as those high priests, to offer up sacrifice, first for his own sins, and then for the people's: for this he did once, when he offered up himself. For the law maketh men high priests which have infirmity; but the word of the oath, which was since the law, *maketh* the Son, who is consecrated for evermore" (Heb. 7:26–28). That's definitely Jesus. Paul leaves no loopholes for someone to deny it is Jesus.

That verse certainly puts a smile on my face. Actually, as one voice, the Father, Son, and Holy Spirit plead with us to come home. Isn't that wonderful! Jesus, the One who lived down here, the One who went through more sorrow that we will ever be able to understand—actually intercedes with the Father for us. How grateful I am. Jesus wants us to ask Him to open our eyes. When we ask, He shows us His care for us. When we won't come to Him, He impresses someone else to pray for us. That's called intercessory prayer.

May God help each of us find a closer walk with Him. Perhaps through reading this book, He may guide your eyes and intellect to see more of His loving influence in your life. It doesn't matter who you are—there have been times for every single person who has ever lived when they have not been able to see God's will clearly, or even wanted to see it. God has loved every person who has ever been born. Each and every person is special in their own unique way.

God is not the one who brings pain and evil. Satan, by disrupting Adam and Eve's trust in God, has brought this misery to the human race. Misery that God never wanted or intended. Satan—the enemy of our soul has picked a fight with God. Satan has freedom of choice too. God gives that freedom to all creation because Love cannot exist without that freedom. All of us are in this battle together. It started in heaven—the most unlikely place. Evil was not God's choice. Look it up (see Rev. 12:7). God did not start that war. It is not God's fault when we believe the devil's lies.

Even though I had an early love experience with God, I haven't had an easy road. But when I look back, I know God has been with me every step of the way. Even when I was blaming Him for all of the trouble I was having! My anger at life had been smoldering for some time. I was married and had three children. And at church one morning, as I sat listening to a sermon where the pastor told how he had been treated very cruelly, my smoldering ember roared into a huge flame of anger. Here is why!

He said, "I am so glad God took me from those cruel people and placed me in a home where I was no longer mistreated." Instantly, my mind screamed out, *Why, God? Why did You allow me to be ripped from a beautiful, peaceful home and given to a stepmother who was very mean to me? Why didn't you work it out so I could stay in my loving grandparents' home?*

Now, I know it was *not* God who made that choice! My dad made it! He did it because he loved his kids and wanted them with him. I am sure he never dreamed it would work out the way it did. The result was what happens when a marriage is a business partnership—he got a supposed mom for his kids, and she got a handyman, and someone to pay the bills. Relationships must be built on love, not just necessity, or perhaps selfish desires. They got married when I was seven years old, and my brother must have been fifteen.

Here are just a few instances of how my stepmother mistreated me. There were many! One day, when I was about eight years old, she literally scared me to death. I had reached my fingers into her mixing bowl and scooped out a hunk of the meatloaf she was making. I quickly stuck it into my mouth. Immediately she screamed at me, "No one puts their fingers into my food when I am fixing it." Then her face turned very sullen. There was a determined set to her jaw when she bellowed— "I'll cut them off."

Quickly, she picked up her butcher knife! I ran as fast as I could to get away from her. She! Right behind me! Knife in hand! Swiftly and forcefully, she brought it down across my fingers. Unbeknown to me, she had brought the dull edge of the knife down across them. Then turning to me with a sneer on her face said, "You're lucky! I used the sharp edge on my kids." I don't believe what she said was true, but I don't know for sure. All I know is I never saw any scars on them.

How terrified I was. And when it hit my hand, it hurt terribly bad. How relieved I was that it didn't cut my fingers off! When I look back on it now, I realize that the Holy Spirit must have whispered into her consciousness, suggesting she use the dull edge of the knife. It could have been so much worse. Surely, God was with me and saved me from her anger. I never thought to tell my dad what she had done. Mistreated kids don't tell. They just think their parents know. I was upset with God for this for many years.

Among the many instances of cruelty, the majority were psychological rather than physical. Two stand out sharply in my mind. One day, I laid my sweater down somewhere when I was playing outside, and I just couldn't find it. I looked everywhere I could think of. So, I had to tell her, and she told me I couldn't come into the house until I found it. Then she added these words— "even if it takes you days to find it!" She knew I was afraid of the dark. So, I continued to search everywhere I could think of, but to no avail. So, when it came time for my dad to come home, I lingered near the door, hoping I could sneak in when he came in.

It never occurred to me that she would have to let me in when he got there. Otherwise, he would know what she had done. I am sure the Holy Spirit must have taken a role in this plight too. Thank You, Lord! I don't think she ever told my dad how she treated me. And I never thought to tell him. Again, kids think their parents know everything. Anyway, I would have been afraid to tell him because of fear of the retaliation she would have heaped on me if he told her what I had said.

Another thing that happened extremely often was her mistreatment of me when I had trouble eating certain types of food. Oatmeal was the worst! It gagged me! And I became sick to my stomach. She raved about its goodness. I realize oatmeal is a very wholesome food. But I was allergic to it. She became extremely angry at me one day for not eating it. I say one day, but she got after me often for not eating something. This day, she slapped me hard across my face. My nose began bleeding profusely. And it hurt terribly. In fact, it left a welt. Yet, God gave me something to smile about. She had a dog named Bugs. He was a beautiful creature. And like all dogs, he liked food. So I would sneak a few bites to him every chance I got.

My other savior was the kitchen sink. Spoonful by spoonful, I washed the food I couldn't eat down the drain. I didn't like using this method. But that is how I got rid of the food that made me sick. I can still feel the tension I had each time I went to the sink. I was so afraid of getting caught. It was self-preservation. I knew I wouldn't get anything else to eat if it stayed on my plate. Whatever I didn't eat, would be served to me at every meal until it was gone—no matter how many days it took me to eat it. God even helps scared little girls.

About six years ago, I found out I have celiac disease. I feel so much better since I do not eat the offending foods. It wasn't allergy after all. I went through years of canker sores so painful I could hardly swallow even sips of water. I thought it was wheat or oat allergy—not knowing canker sores are also a symptom of celiac disease. I can now tolerate oatmeal if it is put up in a gluten-free facility. Oatmeal itself does not contain gluten, but if it is packaged where foods with gluten are packed, it gets contaminated with it.

My dentist understands now—he has a grandchild who had bad canker sores too. And he found recently that the child has celiac disease. He was a valiant man who tried to help me every way he could. As with Benadryl washes because he thought it was food allergy. It was many years ago that he helped me this way. I had grown children. When I look back on all of this, I thank God for helping me understand many of the things which happened. It helped me see God's hand on my behalf for many of those instances.

My stepmother railed against my grandma, too. She told me my grandma didn't love me. She was angry because my grandma told her she would rather I die than come live with her. But it wasn't because my grandma hated me or hated her. Years later, I realized why my stepmother tried to make me believe my grandma didn't love me. It was because my stepmother was hurting. I would have hurt too if someone had said that to me.

But, my grandma wasn't really being mean to her either—she was just being very observant. She sensed how bad my life would be if I got her for my stepmother. Perhaps she hoped my stepmother would listen and change her ways. As I look back on it, I realize that she was probably afraid this woman would destroy my trust in God, and she saw how mistreated I would be. She wanted to save me from physical and psychological trauma. She really did love me and wanted what was best for me. I love her for it. I am glad she intervened the best she could.

Later, I learned how terribly afraid my grandparents really were. As soon as my dad married her, they came to get me, and my grandma and grandpa hid me way out back in the corncrib. But the most telling proof of their concern was when they went to court to get custody of me. They loved my dad, but they did not trust her.

I became a ward of the state. A caseworker came every month to check on me, but I don't recall her ever talking with me. She just checked the home. I did not tell anyone about the cruelty I was experiencing. It just never occurred to me that maybe someone could help me. I didn't tell them for the same reason I didn't tell my dad. My stepmother would have mistreated me even worse if I had tattled. I did not know about the court action until after I was married and had children of my own. I found the legal papers and angry letters my grandparents wrote to her. They had a real battle.

God bless all the children and unhappy marriages of those going through like or worse circumstances right now. The United States was settled by people who fled here to get away from religious persecution. What if our ancestors had not come here? We should be passing on the loving favor. It's a dirty shame those desperate people are being so mistreated. I guess the system that imposes this doesn't stop and think about the fact that we all came from Adam and Eve either. There is no color problem with God. All of us are his children. I am glad Jesus is coming soon.

I pray that the perpetrators will see their wrong and come to know God better—and have a heart that really loves Him. And that the children get comfort from God and come to realize that He hurts when they do. It is my prayer each one finds help, so they do not have to continue to suffer mistreatment. The other book I am writing titled, *The Devil Made Me Do It*, tells us who is responsible for such atrocities, and how God is going to take care of it in the end. I am looking forward to the day when God will permanently destroy all evil.

When I look back on it, I am sure it was after the court intervention that I got to go stay with my grandparents for a week or two every summer. I never told them how bad I was being treated. And they didn't ask. The visit was a treasured relief from the mistreatment I got at home. It was wonderful visiting them.

> *I am looking forward to the day when God will permanently destroy all evil.*

One summer, when I came back from visiting them, my stepmother actually let me sit on her lap a short while. All of us were sitting in the living room together. I wanted her to know I loved her, so I got up the courage to go over and sit on her lap. Wonder of wonders, she let me sit there. I felt so loved, and the love felt so good. But the next morning, I felt like crying. Everything had switched back to normal—the way it had always been. She was screaming at me and telling me how bad and lazy I was. I felt so unloved.

Something else she did was get very angry because I wouldn't honey up to a certain neighbor man. He bought me roller skates and requested she take me to a photographer to get a portrait made for him. She must have told him I wanted skates. I certainly never talked to him. I am amazed she did this! I can't help but wonder whether my dad knew what was going on. I can't picture my very loving, Christian father knowingly allowing her to get pictures of me for this man.

One day, when he came over, he walked up behind me and reached both arms clear around me. Immediately, he began fondling both breasts at the same time. His arms were crisscrossed around me. But I was able to pull away. Instantly, my stepmother's face filled with rage and animosity. The minute he left, she began yelling and screaming at me for not being nice to him. She saw what he was doing! She knew it was wrong! I don't remember what her threats were. But I know I was terribly fearful of physical retaliation from her. But none came. Thank goodness.

She told me I should be ashamed of myself for not being nice to him. She said he was just a lonely old man, looking for love. I look back on it now, and thank God this man never raped me. She should have been protecting me, not placing me in jeopardy. I must have been around fifteen when this took place. From age seven to seventeen, it was a living hell.

She was *not* nice to my father, either. My hope is in seeing my dad someday. My brother is looking forward to that day, too. Our dad really loved Jesus, and he loved my brother and me very much also. He gave his heart totally to his Maker. That's what really counts in life. Not very long before he died, something happened that broke my heart, but I believe God wanted me to know so I could empathize with him. I had come to take my dad and stepmom grocery shopping—something I did twice a month. All the way there, she kept telling me how dumb my dad was. Oh, how it hurt to hear him being mistreated. She claimed he wouldn't be able to tell me how to get to the store if she didn't keep correcting him. I knew better. Every time he told me where to go, she refuted him and proceeded with her name-calling and belittling.

She also told our kids that he was just a crazy old man. That he was mentally deficient. I don't know if your grandpa ever played with you as he did with our children, but he had false teeth, and he would let them drop down in his mouth and then make funny faces to make them laugh. He was playing with them! They loved it. She made these derogatory remarks right in front of the boys. I am so ashamed that I did not stick up for him. I was too afraid of her retaliation and mistreatment to do so. I was protecting myself. Now I know I obeyed the devil. He placed fear in my mind. God wants us to stick up for those who are being mistreated. My dad was being terribly mistreated.

I knew from firsthand experience how detrimental this was to Dad—after all, I, too, had gone through her belittling. She mistreated me psychologically also! She told my teachers I had epilepsy. I didn't! But so what if I did have it?! After all, my head had gone clear through the windshield of my grandpa's car when I was about three years old. I was sitting on my grandma's lap, and Grandpa hit a huge pothole. I can still tell it happened because a third of my eyebrows are missing at the outer edges of my face. But, thank goodness, it did not cause brain damage or scar tissue problems.

I did have a nervous tic, though. It came about when I felt uneasy around my stepsister. I thought she was beautiful. When I first came to live with them, I wanted to look at her and see how pretty she was. She was about the same age as my brother. For some reason, I don't remember my brother ever being there until many years later. But he has told me she was the one who made his life miserable. I don't know how she treated him. I know that he considered it to be very traumatic. I love him so much. He has always been very good to me.

If I looked at her at all, she screamed out, "Mom! Make her stop staring at me." I wasn't staring! I only looked at her if I thought she was looking the other way. When I think back on it, I believe she was mistreated, too. Her mother wasn't very nice to her, either. Not physically harmful, but psychologically so. I felt sorry for her. She could never do anything right in her mother's eyes. When she got older, she took me to the doctor a couple of times when I had nosebleeds. Too bad we didn't talk when we were kids. She even took me to get my hair done at the beauty shop one day. And her mother made fun of her for that, saying, "Anyone can make French braids."

Now, back to my school incident. If I got in a huff with a student at school, and the teacher told my stepmother about it, she would go to school and harass the teacher, telling her she should know better than talk to me about it. Her intervention was much worse than what had already taken place. Right in front of all my classmates, she would tell the teacher she should know better than to talk with me, saying, "You know she is mentally retarded." How embarrassed I was! So I clammed up even more. I had no advocate. I just withdrew from associating with the kids.

When I was in my late forties, I went to the local community college. At that point in time, I had a 4.0 GPA. But when anything was said about it, I made light of it, saying, "The really smart ones are those who can put their knowledge to good use." I still felt so dumb! And I am still wrestling with that emotion. Her cruel words are harming me to this very day. Finally, I went and had a brain scan done. I told the doctor about some funny feelings I had during the scan, and he said they occurred because I was close to fainting.

Later, I found out that feeling took place because of my heart problems. How relieved I was! These experiences help me know how bad my dad must have hurt when my stepmother spat out her cruel words about him. Mental problems are no different than physical problems. Each affects the other. I very well could have had epilepsy from going through that windshield. My head went all the way through it. They drove to the closest farmhouse. They worked on stopping the bleeding for a long time—and panicked because they couldn't get it to stop. I heard it in their voices. I remember hearing them say about me later that my hemoglobin was 5. That's pretty low, and I still battle it. This farmhouse was not near a town. So there was no doctor close by. I realize they were panicking over it.

Another day came when I took them to the store, and she made her usual derogatory remarks. This time, I decided to sit in the car with Dad while she shopped. I wanted to spend time alone with him and empathize. The instant she got out of the car, he blurted out, "Am I crazy?" Tears came to my eyes! The mental pain my dad was experiencing was obviously horrendous. It was awful, and I began crying and hugging him.

As I wrapped my arms around him, I said, "Oh, Daddy, I love you so much! No! You are not mentally ill! If anyone is, it is her." I am so glad he talked with me about his pain. I thank God for impressing me to talk with him. It's a shame we had not talked about our problem sooner. Again, I am sure this was the Holy Spirit interceding on behalf of my very loving father. He was always helping people. He was always good to me and everyone else.

He died soon after that from type I diabetes. It happened on a Sabbath. She was so worried about getting the last little bit of money from him that she took his paycheck to the emergency room, and had him place an x on it for his signature. I was upset. That, too, makes me feel like crying still today. She didn't love him. She just loved his money. God says, "Godliness with contentment is great gain. For we brought nothing into this world, and it is certain we can carry nothing out. And having food and raiment let us be therewith content. But they that will be rich fall into temptation and a snare, and into many foolish and hurtful lusts, which drown men in destruction and perdition. For the love of money is the root of all evil: which while some coveted after, they have erred from the faith, and pierced themselves through with many sorrows" (1 Tim. 6:6–10).

It also grieves me that on my next encounter with her, I was shown she had not given her heart totally to God. I went to see her at a nursing home. I asked her if she had given her heart to Him. I talked to her about the resurrection and how wonderful heaven will be. For a long time, her answer made me feel like I had failed God. But now I know better! Instead, it was God loving her and allowing her to make her own choices in life to the very end. God upheld her freedom to make her own choices in life to the very last moment of her life, as He does for all of us.

Her reply showed me she was still *not* putting God first. She looked at me with anger written all across her face, as she spat out, "Why would I want to go to heaven? None of my children are going to be there." I felt hurt! She was the only mom I had ever known, and she was rejecting me. But that was nominal compared to what she was telling God. Just think how hurt He must have been. He had done everything He could for her, and she was still spurning His love. She didn't care to see Him. She only wanted to see her kids. She died before my next visit a week later. So, I don't know whether she made amends with God. Only God knows.

There is no way she could know whether or not her kids would give their hearts to Jesus in the future. Obviously, she thought they hadn't given their hearts to Him yet. God is fair to every person. I wouldn't be surprised to see some of them there. They were good kids. Donna was very spiritual—just not the same faith. I have no way of knowing whether she thought she was obeying God. He sends His Spirit to each one if they pray and ask for Him. The Holy Spirit helps those who don't know about Him too. God helps everyone know about His great love for them. He speaks through their conscience. What a wonderful God we serve.

They were taken to church. Each one knew about God. God had been introduced to them. They, too, made their choice. I hope they made the right one. Only God can read the heart. No one knows the private conversation of another between them and their Lord. That's God's business—not ours.

> *Only God can read the heart. No one knows the private conversation of another between them and their Lord.*

Look at Paul. I don't think very many people thought he would be saved. Won't they be surprised when they get to heaven, and he is there? As long as there is breath, there is hope. You can read about Paul's life before he was converted in the book of Acts. It tells us what he was like before his conversion. I allowed Satan to lead me around by the nose too. Just as Paul did. But Paul thought he was obeying God. How wrong we can be sometimes. But in the end, Paul listened and was converted. Praise the Lord.

I, too, even when I was no longer under her roof, allowed the devil to hassle me. But after making some mistakes and screaming these words at God, "I hate You. Why did You do this to me?" I finally came through my experiences crippled, but holding God's hand. Here is how my change of attitude came about. The devil still hassles me. He always will because he is evil! That is the nature of selfishness. Look at how Pharaoh resisted all the evidence God sent through Moses. Pharaoh reflected the stubbornness of Satan. He never gives up. But most of all, he causes us trouble because he hates God, and he knows God loves us—every last one of us.

Praise God! He is still trying to teach me to have faith in Him. I needed to understand that it was *not* God who sent me trouble. He knew I needed to know He was right at my elbow—waiting to help me if and when I was willing to place my trust in Him. I had been taking care of my mother-in-law for some time. She was old and very set in her ways. I was having severe back pain, and she was asking me to take her to the bathroom every ten or fifteen minutes all day long. I had to physically lift her on and off the toilet.

This had gone on for at least a week or two. But this particular day, I was in extremely severe physical pain, and I cried out to God, "Lord, please help me!" Immediately, the thought flashed into my mind—go get your Bible. So, I did! Then I felt like God wanted me to just let it open at random. So, that is what I did. I gently set it down on the floor while holding it between both hands, allowing its back binding to rest on the floor. Then, I carefully removed my hands and let it open on its own to wherever the Holy Spirit caused it to open. God chooses to reach each of us in a manner He knows we will listen to. He has a unique plan for each person. That really warms my heart. He is so wonderful.

So! What did this verse tell me? That I should not be complaining and griping about my lot in life! "That at the name of Jesus every knee should bow, of things in heaven, and things in earth, and things under the earth; And that every tongue should confess that Jesus Christ is Lord, to the glory of God the Father. Wherefore, my beloved, as ye have always obeyed, not as in my presence only, but now much more in my absence, *work out your own salvation with fear and trembling. For God worketh in you both to will and to do his good pleasure*" (Phil. 2:10–13, italics supplied).

Then came the clincher! These words bombed me out. I hadn't expected God to correct me. Now I am so glad He did! He said, "Do all things without murmurings and disputings: That ye may be blameless and harmless, the sons of God, without rebuke, in the midst of a crooked and perverse nation, among whom ye shine as lights in the world; Holding forth the word of life; that I may rejoice in the day of Christ, that I have not run in vain, neither laboured in vain" (Phil. 2:14–16). I only saw the words, "Do all things without murmurings and disputings." How hurt I felt! But I listened and said, "I'm sorry, God. I know I am feeling sorry for myself. I will try to stop complaining."

But I was at my wits' end! Finally, I insisted she go to a doctor. They found she had a urinary tract infection. But she tenaciously fought to not drink water. Perhaps, so I would not have to take her to the bathroom so often. I would not have wanted her to do that. It would not be good for her. Praise God; this Bible verse did not cause me to give up. I really did want to do what was right. So I tried it again. And guess what! It opened to Ezekiel 36:26. God knew just what I needed. I believe with all my heart that it was the Holy Spirit who chose where my Bible opened to.

Then, He guided my eyes to these beautiful words. "A new heart also will I give you, and a new spirit will I put within you: And I will take away the stony heart out of your flesh, and I will give you an heart of flesh. And I will put my spirit within you, and cause you to walk in my statutes, and ye shall keep my judgments, and do them" (Ezek. 36:26–27). Just in case you try this, please realize God works individually with each of us. He tailors His answers to take us through what we need to experience in our life to be saved. Each person is special and different. And always be aware that your enemy can bug into God's business. He's a pro at it. But the good news is he can't stand to stop lying. God will never tell you to do something that will disagree with what He says in the Bible. God is in the business of saving people—all who will let Him save them! He always gives freedom of choice.

I had admitted at least part of my wrong. I had been accusing God of not doing His part. Now, God was promising me some help. Often, God waits until we are as low as we can go before He helps us. Actually, He probably just waits till we are willing to listen to Him. I shouldn't have been so upset. But the next verse was a lifesaver. It told me God was willing to help me change if I would give Him permission to change me. So, I told Him how upset I was and that I didn't want to change. But that I gave Him permission to change me anyway. Then, I admitted that I couldn't change overnight. I had truly hit rock-bottom. Now, I had nowhere to go but up. Without hitting that hopeless time in my life, I would never have agreed to the changes I needed. Instead, I would have continued to blame God for all my troubles. Does that sound reminiscent of someone? Adam? Perhaps! Seems to me he was the first one to play the blame game and isn't that what I was doing!

Now that He had my permission to work on my heart, He went into action. It has taken many years and many other mistakes to learn how wonderful God is. But the main thing is I have invited Him into my heart as a permanent resident and have begun learning to trust Him instead of blaming Him. It hasn't been an easy trip by any means—and it probably still won't be—but it has been well worth it. God was answering my prayer. I found it appalling that He used the Holy Spirit to speak to me. Why? Because I was angry with the Spirit!

I accused the Holy Spirit of failing to protect me during most of my life. How wonderful it is that He does not hold such things against us—but is always ready to help us no matter how we have treated Him. He is the one the Father sends to us to guide us. But we must ask God to send Him. So I opened the door of my heart to Him in prayer and asked Him to help me. Then He impressed me to look up this verse. What a help it was. It is Jesus talking. He said, "If ye then, being evil know how to give good gifts unto your children: how much more shall your heavenly Father give the Holy Spirit to them that ask Him" (Luke 11:13).

That's gorgeous! These words tell me I must ask for God's Spirit! Our heavenly Father never forces us to do anything! We refuse to obey Him because of our own stubbornness or lack of knowledge or love for Him. Now, He was telling me He wouldn't force me to obey Him. The verse didn't ask me to do anything. It did not even ask me to change my ways! Most such verses request that we do something, and then God does something for us in return. Not so with this verse that promises a new heart. And look at this one! "But we all, with open face beholding as in a glass the glory of the Lord, are changed into the same image from glory to glory, *even* as by the spirit of the Lord" (2 Cor. 3:18).

I guess God knew I didn't have the will or the energy to obey Him at that point in my life. It took years and many more mistakes before I could willingly turn my life over to Him. I had been bullied and forced too many times. I found I had been rebelling against God, and I didn't even know it. He had to open my eyes and let me see myself as I truly was. I am so glad He met me on level ground. I am so thankful for the beautiful scriptures the Holy Spirit brought to my attention. Truly! Yielding our all to the Holy Spirit is the bottom line for all who are sinking. I am so glad the solution is so simple. All we have to do is give Him permission to work on us. And God caps it off with this promise, "Him that cometh to me I will in no wise cast out" (John 6:37).

Truly it was God who spoke to me through His Word. But this was surprising to me for yet another reason. I also thought it was cruel of the Spirit to lead Jesus into the wilderness to be tempted by the devil. I just didn't understand that if Satan hadn't been allowed to tempt Jesus, then Jesus wouldn't have had to choose whether to obey or disobey His heavenly Father. Just listen to what Jesus went through for us. Cherish the love of Jesus, and the love of His heavenly Father, and the Holy Spirit via the chapters that follow this one.

Everyone's life is at stake. No one is exempt from the temptations of the devil or his deceit. Our God is fair. All have the gift of choice. "For unto us was the gospel preached, as well as unto them: but the word preached did not profit them, not being mixed with faith in them that heard it" (Heb. 4:2). Faith is extremely important, and it is our part of the equation. We choose whether we want to have faith in God. We are free to choose whether to serve our own wants and desires or serve the desires of our Creator. The two decisions are like night versus day.

Jesus had to face every temptation we will ever have to face. Otherwise, Satan would be able to rightly waggle his finger at God, as he did with Job. To be perfectly fair, Jesus had to go through every type of pain we will ever have to experience. Do you know what that means? Each of us are not bombarded with the same temptations. Jesus had to personally experience them all. Wow! What a wonderful Savior—to face all of the sins of every human who ever existed. Yes, for us, who, throughout most of our years, do not appreciate what He is doing and has done to save us.

And what the Father went through too. You fathers know to a small degree how hard it is to see your children suffer. The measures Jesus' heavenly Father went through to allow His Son to die for sinners are off the radar—they are so huge.

CHAPTER TWO

My Leap of Faith

———◆◆◆———

As you just learned in the previous chapter, faith is something I have hassled with most of my life. For some reason, I could not grasp what faith was. And here I was in my seventies, and I was still grappling with it. I studied my Bible, and even wrote about faith and then … can you believe this? That manuscript came up missing. I left a copy of it at our house when we went south for the winter. And while we were there, my computer wore out. I had no paper copy of that book with me. When I got back home, the book was missing. It's like it disappeared in thin air. I have never found it. Obviously, someone didn't want it to be in print. I'll have to ask God about that one someday.

I was experiencing some serious consequences because of having the measles when I was a child. It was the beginning of many hospital visits. They caused me to be depressed and at odds with both my family and my friends. I felt very mistreated. Even when I tried to get support from pastors, they said I was the cause of my problems. They were wrong—I desperately needed counseling and compassion. But I didn't ever get it. God had something else in mind.

The church was having a series of Bible studies on faith. I tried to study them. They didn't help me, either. It was then, when I was again desperately in need of help, that God was able to speak to me. Again, when I had nowhere to go but to God, I listened, and He sent me help. He knew I need His help—not help from someone who would try to intimidate me. Truly, sometimes God is the only one who can help us. And what a counselor He is—perfect.

God is willing to help each of us through our own dark valleys. Yes! It's plural! He alone would be patient with me. He alone will not bully us. He's the best! Just think of the dark valleys Jesus walked through to make salvation possible for each of us. He alone knows our hearts. He alone can personalize it for us. When it seems like things can't get any worse, we need to contemplate how much Jesus went through for us. It puts the spotlight on Him, and makes our problems look more surmountable. Our problems get smaller when we look at His—and that goes a long way in giving courage to face ours.

> *When I was again desperately in need of help, that God was able to speak to me.*

Also, remember! The devil doesn't want us to know what faith is. He strives to blind our eyes, so we don't understand what God is saying. And there's one other thing he does. He makes things look worse than they are. God has promised us victory. Satan doesn't want us to have hope. I hope I remember this the next time I feel overwhelmed with his attacks. That's right! Hopelessness always comes from the devil. He is out to get us—but Jesus won that battle. Praise the Lord. He can see us through.

I now understand that Satan has wanted to destroy my relationship with God from the day I was born. And it is the same concerning each of us. Don't let him do it. He was trying to get me away from my grandparents, so it would be easier for him to destroy me. Everything seemed to go wrong when I went to live with my dad. The devil tried to totally destroy my faith. He tried to get me to stop praying. That way, he would sever my connection with God. It's scary to look back on. He almost won. When I prayed, everything seemed to go wrong. Obviously, I was being tested. God was giving Satan a heyday. He knew I would come through it victoriously. He knows us. Therefore, He can allow things to come our way to strengthen us. Now I know that is how we gain faith. It is through our trials. Why? Because that is what makes us make a choice. God is love—and love is always a choice. I choose to love Him with my whole heart. I pray that will be your choice too.

Little did I know that God was planning to use yet another way to answer my prayers. He just wasn't answering them the way I thought He would. He wasn't making it easy on me. It's too bad I didn't remember the other time I hit rock bottom and recall that God hadn't answered gently that time either. But He answered in a beautiful way—a way that helped me grow closer to Him.

As you know, it certainly wasn't easy street. And, of course, Satan was in the mix both times. When things go wrong, you better believe the devil is the instigator. Now, I know that hardship from Satan will be a lifelong experience. And there's one more thing you need to know about him. He doesn't just pick on those who love Jesus—he even mistreats those who are trying to please him. He's just mean through and through. No matter who you are, you have to deal with him. But the good news is that God wants to save us. And He will—but it won't be easy, no matter which one you choose to obey. Now I choose to serve the Lord. He loves me—the devil hates me.

But! At this time, I finally yielded and did the unthinkable. I stopped praying. And I bet you've already guessed what happened—everything went from bad to worse. I am so thankful the Holy Spirit stayed with me, even though I couldn't feel His presence. God was preparing me for a huge show-and-tell experience. It was then when I knelt to talk to Him and read His Word, that I discovered these words in the worship book I had just picked up to read. They popped out at me at just the right moment. Leave it to God! He is so special. The writer said:

> *Those who do nothing in any way that will displease God,*
> *will know, after presenting their case before Him,*
> *just what course to pursue.*
> (The Desire of Ages, p. 668)

Those words gave me hope. So, I knelt down and promised God I would pray to Him no matter what was happening to me. I promised I would *not* stop praying even if everything continued to go wrong. Now, I had part of the solution! I didn't know it, but God was about to give me something else I needed. I was about to find out how fulfilling, exciting, and yet scary faith can be! I invite you to come along with me on that faith trip. God will bring each of us through our troubles if we accept His gift of faith and totally trust Him even when it seems like everything is going wrong, even when we think we can't stand another moment of the devil's harassment. You are invited to come and take part in my leap of faith. If you so choose!

The very next weekend, as we were leaving church, one of our friends came sauntering up to us as we walked toward our car. Out of breath, he panted these words, "Come see what I found." He opened the trunk of his car and there, before my eyes, were a lot of books.

His next words were, "Would you like to go door to door giving them to people"? I was excited! My heart skipped a beat or two. They were written by the same writer who wrote the words that were changing my life. She, too, likes to help guide people to have a closer walk with Jesus! I sent a quick, silent prayer heavenward. Then, I looked into my husband's eyes and told him, "I would like to do that!" Was he willing? A broad smile spread across my face when he said, "I guess we could."

I was thrilled! So, I sent another prayer heavenward, thanking God for Ronald's positive answer to my prayer. I want everybody to have a chance to know and love God more. And I knew this book upheld Jesus. I knew it also shared steps on how to follow Jesus. What an answer to my prayer this was. So, that very afternoon, we and our friends began doing just that—going door to door, giving people a book that could help them have a closer walk with the Lord.

I can still feel that excitement as I look back on it and realize that something was very different. Now, I know it was none other than the Holy Spirit filling us with trust in God. Trust is another word for faith! It seemed like He was pulling me into a conversation with Himself. Again, I felt wrapped in His love—just as I had from my grandpa's beautiful worship times. So I continued talking to Him in prayer and told Him I trusted Him totally. At that time, I did not realize my trust in Him was called "faith." I was still grappling with the word "faith" and with its meaning. So, after lunch, we and our friends got together to give out the books.

As we chose where to go, I said, "Please, Lord, help me with any distrust I might experience along the way." When I look back on it now, I know what He wanted for me was a closer walk with Him. He always wants to strengthen our faith. He always wants to walk with us and spend time with us. And He always wants us to share our faith with those He guides us to talk with.

So, I proceeded to tell Him I was sure Satan would ramp up his attacks, and dog my footsteps because of the commitment I was making with Him. I had an uneasy feeling that Satan might cause something bad to happen like he did to Esther, Job, and many others. Why? Because I would be stepping on his toes, and he would be mad at me. I was sure he would try to shake the small amount of confidence I had just gained. Then, I admitted to God that Satan was a pro at making me distrust myself.

So, I began pleading with God to help me stay true to Him, even if something bad should happen. I admitted that I could not come to Him by myself and would need to rely totally on Him and the Holy Spirit. Now, I know those words were the ones God the Father wanted to hear me say. Again, I promised I would stick with Him, and I pled with Him to help me stay true to Him. By then, I knew quite a bit about faith and trust. I knew it was our only safety net. But little did I know what lay ahead. I really, truly believed God was in the process of preparing me for something big.

As my husband and I proceeded down the street, we found that many of the people we gave the book to were very interested in it. I noticed after I left to go to the next house that some of them just stood there leafing through it. And they proceeded to stand there reading it. That warmed my heart because I love Jesus, and it made me glad I had given the book to them. I bowed my head and asked God to send the Holy Spirit to them, too, and give them an even closer relationship with Him. We constantly need to recommit ourselves to God, no matter how long we have been His child.

As we continued down the street, there appeared to be an area where there were more dogs than there had been at the beginning of the street. I was afraid my very careful husband would be turning around any moment and telling me we shouldn't go any further. That it was too dangerous. Why? He knew how fearful I am of dogs. But because of the way God was working on my heart, I asked Him to help me know whether He wanted us to continue. I wanted to be sure I was walking in faith—not just doing my own thing.

So, I had a heart-to-heart conversation with God and told Him everyone needed to meet Him. I also admitted I thought it was probably dangerous. Then I asked Him to impress my husband, Ronald, to say "yes" if He wanted us to continue giving people the books. I also admitted to God that physical harm could, and very well might happen to us in this venture for Him. In fact, I felt impressed that I would probably get bitten by a dog, but that I was willing to face that danger if I knew it was His will to continue. I believe God was allowing those impressions to come to me to test my faith.

In fact, I think it was my tiny faith relationship with God that prompted the conversation I was having with God right then. We must trust Him in all things, but at the same time, we must not be presumptuous. He is the only One who knows whether a person is spiritually reachable. I wanted Him, and only Him, to guide me on the path He has planned for me. I never want to do something against His will.

I also admitted I didn't know whether it would be presumptuous for us to keep working despite the increased number of dogs. I told Him I needed to know if He wanted us to do it. That I didn't want to do something foolish. It also flashed through my mind that such an answer to my prayer would give me faith to face last-day events that will occur just before Jesus comes back to earth. The Bible seems to indicate this time is approaching very rapidly. We will need very strong faith in God at that time. Then, the words of one of God's prophets came into my mind. "The just shall live by faith: but if any man draw back, my soul shall have no pleasure in him" (Heb. 10:38). I was in the valley of decision!

It was then that I told God if He wanted me to do it, I needed Him to let me know He did. I told Him I was willing to go through a Daniel experience, or one like the three Hebrew boys went through when they got thrown into the burning fiery furnace if that was His will. I silently told God that if Ronald said "yes," when I asked him what we should do—then I would know it was His will to do it. And I reaffirmed that I wanted Him along to guide our path.

Immediately I saw God go into action! I wasn't prepared for the dramatic way He answered my request. How grateful and thrilled I was and still am for His answer. The instant my prayer ended, my husband turned around and gave me a great big grin. Asking, "Do you see what the street looks like ahead of us"?

A shock went up my spine when Ronald exclaimed, "I was talking to God too."

"Yes," I replied.

Then he said: "There are a lot more dogs down there! Do you still want to keep handing out the books?" And I said to God, "Here we go, Lord." Immediately the Holy Spirit impressed me to tell Ronald everything I just told you, so that is what I did. I told Ronald I had been praying to God too. Then I shared with him the whole conversation I had just had with God.

A shock went up my spine when Ronald exclaimed, "I was talking to God too." Then he smiled broadly—just as he had before. And he said, "I was asking God what to do too. Let's do it!" Boy, was I excited! Again, God's answer was "yes." He wanted us to continue handing out the books. So, we bowed our heads and asked Him to protect us.

I was both thrilled and scared. So, I winged another personal prayer to Him, asking Him to help me with my fears! I told Him I knew fear from lack of faith, and I wanted to trust Him totally. The faith those moments in prayer brought me, and the love God showered on us was terrific. Both of us seemed to have a premonition that there would be a confrontation with a dog. And both of us were willing to continue because God had said, "Yes."

When we got to the end of the street, there was a block of older mobile homes. They were not fancy—but they looked like they were in good shape. In one yard there was a sign saying, "Beware of the Dog." I didn't go into that yard. Carefully, I looked around to make sure, but I believe it would have been presumptuous for me to enter a yard that had a sign saying, "Beware of the Dog." I knew God would have questions about doing that!

I did not want to do something presumptuous or rash. I wanted my actions to be in accordance with His will. So again, I winged yet another prayer to Him. Then, I went across the street from where the sign was. I believe God made sure there was no dog visible in that yard because He wanted me to leave a book at that home. It was a long way to the door—the whole length of the mobile home, and it was a long one—probably sixty or seventy feet or more. I knocked very softly on the door. I did not want to disturb a sleeping dog. No one came to the door.

I had just leaned over and was placing a book on the porch floor when bam! Something bit me on the bottom. When I turned around, I was face to face with a large dog. My guess is he weighed close to a hundred pounds. But I am not good at gauging such things. I knew our cat weighed twenty-five pounds. I only weighed ninety-three pounds myself. But for some reason, I was not afraid, even though he had bitten me!

Perhaps, because he had a peaceful look on his face. Fortunately, he let go. But he watched me closely, and every time I took a step toward the street, he looked into my eyes and edged closer. So, I stood still. It had to be God who took my fear away. I am terribly afraid of dogs. That was my fourth dog bite.

I am still amazed at how calm I was. I just kept repeating, "He bit me," over and over again. I was basically trying to tell Ronald what was going on without raising my voice and startling the dog. But my husband didn't hear me! So, I raised my voice some and told him I had been calling and calling him. Finally, he turned toward me, and in amazement, he said, "Honey! Step back very slowly, and I will get between you and the dog." I argued with him. I didn't want him to get bitten too.

The dog continued to stand there, calmly looking at me. I am positive in my own mind that God was continuing to control that dog. As Ronald slowly eased in front of me, the dog again began edging closer.

Every time I think of what happened next, a chuckle comes up in my throat, for my husband said, "It's OK, doggie! I won't let her bite you!" Again, I believe the words he spoke were impressed upon him by the Holy Spirit. Only God could have caused us to be as calm as we were. I am sure God gave Ronald the words to say—ones He knew would tickle my funny bone and make me laugh. And thus, ease the tension of both us and the dog. If you care to know more about the prevalence of dog bites, you can look it up online at: https://1ref.us/19p (accessed Aug. 5, 2020) and https://1ref.us/19q (accessed Aug. 5, 2020).

The above information further convinces me that God used this experience to help me increase my faith and trust in Him. Earlier, there was a site connected with a report on the number of dog bites treated at hospitals. That site disappeared. So, what you could do is call the hospital in your area to see how prevalent it is in your area. I found the statistics alarming. I believe God would not want me to place myself in possible danger to do something for Him. And I believe Ronald agrees. We should not bring trouble on ourselves. This came about because we believed the Holy Spirit compelled us that God wanted us to give these books to people—and we obeyed.

This experience caused our faith in God to grow immensely. Faith is total trust in God. But we must only do things that God either asks us to do or things He guides us to do through the Holy Spirit. I was impressed that God wanted me to give those books to those people. If there is any indecision on whether the request is from God—then it probably isn't from Him. But the Holy Spirit kept impressing us to do it. God is not wishy-washy. God does not change His mind. And He does not ask us to do things without a good reason. You have probably heard this saying, "He killed two birds with one stone." In this venture God was able to increase our faith, and at the same time, answer the heart cry of someone who wanted a closer walk with Him.

I also believe our prayers need to be silent as much as possible, so Satan can't know how to foul up our conversations with God. He is not out for our good. He is out to deceive and destroy. Ask the Holy Spirit to guide you. Be sure you are not being prompted to do something God would not tell you to do. The devil's promptings are nothing more than him telling us to disobey God. There's a vast difference—and if we know Scripture, the Holy Spirit will open our eyes to the difference. God will never tell us to do something that causes us to disobey His will. He can bring salvation to someone who is searching to know Him better through these means. Our obedience must be done in love to His promptings—not our own desires. The Holy Spirit will never tell us to do something that goes against God's commandments.

As we stood there, at the edge of the road, wondering what to do next, a truck drove up. The driver stopped and just sat there! It was from some workplace and was packed with workers. That company gave its employees a ride to and from work.

I told the driver the dog had bitten me. And, slowly, I pulled my slacks down very discreetly—just enough so I could look at the bite. It didn't look to me like his teeth had even penetrated my skin. I thought only the surface skin was roughed up. But what is even more astounding is that there was no pain. Consequently, I said, "Don't worry. It doesn't look bad!"

But later that afternoon, I began having a lot of pain. In fact, it took six to nine months for the pain to be relieved enough so I could sit down. I believe my perception that the bite was very minor was providential too. I believe that the perception of being minor was given to me by God.

Maybe so it wouldn't cause the owner of the dog to be afraid because his dog had bitten me. I can hardly wait to hear the whole story someday in heaven.

Since I didn't want them to be concerned, I told them everything would be alright. Actually, I thought it would be! The long time it took to heal was very surprising to me. I believe my conversation with them was providential too. Why? Because my words were non-threatening. They looked like they felt at ease. We gave them all of the books we had left, hoping there would be one for each person. I couldn't tell how many men were in the truck. When we were through talking with them, we walked on down the street. As we looked back to see if there was any traffic coming so we could cross the street, we saw a man scolding the dog. It was then that I knew the dog belonged to one of the workers I had just talked with. If I had said the bite was bad, it would have caused him to worry.

That evening, many church members and neighbors told me I should go to the emergency room and have a doctor look at the bite. So, I called my son in Michigan. He agreed and said I should go—that dog bites are very dirty. He said I needed an antibiotic as soon as possible. So, at 7:00 p.m. I finally went.

By then, it was obvious that four of the dog's largest teeth had deeply penetrated my body. I was bleeding profusely under the skin. By the time I got to the hospital, the heart-shaped mark was a deep purple. They measured the bite and took pictures. Later, when I got home, I measured it myself and found that it was four and a half by four and a half inches.

But that was not the end of the miracles. Yes! I say miracles. I believe God caused the dog to bite me in such a way, so I would know He had protected me. I believe He guided the dog to bite at an angle that would make the bite mirror a perfect heart shape. He wanted me to know how much He loved me, and that He had been with me, protecting me the whole time. It could have been so much worse.

God wanted me to know He had been with me just like He was with Daniel in the lion's den and the three Hebrew boys who were thrown into the fiery furnace. Not even a hair of their head was singed. I expect to meet at least one of those men from that street in heaven someday. And, hopefully, many of them! Telling me they had a closer walk with God because of the book I gave them.

God allows things like this to happen if someone can be saved because of it. If we are willing to be His hands and feet, He will use us and send us where He wants us to go. We did not choose which neighborhood to go to. Our friends had already chosen where to go, and he did not know there were many dogs in that neighborhood. I am so thankful, humbled, and awed that God took such care to let me know He loved me that much. Some may say I'm foolish for thinking this way. I don't think I am. I believe God wanted to strengthen my faith. He wanted me to know He will always be with me through thick or thin. It seems like it is getting very close to the time when Jesus will be coming back to take us to heaven. The prophecies concerning His coming have been fulfilled. We may have to face persecution just before He comes back. I believe God will prepare us for whatever lies ahead of us.

He allows trials to come our way because we need to have faith in Him. Tests like this produce faith and help us learn to trust Him more. Even if it's only a little bit of trust. Every little bit by bit adds up. This type of faith will help us obey God—no matter what! Yes, faith that God is with us, even when Satan tries to confuse us with his lies, or if we ourselves cause us to have doubt.

Doubt is a form of unbelief. The question is, do we believe God when He says, "The just shall live by faith" (Heb. 10:38). We are human. We were born sinful. So we have to fight against unbelief. Our wonderful God provided a way to combat doubt when He gave us our measure of faith. Listen to these words; they are truly faith-building. "God hath dealt to every man the measure of faith" (Rom. 12:3). He also says, "By grace are ye saved through faith; and that not of yourselves: it is the gift of God: Not of works, lest any man should boast. For we are his workmanship, created in Christ Jesus unto good works, which God hath before ordained that we should walk in them" (Eph. 2:8–10).

Grace is the most amazing type of love in existence. And it has been available and still is available to everyone who has ever been born. It is undeserved love. You can't buy it. I find the simplest way to look at it is through something people used to do years ago. If a person had trouble paying their bills, they made a way you could have extra time to get the money to pay it with. So when you couldn't pay because of sickness, or some other tragedy, you had an extra period of time to get the money for your monthly payment. And they did not charge late fees. That was generous. It was called the "grace period." The person didn't deserve it. It was a gift of time. That's what grace is—love we don't deserve.

The writer of Romans highlights grace by placing its components of love and faith together. Even though we don't deserve it, God gives it to us anyway because He loves us so much. I invite you to join me in saying, "Thank You," via your own personal love and faith in Him. It's through God's grace and faith alone that we are saved. God's grace + our faith = salvation Trust Them!

> *Grace is the most amazing type of love in existence.*

There is just one more miracle I want to tell you about. When I got home from the hospital, I was shocked to find that the dog had indeed sunk his teeth very deeply into my flesh at all four corners of his mouth. When I removed the pants I was wearing, I looked at them closely for holes where the dog's molars had gone through! Are you ready for this? There were no holes. There wasn't even a thread pulled apart to allow a small tooth to go through the fabric. It was firmly-woven fabric. There should have been four holes. Now that's a miracle. I am saving those pants! They will remain in my closet forever! I am not wearing them! Rather, I am keeping them to remind me of how truly wonderful God is. I am so grateful for His loving care. Thank You, Lord, for Your great love.

Consequently, my main reason for writing this book is to help all of us—myself included—become better acquainted with our God, and know and obey the loving guidelines He gives us for our safety. Together, the three of Them are saving us by welcoming the Holy Spirit into our hearts and lives. Believing and obeying what He shows and tells us, through Bible study and prayer is the most important thing we can do. It connects us to Jesus and helps us really, truly rely on Him and love Him. Because to know Him is to love Him—so knowing Him is extremely important. Thus, it is my desire to point out the love notes He has placed in His Word for each of us. We can't get along without Him or His notes. Jesus' own words illuminate Him and show us His love. He said: *"Think not that I am come to destroy the law, or the prophets: I am not come to destroy, but to fulfil. For verily I say unto you, Till heaven and earth pass, one jot or one tittle shall in no wise pass from the law, till all be fulfilled"* (Matt. 5:17–18).

Do you know what a jot or a tittle is? My Bible tells me in the margin that the dotting of the i or crossing of the t are what a jot and a tittle are. This way, Jesus is verifying that even small changes are important. They can alter the meaning of a verse. Yes, God says He won't even change His Word by removing even just one of those pen marks in His Law.

And look what Paul said under the inspiration of God. "Let your conversation be without covetousness; and be content with such things ye have: for he hath said, 'I will never leave thee, nor forsake thee.' So that we may boldly say, 'The Lord is my helper, and I will not fear what man shall do to me'" (Heb. 13:5–6). This verse is calling Jesus our helper too. And this next verse should also strengthen our courage and faith. Jesus says He will be the same "yesterday, and to day, and for ever" (Heb. 13:8).

The Bible tells us what God has done, and is still doing for us today. He says, "O taste and see that the LORD is good: blessed is the man that trusteth in him" (Ps. 34:8). But all of us must taste and see for ourselves that Jesus is good. That certainly is not a difficult task when we know what Jesus has already done for us.

We, as Christians, desire to be like Jesus. We do not want to be to be deceived. He says, "Beloved, now are we the sons of God, and it doth not yet appear what we shall be: but we know that, when He shall appear, we shall be like Him; for we shall see Him as He is. And every man that hath this hope in himself purifieth himself, even as He is pure" (1 John 3:2–3). Now that's a real WOW!

It takes faith. I am so glad God gives us what I call our starter faith. Faith has to be exercised. You can't exercise something you do not have, but God assures us that He has given each of us a measure of faith. Exercising that measure increases it. That's what I was doing. Faith is one of many gifts given us through our conscience and the gift of the Holy Spirit. It is crucial that we know God's will. A godly conscience is increased by reading the Bible and knowing God's will. As we exercise the faith God gives us, it will become easier and easier to believe and accept and obey His will.

Faith is not presumption. We can't just presume God said something—we must know, via God's Word, that God said it. Faith is total trust in God. When Noah and his family got into that boat, it showed their faith. It was their faith that caused them to go into the boat. It takes a lot of grit to do what they did. After all! They were not anywhere near a body of water. They were being taunted and laughed at. And our longsuffering God had Noah preach to those people for a hundred and twenty years (see Gen. 6:3). It probably seemed like forever. I am sure they taunted him concerning the length of time. Can't you hear their jeers and taunts? It's still that way today. "As it was in the days of Noah, so it will be at the coming of the Son of man" (Matt. 24:37, NIV).

If we clasp God's hand tightly by following in Jesus' footprints, and listen to the pleading voice of the Holy Spirit, we will have an exciting journey, one that will last the rest of our lives. We must be in prayer with Him. He loves it when we spend time with Him. Are you ready for an adventure? Here it comes! It's ready to happen! We already love Him, but as we spend more time with Him, we will fall more deeply in love with Him, and we will never be the same again! Praise the Lord! Here is the key! It is by looking at Him, that we become changed (see 2 Cor. 3:18). God was with Noah, and He will be with us.

What do you say we get better acquainted with our God. Let's learn what the threads of His love really are. Every time we open our Bible, we will be learning about Him, and about His character of love. This is true until the day He comes to take us home with Him. Have you looked at Him today? Take a long look! He can save your life if you let Him. He has promised to see you through—but it won't be easy. It wasn't easy for all of His children down through the ages, but They did it anyway. What a loving God we serve.

CHAPTER THREE

The Reason— God's Love Story

———◆●◆———

The Bible really does contain a love story! It's the greatest love story ever told or written. His love story gives us the history of God's love for every creature. But He has an enemy! And! Can you believe this? God's love story even includes His love for those who do not love Him. How dare I say this? I can say it because the Bible tells me, "The Lord is not slack concerning His promise, as some men count slackness; but is long suffering to us-ward, not willing that any perish, but that all should come to repentance" (2 Peter 3:9).

Do you realize the Bible contains the history of God's love for every creature He has ever created—human, angelic, and all others in between— even the animals! Every created thing came from the hand of one Creator. I am so glad there is only one true God, and that He is the *only* Creator who has ever existed. Everything that has ever been created came from Him. Thus, there is continuity throughout all of creation. Everything was created with the same loving care. All abide under the same loving laws. Just as the Creator Himself is love, so are His laws rules of love. They teach us how to love God, ourselves, our fellowmen, and all other creatures. Mainly, God wants to tell us how to win the battle with His and our enemy—Satan. And we gain that victory through love.

Thus, it is of utmost importance we understand what God's laws of love are all about, and why He formulated them the way He did! I know what I am saying may come across as ridiculous to some, but we really must know God's laws. You are probably thinking, His laws are simple and easy to understand. You are right! They are easy to read! And they aren't complicated! Anyone can understand them. Our God of love wouldn't have it any other way.

Then He brought me hope with these thoughts. "Was Eve a kindergartner?" I resoundingly exclaimed. No! Eve was fresh from the hand of God. Created perfect. Brilliant in intellect. But on her own, she was no match for God's enemy whom she was about to encounter. He is the same one who was causing me trouble. And I could go on naming every person who has ever been born—since he has caused every single being on planet earth much grief. At times, we, too, feel just as confident as she did. But because of our heritage, the heritage passed down to us as a result of her sin, we also fail to grasp the depth of the devil's cunning and deceit. He can turn a simple thing into a nightmare in the blink of an eye just because of all of the baggage we carry caused by her sin.

Each person can only know through their own unique experiences the depth to which sin can take them. Each person's experience is his or her own. Many times, I have failed to grasp the enormity of Satan's temptations. So, we need to think seriously about these issues. I need to think seriously about my own plight with Satan and with sin. I need to realize that I, too, am no match for the devil. Whether I believe it or not, he is my enemy. Yes! This is true for every last person on earth. There is a battle going on right now, just as there was in that garden long ago.

It's not trivial. It's no laughing matter. The business at hand is dead serious for every one of us. Just as it was for Adam and Eve. Because of Eve's lack of concern for herself, and also for her husband's safety, we too are now on death row, so to speak. Actually, we are in a war between good and evil. That's more than serious, and it makes it extremely important that we love and believe what God says, We must not believe our own ideas or those of other people; especially ideas from people who believe things that disagree with God's Word.

We must only believe the words of our one true God. We must place our hand in His and be much on our knees in prayer, placing every person He puts in our path under His care. We must be joining our hearts to His and interceding on behalf of others, asking God to speak to them through the Holy Spirit. That gives God permission to work with them, and it's called intercessory prayer. God desires to send His Helper, the Holy Spirit, to every person. Just listen to these beautiful verses: "Likewise the Spirit also helpeth our infirmities: for we know not what we should pray for as we ought: but the Spirit maketh intercession for us with groanings which cannot be uttered. And he that searcheth the hearts knoweth what is the mind of the Spirit, because he maketh intercession for the saints according to the will of God" (Rom. 8:26–27). God desires to send His Helper, the Holy Spirit, to every single person. I find that very comforting.

> *Although God may do some dramatic things to get our attention, He is not like our enemy, Satan, who bullies his way into our business.*

Although God may do some dramatic things to get our attention, He is not like our enemy, Satan, who bullies his way into our business. God pleads with us through the Holy Spirit and woos us to Himself through His words in the Bible. We get to know God through His words and acts of love. God is gentle, kind, and peaceable. He shows us how much He loves us and then waits for us to invite Him into our hearts. Jesus' counsel to us is, "Ask, and it shall be given you; seek, and ye shall find; knock, and it shall be opened unto you" (Luke 11:9). I had asked. I was determined to have love and faith in God. We must do our part. We must ask, seek, and knock.

Consequently, my main reason for writing this book is to help all of us, myself included, become better acquainted with our God, and know and obey the loving guidelines He gives us for our safety. We must learn to really, truly love Him. Why? Because to know Him is to love Him—so knowing Him is extremely important! It is my desire to point out the special love notes He has placed in His Word for each reader. His own words will illuminate Him and show us His love.

If we clasp God's hand tightly, follow in Jesus' footsteps, and listen to the pleading voice of the Holy Spirit, we will have an exciting journey that will last the rest of our lives. We must be much in prayer with Him. He loves to spend time with us. Are you ready for an adventure? Here it comes! It's ready to happen! We already love Him, but as we spend more time with Him, we will fall more deeply in love with Him, and we will never be the same again. Praise the Lord. Here is the key. It is by looking at Him—through talking with Him in prayer—through learning what He went through for us from the pages of our Bible—that we become changed!

What do you say we get better acquainted with our God? Let's learn what the threads of His love are! Every time we open our Bible, we will be learning about Him and His character of love. Yes, until the very day He comes to take us home with Him. Have you looked at Him today? He can save your life—if you let Him. He has promised to see you through to the end, but it won't be easy. It wasn't easy for Him, but He did it anyway. Jesus will bring each of us through our troubles if we have faith in Him and totally trust Him—no matter how bad things are—or how bad they look. God bless you as you make your decision.

CHAPTER FOUR

God's Way is the Best Way

———◆◆◆———

The subject of my book concerns our of worship of God. It is given to us through the fourth commandment in His Law. which tells us that God is our Creator, and that *He is the only one we are to worship*. Let's just quickly review that command. It is the one a lot of people have been told has been done away with. Today, most people keep the first day of the week holy. They say they are doing it in honor of Jesus' resurrection. But is there anywhere in the Bible that tells us Jesus told them to change God's day of worship to a different day?

Come! Let's search our Bible and see what God says about it. Has He changed it or done away with it? What God says is of utmost importance. In fact, it's a matter of life and death. Here is His Law. It begins with the word, "remember." That means—don't forget. What are we to remember? *"Remember the sabbath day, to keep it holy"* (Exod. 20:8).

Then God tells us which days in the week belong to us, to do whatever we want to do on them. There are six of them. God only reserved one day a week for Himself. He was very generous with us. He gave us six days, and we can do whatever we want on them. We do not serve a selfish God—He is very generous. He says, *"Six days shalt thou labour, and do all thy work"* (Exod. 20:9).

Quickly, I reached for my Bible and scanned the creation story. Chapter two gives us the account of how God ended His work. The seventh day of the week is His special day. He wants to spend that day with us. Yes, it's the Lord's Day. It's His Sabbath. He is the Lord of it. He is the one who decided what was to be done on that day. For God says, "But he seventh day is the sabbath of the LORD thy God" (Exod. 20:10). It's special to God. And He says it this way in the creation story:

"And on the seventh day God ended His work which He had made; and He rested on the seventh day which He had made. And God blessed the seventh day, and sanctified it: because that in it He had rested from all His work which God created and made" (Gen. 2:2–3). Are you interested in knowing who that Lord is? God doesn't leave us in the dark as to who created us or our days of the week. He says, *"And to make all men see what is the fellowship of the mystery, which from the beginning of the world hath been hid in God, who created all things by Jesus Christ"* (Eph. 3:9). That's right! It's Jesus—the one who died to pay for our sins who created us. WOW! What love! What devotion! And He only asks us to love—for love is what the commandments ask us to do.

And love is what He wants to do on His holy day. He wants to spend quality time with us on that day and love us in a special way. It is the only day He has ever set aside for us to worship Him on. It was also the only day Jesus made holy when He created our world. It was a gift in time He would spend with the ones He had created! How much more special could it be? None of the other days of the week were ever made holy by God. Thus! No other day can take the place of His holy Sabbath day. He only claimed the seventh day of the week as His day.

And right away, He told mankind how and why He wanted them to keep it holy. He said: "in it thou shalt not do any work, thou, nor thy son, nor thy daughter, nor thy manservant, nor thy maidservant, nor thy cattle, nor thy stranger that is within thy gates: For in *six* days the Lord made heaven and earth, the sea, and all that in them is, *and rested the seventh day: ... and hallowed it" (Exod. 20:10–11, italics supplied).*

We tell Him, thank You, when we worship Him on that day. And our worship of Him on the day He tells us to worship confirms that we love Him and that He is our God—that He is the One we love. We need to pause and realize that when we do not do what He tells us to do, we are disobeying Him—that's not an act of love. I've been there and done that. I put my wants ahead of His wisdom. We need to pause and picture how bad it makes us feel when our children do not want to spend time with us. Remember! He took on human nature. He hurts the same way we hurt, only more intensely, and it's kind of like saying we don't consider that day special. Ouch! But don't listen to me. He's the One we need to listen to. So let's take a walk through the Bible and see what God says about His holy day.

Nowhere does God tell us He changed the holiness of the seventh day of the week to a different day. To be legitimate, since it is a law, He would have to nullify that part of His Law. In other words, abolish it. And then, if He still wanted to have a special weekly day to spend with us, He would have appoint another day of the week and hallow it to take its place—to make it legal. If you can find such a law in the Bible—changed by God—I will gladly change and worship Him on that day. Please let me know if you find such a command of God. I want to serve Him.

I am going to let Jesus do most of the talking as we take this walk. He, His Father, and the Holy Spirit are the only Ones who can legally write a new law to take the place of the old one. Why? Because They are the authors of the original law. I like that; for if we can believe anyone, it is God who we can believe. We certainly do not want to believe the enemy of our souls—the devil. He's the real culprit when we are truly deceived.

I love you, my brothers and sisters. Each of us has to determine for ourselves what our choice will be. I'm only going to share what God says about it. We each need to hold His hand as we take this walk—myself included. He loves all of us very much. He won't get upset if we have a hard time figuring it out—I certainly have been there and done that, as you already know. And I know you love Him or you wouldn't be reading this book. I hope you enjoy the journey. I am going to begin with Genesis and end with Revelation. But let me share a couple verses for background first.

Do you realize that Jesus calls us brother and sister? And what is His criteria? Matthew says, "While He yet talked to the people, behold, his mother and his brethren stood without, desiring to speak with him. Then one of them said unto him, Behold, thy mother and thy brethren stand without, desiring to speak with thee. But he answered and said unto him that told him, Who is my mother? and who are my brethren? And he stretched forth his hand toward his disciples, and said, Behold my mother and my brethren! For whosoever shall do the will of my Father which is in heaven, the same is my brother, and sister, and mother" (Matt. 12:46–50). Isn't that heartwarming? If we obey God, we are part of Jesus' family.

I think most Bible scholars agree that it was most likely Moses who wrote the first five books of the Bible. And he did it under the inspiration of God. And our God spoke to His prophets and said, "Knowing this first, that no prophecy of the scripture is of any private interpretation. For the prophecy came not in old time by the will of man: but holy men of God spake as they were moved by the Holy Ghost" (2 Peter 1:20–21). Isn't that comforting? It was God the Holy Spirit, who conversed with the prophets. Moses certainly was a holy man. Both Moses and Peter went through a lot of harassment to get to get to honor God.

That means it would be through Moses that God tells us about the creation of our world. Concerning the last day of the week, Moses shares this truth: "And on the seventh day God ended his work which he had made; and he rested on the seventh day from all his work which he had made. And God blessed the seventh day, and sanctified it: because that in it he had rested from all his work which God created and made" (Gen. 2:2–3).

I want to combine the old and the new as we look at things. So, let's skip ahead and get Ecclesiastes' take on the unchangeableness and solidarity of God's law. He says, "Let us hear the conclusion of the whole matter: Fear God, and keep his commandments: for *this is the whole duty of man*. For God shall bring every work into judgment, with every secret thing, whether it be good, or whether it be evil" (Eccl. 12:13–14, italics supplied). They will not get away with their disobedience to God's Law. God does not tolerate deceit. All will have to own up to their trickery. Jesus tops it off with these words! "But I say unto you, that every idle word that men shall speak, they shall give account in the day of judgment. For by thy words thou shalt be justified, and by thy words thou shalt be condemned" (Matt. 12:36–37). That gives me peace of mind. All I have to do to be on God's side is ask Him to forgive me and then cheerfully obey Him.

Now, let's quickly flip through God's account of His creation of Adam and Eve and Jesus giving Adam the breath of life. First, let's look at what Isaiah told the people in his day concerning God's holy Sabbath. The Lord told Isaiah He still expected people to keep the Sabbath holy at his time in history. The message is from Jesus. He says, "If thou turn away thy foot from the sabbath, from doing thy pleasure on my holy day; and call the sabbath a delight, the holy of the LORD, honourable; and shall honor him, not doing thine own ways, nor finding thine own pleasure, nor speaking thine own words: then shalt thou delight thyself in the LORD; and I will cause thee to ride upon the high places of the earth, and feed thee with the heritage of Jacob thy father: for the mouth of the LORD hath spoken it" (Isa. 58:13–14).

He created a special day for the purpose of not only spending time with us—but also a time for us to worship Him, and tell Him how much we love Him.

It was Jesus who gave Adam the breath of life. God doesn't leave us in the dark as to who created us either. "And to make all men see what is the fellowship of the mystery, which from the beginning of the world hath been hid in God, who created all things by Jesus Christ" (Eph. 3:9). Isn't that beautiful! Jesus, the One who created us! Also, He created a special day for the purpose of not only spending time with us—but also a time for us to worship Him, and tell Him how much we love Him.

How do we worship God? Obedience to His will is an act of worship. So Jesus instituted worship at the same time He created us. Why do you think He was so quick to do that? Have you noticed that at the same time Jesus showed Adam his garden home, He gave him some very special instructions. What were they? "Of every tree of the garden thou mayest freely eat: But of the tree of the knowledge of good and evil, thou shalt not eat of it: for in the day that thou eatest thereof thou shalt surely die:" (Gen. 2:16–17). Why do you think Jesus was in such a hurry to do that? It was because Jesus knew His enemy would invade that garden. Not eating that fruit was a safeguard He gave Adam. What kind of a God would Jesus have been if He hadn't counseled Adam immediately! Certainly not a God I would want to worship. I think it is interesting that God didn't tell Adam why he was so specific. Adam had never seen something die. He was innocent. But to be truly obedient, he should obey God, even if he didn't know what death was all about. I am sure Adam knew it would be bad if he did touch it. If he loved Jesus, he just needed to obey Jesus' instruction.

God told Adam exactly what He expected of him and informed him of the dire consequences, should he disobey. He instructed Adam right up front, before anything could happen. Jesus needed to be upfront with Adam, Eve, and all of us on such a serious matter as our worship of Him. Yes! I call Adam's obedience at that time an act of worship. Jesus knew His enemy would come and tempt them to disobey Him. He instructed him right up front before anything could happen. I think probably Satan's favorite lie concerns our worship of God. He is jealous of Jesus.

He is our common enemy. Mark tells us the battle is horrendous! For he says, speaking of the coming of Jesus—"Then if any man say to you, Lo, here is Christ; or, lo, he is there; believe him not" (Mark 13:21). If we don't know what God says, we will truly be deceived. But Jesus gives us hope, saying, "False Christ's and false prophets shall rise, and shall shew signs and wonders, to seduce, if it were possible, even the elect" (Mark

13:22). The elect will be obeying God. They will not be deceived. They will know what God has said and will not be seduced. They will love and obey Him. Jesus will not come secretly. Look up Mark 13:26, 32–33.

Satan knows he deserves the punishment which is coming his way—most of us know too—for the Holy Spirit works on our hearts. Then we feel guilty. If Satan had asked God to forgive him, God would have, if he was sorry for his sin and asked for forgiveness. That's just who God is—always ready to forgive—if there is real repentance. God wants us to recognize our wrongs. May I repeat—God does not force our choices. God is love. True love always gives freedom of choice. So, allow me to explain what this book is about! From Genesis to Revelation there is not a single word about changing the seventh-day Sabbath to the first day of the week. In my book I trace what God says will happen to our world because of Lucifer's sin. I am asking God to do the talking. He is the only One who can tell it right! That is why I have used so many Bible verses. I don't want to tell it. I want God to tell it.

I have prayed for every person who will be deciding whether to read on from this point in my book. Yes! I am praying for each of you. God wouldn't have it any other way. He leaves every one of us free to make our own choices. It is our choice to believe God or Satan, the enemy of our souls. He is still the slick liar he was in that garden long ago. I hope each and every one of you will continue reading and hear God out. For He is the One I am quoting! Trusting God is a life and death matter as Adam and Eve discovered in the Garden of Eden. We will never truly obey unless we truly trust. If we love Jesus and trust His wisdom, we will keep His commandments—all of them.

Most people have been told from their birth that the fourth commandment was nailed to the cross. But, was it God who said that? In my mind the answer is clearly a resounding "No!" But you must not listen to me. God is the one we each must listen to. We will never be sorry for listening to Him. He truly loves us. Come and find out *what was really nailed to the cross!* It was a law! But what law? And don't take my word for it. Study out what I have said for yourself, and verify it with God's Word. Maybe you will find texts I didn't. I will follow history's timeline. It is when we get to the time close to Jesus' crucifixion that I talk about what was really nailed to the cross. I have chosen to put the chapters together in that sequence because I believe it will be more understandable if we begin with creation and study it in the sequence it took place.

We need to listen to God as He speaks to our hearts. And be aware that the devil will try to confuse us as he did me. He will contradict God at every turn, as God speaks to you through the Holy Spirit. He will be insinuating in your other ear—catch him in his lies. God always tells the truth. "The truth shall make you free" (John 8:32). If you decide not to do anything which will displease God, you will be led to the truth. God will give you the strength to follow Him, and He will help you understand what He is saying. Your life depends on it. Stick totally to God's words; they will never let you down. Even pastors need to be sure they are not being tricked by Satan—and thus misleading their parishioners. Pray for them.

Remember! One-third of the angels believed Lucifer's lies. Certainly, we are in as dire need as they were. God says, "Fear them not therefore: for there is nothing covered, that shall not be revealed; and hid, that shall not be known. What I tell you in darkness, that speak ye in light: and what ye hear in the ear, that preach ye upon the housetops. And fear not them which kill the body, but are not able to kill the soul: but rather fear him which is able to destroy both soul and body in hell" (Matt. 10:26–28).

I am so thankful for the times in my life when God loved me enough to let me know it was Satan who was placing fear in my mind. God never gives us a spirit of fear. Now, I know my love for God was impaired, and He drew me closer. It took away the fear I had of hurting Him. He does that over and over again for each of us as we walk and talk with Him. God says, "There is no fear in love; but perfect love casteth out fear: because fear hath torment. He that feareth is not made perfect in love" (1 John 4:18).

It is Satan who tries to instill fear in our hearts. He does not want us to understand God's Word. He is still planning to overthrow God's government. You see! He has tricked himself into believing his own lies—that he will someday totally overthrow God's kingdom. He thinks that will keep him from having to burn up in the lake of fire God has planned for him. Matthew tells us about it. He says, "Then shall he say unto them on the left hand, Depart from me, ye cursed, into everlasting fire, *prepared for the devil and his angels*" (Matt. 25:41, italics supplied). By the way—it will only burn as long as there is something left to burn. That's a whole other issue. Our God is a lover—not cruel and hateful.

None of us have to burn in that fire—it's not prepared for us. If we do burn in it—it will be because we chose to burn in it. I feel so much better now that I have followed God's bidding. Since I am depending on His Spirit to guide us, I can just relax and let God do His Word. He knows each person's heart. If you ask Him, He will guide you into all truth. God bless you as you read and commune with Him. Above all, ask God for His guidance and for protection from any thoughts Satan may place in your mind. I hope you enjoy the trip.

Remember! Stay close to God, not some friend, family member, or even your pastor. They are all sinners, just like us. They become tricked by the devil just as we do. We need to keep our pastors in our prayers. They have a huge job to do for God, and they are not exempt from Satan's heckling. In fact, he just loves to mess our pastors up—just think how many people he can destroy, by leading just one pastor astray. I encourage you to pray for them and for all of us.

> *We need to keep our pastors in our prayers. They have a huge job to do for God, and they are not exempt from Satan's heckling.*

Pray that God will be your pastor's ultimate guide and yours too. Pray that God will counsel both you and your pastor as you read. God says, "Trust ye not in a friend, put ye not confidence in a guide: keep the doors of thy mouth from her that lieth in thy bosom. For the son dishonoureth the father, the daughter riseth up against her mother, the daughter in law against her mother in law; and a man's enemies are the men of his own house. Therefore I will look unto the LORD; I will wait for the God of my salvation: my God will hear me" (Micah 7:5–7). "It is better to trust in the LORD than to put confidence in princes" (Ps.118:9).

I am so thankful Jesus was willing to bear the agony of the cross, also all the cruelty of mankind, and all the terrible fury of Satan bombarded Him with. I also praise the Father for Jesus to make that choice. But that's just the way the Father is! Jesus chose to be made like us, and experience every cruelty any of us will have to face. Why? Let's look and see.

Paul says, "Forasmuch then as the children are partakers of flesh and blood, he also himself likewise took part of the same; that through death he might destroy him that had the power of death, that is, the devil; And delivereth them who through fear of death were all their lifetime subject to bondage. For verily he took not on him the nature of angels; but he took on him the seed of Abraham. Wherefore in all things it behooved him to be made like unto his brethren, that he might be a merciful and faithful high priest in things pertaining to God, to make reconciliation for the sins of the people. For in that He Himself has suffered being tempted, he is able to succor them that are tempted" (Heb. 2:14–18).

Jesus knows how much we hurt and how we feel because He went through the experiences we are going through. Yes! He faced the torture of Satan, but He didn't deserve it. He experienced our sins for us. What love! What compassion! That the Son of God would do that for us. How can we stand to not love Him? We can never thank Him too much. Really, we thank Him too little. Without His gift of facing what we have to experience, we would have no hope. Without His victorious show and tell of the sins of all mankind and the trials of our faith, sin would never have ended. That would be hell without end. I don't think there is a single person who would want that. Especially Jesus.

Stop and soak in how amazing Jesus' gift is. And how amazing it is that it is available for each one of us. Just the gift of knowing this mess will end someday is breathtaking, but going to heaven and living forever with God is priceless—just being in His presence is mind-boggling. It's more than worth suffering for.

I hope these tests whetted your appetite to find more of the truth about whether His holy day is still the same day of the week Jesus kept. Come and find out more about the scope of mankind's journey. Learn more about the reality of God's holy law—the Ten Commandments. Your life depends on it. We can know for sure whether we are keeping the right day of the week holy. We need to know, without a doubt, the truth. Are you ready? If you are, let's go and contemplate the reality of those thirty-some years Jesus suffered to pay for our sins!

CHAPTER FIVE

A Gift from God for Our Day—John at Patmos

———◆◆◆———

John was a beloved disciple of Jesus. Just a short time before he died, God gave him a very important vision. He was Jesus' youngest disciple. Consequently, he was still alive quite a few years after the other disciples had passed away. I believe God gave John this particular vision both for John's benefit and ours—people who may still be living when Jesus comes back to earth. John, too, lived at a very special time in earth's history. He lived for many years after Jesus' crucifixion. But! What is most important is that God allowed John to know the Ten Commandments were not done away with when Jesus died on the cross.

We are living in the last days of earth's history! The years just before Jesus return to this earth will face an unprecedented barrage of attacks from Satan. Why? Because of their loyalty to Jesus. That is why John was in trouble too! The Jewish religious leaders harbored great anger toward him, and they exhibited it in dangerous, outrageous ways. It was because he talked to the Jewish people about Jesus being the Messiah. Therefore, they wanted to shut his mouth because Jesus' words convicted the hearts of many, many people. John's witness of Jesus caused many Jews to accept Jesus as their Messiah.

Isn't it amazing that it was the religious leaders who refused to accept Jesus as their Savior? Their refusal to accept Him made them more susceptible to Satan's deceit! This is why they fell prey to the devil's lies. He was able to convince them to end John's life. John's character emulated the character of his precious Savior. John called Jesus the Lamb of God, and many people believed what he said. He led them to worship Jesus as the Son of God. John's enemies just couldn't stand to have Jesus receive praise. What a shame! The very ones God chose for spreading the gospel of Christ were refusing to accept Him as their Savior.

Yes, and they misrepresented God's holy Sabbath day. They tampered with God's law—the one concerning how to keep the Sabbath holy. In fact, they constructed a huge number of extremely strict laws concerning the keeping of it. There were so many rules that the Sabbath became a burden. Many of the Sabbath rules conflicted with other Sabbath rules. So, it became impossible to keep one law without disobeying another. Consequently, these Jewish religious leaders were leading many, many people to go astray. And they were also making the Sabbath a distasteful, burdensome day, rather than the delight God intended it to be. It's a dangerous thing to tamper with God's law.

This happened more than fifty years after Jesus went to heaven. God knew that many of the religious leaders in our day would misrepresent the Sabbath too. But the Bible says, "For as the new heavens and the new earth, which I will make, shall remain before me, saith the LORD, so shall your seed and your name remain" (Isa. 66:22). What a forgiving and just God we serve. He doesn't cut the children of wicked parents off because of what the parents do. "And it shall come to pass, that from one new moon to another, and from one sabbath to another, shall all flesh come to worship before me, saith the LORD" (Isa. 66:23).

This teaching tells us God's holy Sabbath day will never end. This verse is talking about when God re-creates our earth anew. Then He gave His disciple, John, a very important vision. One which showed John that God's holy law still resides in His holy temple in heaven. This means that it still resided there after Jesus died on the cross. In fact, it still resides there to this very day. Thus, that vision also refutes the claim that says His Sabbath command was nailed to the cross. This truth boosts our faith in God's unchanging law. When we read about the vision God gave John, we realize what a great gift that vision was. It confirms that the Sabbath was not done away with at the cross. And it confirms that we will be keeping the Sabbath holy with Jesus when He comes and lives with us in the earth made new.

It's hard to stay cool-headed when people are lying about you and trying to kill you, but through it all, John stayed true to his Lord. His testimony was eloquent and powerful. Not because he was doing great things by human standards! No! The things that really counted were his honesty and his love for God. John obeyed God's commandments, even unto death. And John loved his neighbors, as God's tells us to do in His Ten-Commandment law. In God's eyes love through obedience is golden.

The same is true today. When people are obeying God, it irritates and angers those who *do not* obey Him. For when they see a person lovingly obeying Him, they see the contrast between themselves and anyone who is really doing His will. It bothers their conscience. Living as Jesus would live is the most powerful witness a person can have. But! Often, the more powerful a persons' witness is, the more upset their enemies become. That's what happened to John.

Their hatred steadily grew. Finally, they were able to succeed in getting John thrown into a pot of boiling oil. He was an amazing disciple of Jesus. His allegiance never wavered. It just grew stronger. Because of his witness, while he was in that pot of oil, God saw to it that he was removed from it. What is even more amazing is that the same men who threw him into that caldron took him out of it. Then they banished him to a barren island called Patmos. We too may experience our Patmos, and if we do, God will be with us to the end just as He was with John. These stories in the Bible are given to us to give us courage, hope, and faith in God. Satan is nasty. He wants to destroy every one of us.

This island was far out at sea, and devoid of vegetation. It was where they sent the vilest criminals. For John, his stay on that island turned out to be a gift from heaven. Even though he was away from family and friends, he was in close contact with angels and his God. It was the angels, and the Holy Spirit, who helped John hold onto his strong contact with his Savior. Why was this imprisonment of John a God-send? Because the Jews were unable to persecute him while he was there. They thought they had bested him! But how wrong they were!

Daily, John turned from all of the sins of which the Holy Spirit convicted him, and he continued to trust in God's grace. That's when God can do great things with and for a person. That's when spiritual growth takes place! Times like these really cause the devil to get busy. Relentlessly, John resisted Satan. There's a song which goes like this: "Trust and obey, for there's no other way, to be happy in Jesus, but to trust and obey." In fact, John obeyed God to the point of death. Thus, God was able to trust him to do amazing things for him.

While he was there, he was among men who desperately needed their sins forgiven! These men were on death row! That's when John did some of his greatest work for the Lord. It was a special work God handpicked just for him. I believe it was God's will that John was placed on that island. God knew it would become a haven for him away from the men who wanted to kill him. There John had peace and time! Time to witness to men who were outcasts of society. Men no one else could or would help because they, too, had been banished from society. It also gave John time to do the writing God wanted him to do. Someday, I would like to talk to John and ask him whether he realized that it was a good thing from the start. If it had been me, I'm afraid I would have thought the devil was getting his own way with my life. Just think how scary it would be to get thrown into a pot of hot oil.

Amazingly, from that island prison, John wrote the book of Revelation. God gave him vision after vision. Once he settled in, he must have realized he finally had peace and freedom to do what God asked him to do. Then he wrote these words to his family and friends back home. "I John, who also am your brother, and companion in tribulation, and in the kingdom and patience of Jesus Christ, was on the isle that is called Patmos, for the word of God, and for the testimony of Jesus Christ" (Rev. 1:9).

Yes, John knew why he was there. But before John realized what God was doing, his life must have looked very bleak and frightening. I'm sure Satan told him he was a failure in life and tried to get him to believe that God was mistreating him and that he had failed God miserably. What lies they were! John was no failure. We are so blessed because of John's willingness to do what God asked him to do. He joined that throng of great men who stood up for their Lord, and their example is a witness of what God will do for all who love Him.

John never stopped loving and honoring God. God revealed deep things to him about future world events. Yes, the very history we are watching unfold right now in our day. God placed John on that island so he could testify about God's Son Jesus. The book of Revelation was written to reveal Jesus Christ. Just look at how John began that book of the Bible! "The Revelation of Jesus Christ, which God gave unto him, to shew unto His servants things which must shortly come to pass; and He sent and signified it by His angel unto His servant John: Who bare record of the word of God, and of the testimony of Jesus Christ, and of all things that he saw" (Rev. 1:1–2).

By the time you get to chapter eleven in the book of Revelation, John shares these astounding words—words Satan wishes he could obliterate. "Then the temple of God was opened in heaven, and there was seen in His temple the ark of his testament" (Rev. 11:19). The message in this chapter paints afresh the unchanging character of God. This verse is part of a prophecy, but what I want you to notice is what John saw. God only allowed him to see one small area of His holy temple. Can you image that! Through a vision John was actually looking straight into the holy temple of God in heaven. It's as if God gave him tunnel vision! God had things on His heart He wanted John to share with us.

God knew the people of our day would need confirmation that God's law really does still reside in His heavenly temple. His law is still binding, and He still lives and rules with the same set of rules as He has always had. That His law has not been changed! That He has not done away with it! That He really does expect us to obey it! God wanted to affirm that He still extends mercy to those who disobey Him and fall into sin. Let's look at that vision! John saw a very special piece of furniture called *"the ark of His testament"* (Rev. 11:19). This ark is both a resting place for God's law and a platform for His throne. Yes! The ark of His testament is what holds God's Ten Commandments, and the ark of His testament is covered with the mercy seat. This platform is where God's throne rests. God's throne and His law are inseparable. His throne is called the mercy seat, and that seat still sits on the ark of His testament. Inside that ark is God's law of love—the Ten Commandments.

When God told the children of Israel how to make a sanctuary on earth, He told them He wanted them to make it just like the one in heaven. Let's look at some of the texts about it again. As you read these verses, take in its beauty. God said, "Let them make Me a sanctuary; that I may dwell among them" (Exod. 25:8). What love He had that He wanted and still wants to dwell among rebellious people. "According to all that I shew thee, after the pattern of the tabernacle, and the pattern of all the instruments thereof, even so shall ye make it" (Exod. 25:9).

> *God knew the people of our day would need confirmation that God's law really does still reside in His heavenly temple. His law is still binding.*

"And they shall make an ark of shittim wood: two cubits and a half shall be the length thereof, and a cubit and a half the breadth thereof, and a cubit and a half the height thereof. And thou shalt overlay it with pure gold, within and without shalt thou overlay it, and shalt make upon it a crown of gold round about. And thou shalt cast four rings of gold for it, and put them in the four corners thereof; and two rings shall be in the one side of it, and two rings in the other side of it. And thou shalt make staves of shittim wood, and overlay them with gold. And thou shalt put the staves into the rings by the sides of the ark, that the ark may be borne with them. The staves shall be in the rings of the ark: they shall not be taken from it. And thou shalt put into the ark the testimony which I shall give thee. And thou shalt make a mercy seat of pure gold: two cubits and a half shall be the length thereof, and a cubit and a half the breadth thereof. And thou shalt make two cherubim of gold, of beaten work shalt thou make them, in the two ends of the mercy seat. And make one cherub on the one end, and the other cherub on the other end: even of the mercy seat shall ye make the cherubims on the two ends thereof. And the cherubims shall stretch forth their wings on high, covering the mercy seat with their wings, and their faces shall look one to another; toward the mercy seat shall the faces of the cherubims be. And thou shalt put the mercy seat above upon the ark; and in the ark thou shalt put the testimony that I shall give thee. <u>And there I will meet with thee, and I will commune with thee</u> from above the mercy seat, from between the two cherubims which are upon the ark of the testimony, of all things which I will give thee in commandment unto the children of Israel" (Exod. 25:22, emphasis supplied).

What precious meetings these must have been for Moses while they were in the wilderness. It gave him a visual picture of just how it was in heaven. And how precious it is still today. We can meet with God through the Holy Spirit as we talk with Him in prayer. Yes, God still meets with His people today when they kneel before Him and choose to talk with Him. Right now! Jesus is at that throne of mercy, waiting for us to come to Him in prayer as His child. "Now of the things which we have spoken this is the sum: We have such an high Priest, who is set on the right hand of the throne of the majesty in the heavens; A minister of the sanctuary, and of the true tabernacle, *which the Lord pitched, and not man*" (Heb. 8:1–2, italics supplied).

The tabernacle on earth was only a copy of the true tabernacle which resides in heaven itself. "It was therefore necessary that the patterns of things in the heavens should be purified with these; but the heavenly things themselves with better sacrifices than these. For Christ is not entered into the holy places made with hands, which are the figures of the true; but into heaven itself, now to appear in the presence of God for us" (Heb. 9:23–24).

That's right! This is where Jesus is right now. God wanted John to know the ark that houses His ten-commandment law is still in His heavenly temple. That everything is the same as it has always been from eternity. What a gift this was for John! He was going through horrendous hardships. God knew John needed this affirmation. He knew we would need it too, in the last days of earth's history, when men would say his fourth commandment law had been nailed to the cross.

This vision is not only important because it reveals that God's law of love has existed from eternity—but also, that it still exists in heaven today. That is why God had John write the book of Revelation. It was to reveal what Jesus is doing for us right now—this very day. Yes! He is in that heavenly temple at this very moment. He is going over the books and getting the evidence ready for that last day in court. It is then that He will judge everyone on earth *"by the law of liberty"*—God's ten-commandment law.

Some say that the existence of God's ten-commandment law began at Sinai! But this shows that His law is, and was, in heaven before God gave it to the Israelites at Sinai. It has *always* been in existence. God has always been a God of love. This also proves that God rules the whole universe with the same laws as He rules heaven. Yes! John verifies that God's ten-commandment law will still be in effect when God presides over that final judgment. Remember—God says to us just as Jesus did, "I change not." (Mal. 3:6). "One jot or one title shall in no wise pass from the law, till all be fulfilled" (Matt. 5:18).

James makes sure we know what law we will be judged by at the end of time, and it doesn't take a rocket scientist to figure out this judgment is still in the future. This proves that the fourth commandment will still be in existence when that final judgment takes place. Listen to James' description of it. "If ye fulfill the royal law according to the scripture, Thou shalt love thy neighbour as thyself, ye do well: But if ye have respect to persons, ye commit sin, and are convinced of the law as transgressors. For whosoever shall keep the whole law, and yet offend in one point, he is guilty of all. For he that said, Do not commit adultery, said also, Do not kill. Now if thou commit no adultery, yet if thou kill, thou art become a transgressor of the law. So speak ye, and so do, as they that shall be judged by the law of liberty" (James 2:8–12). That's right! If a person only breaks one commandment, they have broken God's law.

Finally, in Revelation, Jesus told John to write this. That means if we only nail one of His commandments to the cross and do not do what it asks us to do, we have disobeyed God's law, and are guilty of disobeying the whole law. That's extremely serious! "And I saw a great white throne, and him that sat on it, from whose face the earth and the heaven fled away; and there was found no place for them. And I saw the dead, small and great, stand before God; and the books were opened: and another book was opened, which is the book of life: and the dead were judged out of those things which were written in the books, according to their works. And the sea gave up the dead which were in it; And death and hell" (the grave) "delivered up the dead which were in them: and they were judged every man according to their works. And death and hell were cast into the lake of fire. This is the second death. *And whosoever was not found written in the book of life* was cast into the lake of fire" (Rev. 20:11–15, italics supplied).

Yes, our faith always will bear the fruit of good works. True faith never fails to produce good behavior in harmony with God's ten commandments. We must trust God, and then we will surely obey God. Our works show God whether or not we love Him. It's important to tell God we love Him. The dead people these verses are talking about are all of the wicked who died before Jesus' second coming, plus those who were destroyed "With the brightness of his coming" (2 Thess. 2:8). These verses are talking about those who will receive the punishment of the second death. It will take place after the righteous have been in heaven for a thousand years. These people who die the second death are those who will not tell

God they love or trust Him by obeying all of His commandments. They the ones who will be destroyed at the brightness of Jesus coming when He comes to earth the second time.

Remember! God's law is a perfect reflection of His character. His rules tell us how to love Him and how to love our fellowmen! That is why His throne is called the mercy seat. It is where our great High Priest, Jesus Christ, sits next to His Father. The Father is waiting there for us to come to Him in prayer. He graciously takes time to listen to all of our joys and sorrows when no one else will. He wants us to confide in Him. Yes, when no one else will even speak to us, God listens and sends the Holy Spirit to guide and comfort us. That is if we ask Him to send the Spirit. The Holy Spirit won't scold or make light of what we think or say; neither will He try to force us to obey. How comforting that is!

We are extremely valuable in God's sight. He wants to save us. Remember! He won't let anything happen to us that we can't bear if we trust Him and believe that He will make it possible for us to bear it through His way of escape. It is the devil who tempts us to believe God doesn't care. God says, "There hath no temptation taken you but such as is common to man: but God is faithful, who will not suffer you to be tempted above that ye are able; but will with the temptation also make a way of escape, that ye may be able to bear it" (1 Cor. 10:13).

That knowledge comes to us both through the Holy Spirit, and through the knowledge we gain by reading our Bible. Yes, God is for us. That's why Paul says, "Let us therefore come boldly unto the throne of grace, that we may obtain mercy, and find grace to help in time of need" (Heb. 4:16). And he also says, "If God be for us, who can be against us? He that spared not His own Son, but delivered Him up for us all, how shall He not with Him also freely give us all things" (Rom. 8:31–32)?

None of us deserve that kind of love. But God still offers it to us because He loves us so much. God wants us to run boldly to Him and throw ourselves into His arms, and when we do, He promises to give us the special love He has—the kind of love that is just for sinners. Only sinners need grace. We need grace because we have sinned. God pours grace on us by forgiving us. Love is not something that can be expected or required. True love comes from the heart. Love begets love! God says that *"We love Him, because He first loved us."* (1 John 4:19) Isn't that wonderful? We love Him because we know He loves us. God loves everyone. He is just waiting for us to come to Him. His arms are open wide. But we must stop trusting the devil's lies and forsake him.

Those who do not sin do not need grace. There are holy beings on unfallen worlds who do not need grace. They have already passed the test of faith and trust. Grace is a manifestation of God's love for His children who have disobeyed Him. The beings on those other worlds stayed faithful to Him, so don't need the grace of forgiveness. Our world is *not* the only world God made. We know this because Paul wrote these words; saying, "God, who at sundry times and in divers manners spake in time past unto the fathers by the prophets, hath in these last days spoken to us by His Son, whom He hath appointed heir of all things, by whom also He made the *worlds*" (Heb. 1:1–2, italics supplied).

Grace is that special deep love God showers on those who love themselves more than they love Him. Sinners! That's us! I am so glad we serve a God who is love—a God who loves sinners! Grace offers a second chance to sinners. That second chance is right now—not way off in the future. God's offer of a second chance began the day Eve sinned. We must believe what God says we are to do to be saved. We must give our hearts totally to Him, confess our sins, and ask Him to forgive us for sinning against Him. Yes, sin is always against God. God's grace is not in some distant future—at a set time. It is available every day of our lives. But! Tomorrow could be too late! We could get killed in an accident, so tomorrow would never get here for us. You can't come to Jesus when you are dead. The first lie Satan told Eve was that she wouldn't die if she ate the fruit from the tree of the knowledge of good and evil. And it is still a lie today. (Gen. 3:4). No! That tree is not here. But the Ten Commandments are here. Just knowing that we will be judged by the whole law of God at the end of time, tells us that the fourth commandment is still binding and in existence.

The persecution John received for loving God was ferocious. But he did his part. So God gave John love pats to share with us. People cannot understand what someone else is going through until they have faced the same type of trial themselves. Even then, we can't really know another's pain. Each person's experience is his own. But when we face those same kinds of trials, we can understand in a small way what they felt. Then we can empathize with them. Jesus did that! He went through the same trials we must go through. He walked our walk and has shared in our trials.

With our hand in His, we, too, can walk that walk. We can know the Father, Son, and Holy Spirit are with us even in our darkest hours. Oh yes, the devil will be whispering doubts in our ears. But I choose to believe God. My Bible tells me how much They care. We can believe God's love without a doubt. God really does care. It is so comforting that God gives us this picture, confirming what Jesus is doing right now. I am so glad Jesus is our Great High Priest. The Bible says, "For we have not a high priest which cannot be touched with the feeling of our infirmities; but was in all points tempted like as we are, yet without sin" (Heb. 4:15).

Many people have been told and are still being told that the Ten Commandments are no longer binding. Many claim that when Jesus died on the cross, those old laws were done away with. Therefore, according to them, we don't need to keep that old rule of love anymore. That doesn't make sense. Why in the world would God ever say we didn't need to love Him anymore? When you hear such a lie, you need to put your hands over your ears, go to God in prayer, and find the answer in your Bible. You also need to pray for the

> *People cannot understand what someone else is going through until they have faced the same type of trial themselves. Even then, we can't really know another's pain.*

person who said that to you. For they have been deceived by our common enemy, the devil. All of us have lied many times. No one is exempt. That's because all of us are daily deceived by the devil. Not one of us should be hard on another person for lying.

All of us have lied because we have been deceived by our enemy. Let the Bible answer your questions. Because that's God talking! It's God's enemy, the devil, deceiving you and saying those untrue things, chewing at the ears of God's people. It makes God sad because He loves all of us. He hurts when He sees even one person being deceived by Satan. Every last one of us falls into that trap—actually, we fall into it often. God says to us, *"If you love Me, keep My commandments"* (John 14:15, NKJV, italics supplied). Do you love Him?

Remember, Jesus, our High Priest, is still the same as He always was. Praise God! And His Father is still the same too. He doesn't ask us to go by one set of rules while He and all the heavenly beings are using a different set. Isn't it wonderful that God showed John this truth about His love, so that this very day, we can be assured that those same laws really do still reside in His heavenly temple? And that God still rules with the same laws that have come down to us from antiquity.

They are the most wonderful laws ever to be written, and they were written by the finger of God. Imagine that! God did not trust someone else to write such an important document—a document that contains the rules which guide us through life—the life here and now—and our future life too. Those commands tell us how to shun evil. I'm so glad God wrote it with His own hand, and that He told us He did. Knowing this should give us solid trust in His Word. "And the tables were the work of God, and the writing was the writing of God, graven upon the tables" (Exod. 31:18).

As we continue to look at God's love for us, we will see many more views of the beautiful picture of His great love. As God weaves the intricate pattern of His love, His Word will contain the truth for us. His Word, the Bible, is the only safe guide for us to follow. Everything we are told and everything we read must be tested by God's Word. If it does not agree with the Bible, it is untrue. It is a lie of the devil. For God says, "To the law and to the testimony: if they speak not according to this word, it is because there is no light in them" (Isa. 8:20).

Absolutely none! Through the pages of His Word, He will continue to give us an even closer look at His love for us. Yes, for us in our day! And yes! God wants us to obey His whole law today. Not even one word has been deleted from it. See you in the next chapter. It, too, is about God's holy day—the Sabbath.

CHAPTER SIX

The First Sabbath on Earth

———◆•◆———

The Bible begins with God telling us how He created our world and everything in it. He carefully tells us that He created it in six days. God was very explicit. Notice! He had already provided a formless, dark, empty mass with water on it before He began perfecting it to be our home. He called it "Earth." "In the beginning God created the heaven and the earth. And the earth was without form, and void; and darkness was upon the face of the deep" (Gen. 1:1).

Isn't it interesting that the first holy Being mentioned in the Bible by name is the Holy Spirit? He played an active role in creating our world and us. The word *"God"* in this verse is in the plural tense. It includes all three of the holy Beings who are our One God. They are one in three and three in one. We cannot penetrate this mystery of the Godhead. But we can accept it by faith because it is revealed to us. From a human standpoint, we cannot explain the unexplainable. But we can enjoy the triune God by faith. We all appreciate gravity. Without it, life would cease to exist. But the brightest minds cannot explain it. The Hebrew word for God, according to Strong's Concordance, is *'Elohim.'* It is #430 in the

Hebrew Dictionary at the back of the book. Here is the definition it gives: "God (plural of majesty: plural in form but singular in meaning, with a focus on great power."

Even when the words *"Spirit of God"* are used, the plural form of the word *"God"* is used. As One, They created our world. All three were present, and each one was doing His respective job. *"And the Spirit of God moved upon the face of the waters"* (Gen.1:2). According to the Strongest Strong's Concordance of the Bible, the words "without form" indicates "empty space," #8414. The word "void" also means "emptiness, desolation; and is associated with chaos." Thus, "emptiness #922" and void are "a state of total chaos and emptiness." And Strong's Concordance says "deep" means "the sea or ocean," "the deep, depths, with the associative meanings of darkness and secrecy." Webster's New World College Dictionary, Fourth Ed., also gives many meanings of the word "deep," "the sea or ocean," one of which is "a deep place or any of the deepest parts, as in water or earth." I find it interesting that depth refers to all three—water, earth, and space.

Yes! It was dark. There was no light at all. This was the condition of the mass before God began perfecting it for us to live on. The darkness was already present before He began changing it into a livable place. Then God made light. Notice also that God spoke the light into existence. He said, *"Let there be light: and there was light"* (Gen. 1:3). I believe it is very important that we take note that the first day of creation began before God created light. He also created the heaven to surround the earth. Then, after all of that was done, *"God divided the light from the darkness. And God called the light Day, and the darkness He called Night. And the evening and the morning were the first day"* (Gen. 1:4–5) Did you notice that God mentioned the word "evening" first. He called the dark part of the day evening. This information is very important, as you will see. Yes, creation began with the original darkness that was upon the face of the deep. It was as if the sun had just sunk below the horizon of the earth. Thus, this beginning darkness was part of the first day. The reason this is important is because it is that darkness that shows us when day begins, and also when it ends. Thus, it also shows us when the Sabbath, the seventh day, began and ended.

This was an extremely important thing God did on that first day. There was something else important about it. For it also marked out and set in motion the amount of time Jesus would need on the fourth day. That day would be a very special day too! For on that day, He would create His built-in time clock. Thus, He created each night and day to be twenty-four hours long—just the amount of time He would need when He made the sun, moon, and stars and placed them in their circuits. Yes, He planned to make those heavenly bodies on the fourth day of the week! Consequently, God had already chosen the timing of the fourth day. Everything was ready for Him to place His lights in the sky.

Those lights were not created just to separate the days from the nights. They were to have many functions. What is their function? God said "Let there be lights in the firmament of the heaven to divide the day from the night; Let them be for signs, and for seasons, and for days, and years: Let them be for lights in the firmament of the heaven to give light upon the earth: and it was so. And God made two great lights; the greater light to rule the day, and the lesser light to rule the night: He made the stars also" (Gen. 1:14–16).

Those heavenly bodies have always provided and will always continue to provide us with a correct clock and a matching calendar. God set them in motion purposely to provide days, nights, months, years, seasons, and times. And yes again, God allotted Himself one whole week for creating and celebrating the birth of the world we live in. He created everything He knew we would need for enjoying life to its fullest.

He also tells us how He created all of the living creatures—including us. I'm so glad God has shared our beginnings with us. On the sixth day of the week, the day we now call Friday, God finished creating us and our world. How do we know? He says so! First, He created the living creatures. Then He created Adam. "And the LORD God formed man of the dust of the ground" (Gen. 2:7). "And out of the ground the LORD God formed every beast of the field, and every fowl of the air; and brought them unto

Adam to see what he would call them" (Gen. 2:19). Then, Jesus did surgery on Adam and took out one of his ribs. "And the Lord God caused a deep sleep to fall upon Adam, and he slept: and he took one of his ribs, and closed up the flesh instead thereof" (Gen. 2:21). Then He created a wife for Adam. "And the rib, which the Lord God had taken from man, made He a woman, and brought her unto the man" (Gen. 2:22).

The writer of the Bible tells us Jesus was pleased with His work. "And God saw every thing that He had made, and, behold, it was very good. And the evening and the morning were the sixth day. Thus the heavens and the earth were finished, and all the host of them" (Gen. 1:31–2:1).

Notice what God did next! "And on the seventh day God ended His work which He had made; and He rested on the seventh day from all His work which He had made" (Gen. 2:2). That's right! On the very next day—the seventh and last day in the week, there was no more work to do. God had made everything He wanted to make. Then He did something very special. On the seventh and last day of the week, He was free to relax, rest, and enjoy the work of His hands. Yes, the very first week on earth was complete when that special day came to a close. He enjoyed it by spending time with the people and other creatures He had formed. They relaxed together and enjoyed each other's company.

Notice God had already become acquainted with them the day before when He created them. He had given them His glory and blessed them. They were like Him. Now, He would show them around and tell them how they and their world came into existence. Then they would know that He was the One who had made them. They would know that He loved them and that they could love and trust Him back. "So God created man in His own image, in the image of God created He him; male and female created He them" (Gen. 1:27).

Listen to the words God told Adam and Eve that sixth day we call Friday, as He explained the purpose of the seventh day of the week to them. He wanted them to know the seventh day of every week would remain special throughout eternity. A day when He could spend time with them—and enjoy each other's companionship. It is still the day God wants us to worship Him, and spend time alone with Him. He knew someday He would come and be one of us—His family and our Creator.

Yes, the seventh day of each week is still a day when we can have a special date with God. He did no creative work at all on that day. Now, week after week, He still saves that day so that we can have special time together with Him and with each other. So, what did God do that first Sabbath? All He had left to do were three things, and He tells us what they were. First of all, the Bible says, "God *blessed* the seventh day" (Gen. 2:3). And He "sanctified it" (Gen. 2:3). When something is sanctified, it is made holy. God alone is able to make something holy. Man cannot do that. Look how God puts it in Exodus 20:11. "For in six days the Lord made heaven and earth, the sea, and all that in them is, and rested the seventh day: wherefore the Lord blessed the sabbath day, and hallowed it" (*Exod. 20:11*). He made it holy.

> *The seventh day of each week is still a day when we can have a special date with God.*

Yes! His seventh-day Sabbath is a special day of rest. It comes at the end of every single week. It has remained at the end of every week ever since God created it. He always spends time with mankind if they will spend it with Him. It is the only day of the week He made holy. Yes, the choice to spend time with God is always up to us. He never tries to force us to keep that date with Him. One of the ways He placed a special blessing on that seventh day of the week was when He made it holy. It is the only day of the week that He says He blessed. That, in itself, makes it special and unique. And He makes sure we know it is a holy day—and that He is the one who made it holy.

He also makes sure we know that we are to rest from our work every Sabbath. Why? Because rest and sanctity go together. When we rest on it, we honor its holiness, and we, too, set it aside for a holy use. God says, "*Six days may work be done; but the seventh is the sabbath of rest*"

(Exod. 31:15). The very meaning of the word "Sabbath" is "rest." It doesn't matter who or what is resting. When a field is not planted, it enjoys a sabbath. In other words, it enjoys a rest. Everything needs rest, and God has made provision for that needed rest. "Six years thou shalt sow thy field, and six years thou shalt prune thy vineyard, and gather in the fruit thereof; But in the seventh year shall be a sabbath of rest unto the land, a sabbath for the Lord: thou shalt neither sow thy field, nor prune thy vineyard. That which groweth of its own accord of thy harvest thou shalt not reap, neither gather the grapes of thy vineyard undressed: for it is a year of rest unto the land" (Lev. 25:3–5).

The next thing God did on the holy Sabbath day was place another special blessing on it. How did He bless it? He placed His blessing on it when He *"sanctified it"* (Gen. 2:3). Blessing the Sabbath and sanctifying it go hand in hand. Why did God sanctify it? *"Because that in it he had rested from all his work which God created and made"* (Gen. 2:3). But! How does one sanctify something? Since God says He sanctified the seventh day of the week, it seems like we need to know what that word means. The Bible tells us that sanctifying something is a very special act. God also sanctifies people and things. It simply means someone or something has been set apart as special, to be used for a special holy purpose.

Are you aware of what God just did when He asked Adam and Eve to rest with Him on His holy day? He performed His first show and tell. Instead of just telling them He wanted them to rest on that day—He rested with them. By resting on that first Sabbath, He showed all of us down through the ages how to keep that day holy. God made it holy because He wants it to be a special day. It is a day He wants us to keep holy with Him—now and throughout eternity. It brings a smile to my face when I think about God resting on and enjoying the Sabbath at the same time I am. The very first week was complete when that first Sabbath day came to a close. God is always resting on it when we are. But that's not all that is important about that first Sabbath. He showed us how we could honor Him.

When we rest on His special day, we are honoring Him. He gave Adam and Eve, and every person born thereafter, an example of how important the Sabbath was, and still is to Him. Yes, still, today, He wants us to honor Him by resting from our work just as He rested from His. This will become very clear as we trace the Sabbath throughout history. Resting on that day was an act of love from God to His people, and it is an act of love from us to Him when we keep it holy with Him as He has told us to do. When you love someone, you want to spend time with them. God spent time with Adam and Eve, and they spent time with Jesus—the One who actually formed them from the dust of the earth. That's what God wants us to do every Sabbath. He wants us to spend time with Him.

There is only one Sabbath each week, and He tells us which day of the week is the Sabbath. God echoes the words of Genesis 2:3 in His Sabbath command. He told them and He still tells us which day of the week was and still is His holy Sabbath day. His act of resting on it was also part of His blessing of it. In His fourth commandment, He tells us whose day it is. Whose day does He say the Sabbath is? He says, "the seventh day is the Sabbath of the LORD thy God:" (Exod. 20:10).

The seventh day of every week is the Lord's rest day—His Sabbath. He is the one who placed a special blessing on it. He is the one who made it holy. *No one* can make any day holy, and neither can anyone remove the solemnity which God placed on the seventh day of the week. It is the only day of the week God made holy. Also, it is the only day of the week which is a commandment in God's holy law. That's right! The command to keep the seventh day of the week holy is the fourth command in His law—the Ten Commandments.

Nowhere in the Bible does God ever say He removed His blessing, or the holiness of His special holy day. Not only did God place a blessing on the seventh day of the week but He blesses the people who honor Him by keeping it holy. The seventh-day Sabbath will always be holy and blessed by God. Remember, Malachi a prophet of God says that God never changes. Why doesn't God change? He doesn't change His mind or His law because "the law of the Lord is perfect" (Ps. 19:7). One only needs to change something if they haven't done a perfect job of creating it. One can't improve something that is already perfect. If it's perfect, to change it would mar it. "As for God, his way is perfect; the word of the Lord is tried: he is a buckler to them that trust in him" (2 Sam. 22:31).

What message do we send God and other people when we do what God asks us to do and go to church on the day He set aside for us to go to church on? We tell them we believe that what He tells us to do is very important. Yes, we believe He really does set it aside for us to rest on with Him. We say we really do believe He wants us to use it for that holy purpose. This affirmation is very important to God. He wants all of us to be saved. And when we keep the Sabbath holy, we show we accept Him as our Lord and Master. Our God! And that we want to witness for Him.

There is nothing more important than telling someone God loves them. He wants us to tell them this by the way we live and by whatever way He chooses for us to do it. Yes, it's as simple as that! God isn't a hard taskmaster! He makes things very easy to do and understand. What a wonderful, loving God He is. He just wants us to love Him. Listen to what He told the children of Israel. When we obey Him it verifies that we believe He has set us aside for a holy purpose too. He is the one who sets us apart. He is the one who makes us holy. He is also the one who sanctifies us. Listen to God's words to the children of Israel many years later. *"Verily my sabbaths ye shall keep: for it is a sign between me and you throughout your generations; that ye may know that I am the Lord that doth sanctify you"* (Exod. 31:13).

He is saying, I am the one who sanctifies you. I am the one who makes you holy. I am the one who gives you special ways to serve Me. *"Ye shall keep the Sabbath therefore; for it is holy unto you"* (Exod. 31:14). Yes, God sanctifies us, and He makes us holy. He says keeping the seventh-day Sabbath holy is a sign that we know He is the one who "sanctifies" us, and that He is the one who makes us holy. So every time I go to church on His day, I am telling Him that I believe Him and trust Him. Listen to these verses as God talks to Ezekiel about how He saved Israel, and that then they turned away from Him. It was just like it is in our day. His words are still good for us today. You see, God grieves for us just as He did for those people back in Ezekiel's day.

Here is what God did for His people when they were in the wilderness. These verses are almost an exact quote from what God told the children of Israel in the book of Exodus. God was grieving because the ones He gave these words to back then, still needed to repent and turn to Him. They had gone back into idol worship. He was calling them back to worshipping Him. He said, *"Moreover also I gave them my sabbaths, to be a sign between me and them, that they might know that I am the Lord that sanctify them"* (Ezek. 20:12)

He leaves no doubt in anyone's mind as to who it is that sanctifies us. God wants us to know that He is the One who sanctifies us. God wants to sanctify us. In fact, He is eager to sanctify us. Yes, we, who are living right now. He wants to set us apart for a holy use just as He did those people back then. He gives us a chance to be His child. He says to us, as He said to them, *"Walk ye not in the statutes of your fathers, neither observe their judgments, nor defile yourselves with their idols: I am the Lord your God; walk in my statutes, and keep my judgments, and do them; And hallow my sabbaths; and they shall be a sign between me and you, that ye may know that I am the Lord your God"* (Ezek. 20:18–20).

Yes, keeping the seventh day of the week holy is a sign to God and to everyone that we know He is our Lord. We must place our trust in what God says—not in what any human beings say. Why? We humans make mistakes. And we will continue to make mistakes until almost the very day Jesus comes to take us home with Him. A very few days, or weeks before He comes, our fate will be sealed, as we all know! The day of Jesus' coming is approaching very quickly. Most of us are all looking forward to it. Here are some of the ways we learn God's will and are sanctified: Jesus prayed to His Father, saying, *"Sanctify them through thy truth: thy word is truth" (John 17:17)*. And God uses other words to ask us to sanctify ourselves, like "set" ourselves apart so He can use us. *"I am the Lord your God: ye shall therefore sanctify yourselves, and ye shall be holy; for I am holy"* (Lev. 11:44).

How do we sanctify ourselves? We sanctify ourselves when we choose to belong to God and worship Him on His holy day. The seventh day of the week received His divine favor. *Strong's Concordance Dictionary* says "holy" means to "set apart as dedicated to God." The reason we should keep it holy is because it is holy. It was God who made it holy. No one can change the holiness of the seventh day of the week. Man cannot undo what God has done. God will never change it.

Paul told King Agrippa about his conversion and witnessed to him concerning what Jesus had said to him. Here are Jesus' words to Paul, *"But rise, and stand upon thy feet: for I have appeared unto thee for this purpose" (Acts 26:16)*. Then, Jesus told Paul what He wanted him to do: *"To open their eyes, and to turn them from darkness to light, and from the power of Satan unto God, that they may receive forgiveness of sins, and inheritance among them which are sanctified by faith that is in me"* (Acts 26:18). We, too, receive forgiveness of sins by having faith in God. It is also Paul who tells us that God made him a minister so *"that the offering up of the Gentiles might be acceptable, being sanctified by the Holy Ghost." (Rom. 15:16)*

All of us who are not Jewish are Gentiles by natural birth. What is it that makes us acceptable? We become acceptable as we listen to and obey the instructions of the Holy Ghost. We are Jews only by adoption and new birth. God says to us, as He said to them, that He wants us to sanctify the Sabbath by keeping it holy. How about that! When we Gentiles keep the Sabbath holy, we sanctify it by setting it apart so we can keep it holy, and we are sanctified. How? We choose to come apart to be used by God. He says, *"Keep the sabbath day to sanctify it, as the LORD thy God hath commanded thee" (Deut. 5:12)*.

Since no one can remove the sanctity of the seventh day of the week, and since only God can remove its blessing, holiness, and sanctity, wouldn't you say, when someone tells us to do something different other than what the Bible says, we should continue to obey God. In fact, that is what God tells us we should do through the words of Peter. God says, *"We ought to obey God rather than men" (Acts 5:29)*.

We serve a just God. He doesn't suddenly form a law after we have done something wrong, and then accuse us of disobeying it. God is upfront. He made His rules known to Adam and Eve way before they were tempted by Satan and before Satan tried to get them to distrust God. Our God does not expect the impossible. His rules are **not** made so He can punish us when we displease Him. They are rules that show us how we can be safe. They show us how much He loves us and how we can love Him back.

They are rules of love for another reason. God's rules give us freedom of choice. God did not tell Adam and Eve they had to obey His rules. God's rules always give us freedom of choice. He never tries to force anyone to love Him. Why? Because, if force is involved, there is no love. Why is there no love when force is used? It is because force destroys love. God cannot force us to obey Him and still be a God of love. But! He has done everything He can to show us He really does love us. It was an act of love on God's part that first seventh day when He showed Adam and Eve how to love Him through keeping His day holy. Timothy tells us, *"Study to shew thyself approved unto God, a workman that needeth not to be ashamed, rightly dividing the word of truth" (2 Tim. 2:15)*. He also says, *"The Lord knoweth them that are his. And, let every one that nameth the name of Christ depart from iniquity" (2 Tim. 2:19)*. Then he gives this encouragement: *"If a man therefore purge himself from these, he shall be a vessel unto honor, sanctified, and meet for the master's use, and prepared unto every good work" (2 Tim. 2:21)*.

> *He doesn't suddenly form a law after we have done something wrong, and then accuse us of disobeying it.*

All Christians want God to be the Lord of their life. They want to obey Him because they love Him. He is a wonderful, caring God. Our instruction book is the Bible. We should be asking God, "Help us to study it more, so we can give our hearts totally to You." Every time we read the Bible, we learn more new ways to tell God how much we love Him. God leads us gently. Yes, every last one of us is led by God—if we want to be. I'm so glad!

Don't you think we should do what God says? And let Him know how very much we love Him!

Our loving obedience to Him scares Satan. Then he gets busier than ever. If Satan were smart, he would be running really scared right now! He should almost feel the fire, but he won't let himself believe the truth—that his death will be very soon. Praise God! Satan's death cannot come too soon! It won't be long until he will no longer be causing people to believe his lies. Soon, God's people will no longer have to go through undeserved harassment. Our last days on earth won't be pretty! But God will see us through them. Thank You, Lord, for all You have done, are still doing, and will do in the future for us.

CHAPTER SEVEN

God's Official Seal

———•••———

Every legal document has an official seal or mark placed on it. The presence of that seal is what assures us that the document is legal. The seal confirms that the law the seal is attached to was written by someone who had the authority to write it. The seal also verifies that the document is in conformity with the laws of the government from which it was issued. This solidifies the fact that it can be enforced by the court of law in that particular place. The Ten Commandments are the laws of God's government. Since God is the Creator of everything, His seal covers heaven, earth, the sea, and every creature in them. The Sabbath command is a covenant agreement. It is the official seal of God's law. Let's look at it.

A. An official seal always contains the name of the officer in command—it's ruler. In this case it is "the LORD thy God." *(Exod. 20:2)*

In the United States, the officer in command is our president. He, or she, is the commander-in-chief. They have the authority to rule our nation through override, or whatever is necessary, during special times. B. An official seal also contains the occupation, or title, of the one in command; in this case, "Creator" is the occupation of our God. "The Lord made heaven and earth" *(Exod. 20:11)*. He created them. The title for our president is "commander-in-chief." He heads our nation. C. The last identifying mark of an official seal is the name of the territory or area he or she rules. God's territory is vast. Our earth is only a small speck in comparison to it. For God rules, "heaven and earth, the sea, and all that in them is." *(Exod. 20:11)* He is the Creator of everything. All are under His rule—people, angels, animals, birds, fish, crawly things, insects—all living flesh. Whereas, our president's jurisdiction is only the United States of America.

God's seal of His authority is nestled right in the center of His law. It is in His fourth commandment. That command tells us who our Ruler is; also it gives us His occupation, and thirdly, it tells us the boundaries of His territory. He rules everything—there are no boundaries to God's rule.

The Ten Commandments are the laws of God's domain. I find it very comforting that He rules everything and every creature with His ten laws that describe what love is. It tells me that God is faithful, and it shows me that He intends to keep His promises. He promises to always be a loving Ruler. He doesn't say one thing and do another. He always keeps His promises! And He always will! His law, or seal, tells me I can trust Him with my life here and know that His promise of salvation is sure. All I have to do is keep my part of the covenant.

God's law should be central in our lives just as His seal is central in His law. Why is it the fourth commandment in His law that houses His official seal? It is because the fourth command declares His name, His occupation, and the territory He rules. He is the Lord our God. He created us. He rules the whole universe with His loving commands. Why would anyone want to do away with them? I hate to think of what the world would be like without those laws of love. It's bad enough as it is! I'll be so glad when the battle is over! It won't be long!

When every man, woman, and child has made their decision to either accept or reject God as the ruler of their life, the battle will be over. Then God will say, "He that is unjust, let him be unjust still: and he which is filthy, let him be filthy still: and he that is righteous, let him be righteous still: and he that is holy, let him be holy still. And, behold, I come quickly; and my reward is with me, to give every man according as his work shall be" (Rev. 22:11–12).

It is looking more like the days of the flood and Sodom every day. We can certainly see right now that the devil is doing what God said he would do. Just look at the loving counsel God gives us. He says, "God resisteth the proud, and giveth grace to the humble. Humble yourselves therefore under the mighty hand of God, that he may exalt you in due time: Casting all your care upon him; for he careth for you. Be sober, be vigilant; because your adversary the devil, as a roaring lion, walketh about, seeking whom he may devour: whom resist stedfast in the faith, knowing that the same afflictions are accomplished in your brethren that are in the world" (1 Peter 5:5–9).

Did you notice what Peter said about those who are not obeying God? We all suffer from the same afflictions. God allows affliction to come on all of us. Sometimes I think we tend to think the wicked don't suffer—but this verse says they do. Satan isn't choosy about who he afflicts. What a taskmaster! Imagine that! He even sends affliction on those who are doing what he wants them to do. Wouldn't you think that would cause those who honor him to get upset and turn to God? I would! But, as we see, usually the opposite happens. Now that's hard to understand. But it tells me that no matter who I choose for the master of my life, I will be afflicted. At least those who love God will go to heaven in the end. I can't imagine why anyone would want to serve Satan and end up with double affliction. To me, heaven looks a lot better than hell. I'd rather serve someone who loves me, instead of someone who is trying to destroy my God and me.

Jesus told His disciples that the temple in Jerusalem would be destroyed. They thought surely it would take place at the end of the world, so they asked Jesus when that would happen, and what sign they should look for when those things began happening. He gave them a long list of signs, which will tell us how to know when His coming is almost ready to take place. Then He so graciously assured them, "When these things come to pass, then look up, and lift up your heads; for your redemption draweth nigh" (Luke 21:28).

It bears repeating, that God's law is so important He wrote it Himself. He didn't want anybody to be able to claim some scribe made a mistake when they wrote His law down for Him. Or that the law had been tampered with. God did not want anyone to tamper with His seal. God wrote His law on two tablets of stone, signifying that it is perpetual and tamper-proof. Stone lasts forever. He wrote it Himself—so everyone could be sure it is still the same in our day, as it was the day He wrote it. Look it up for yourself. It's in Exodus 31:18.

CHAPTER EIGHT

No Other Gods

———•••———

I believe now is a good time to take a closer look at God's commandments. Remember, it was James who called the Ten Commandment law by the title "the royal law" (James 2:8). We looked at it in chapter three. And he was the one who said, even if you only break one command, you are guilty of breaking all of them. The royal law, as we saw in chapter three, is God's ten-commandment law. So let's take a good look at God's first commandment. It says,

1. "Thou shalt have no other gods *before Me*" (Exod. 20:3 italics supplied). When God spoke this command, He was telling everyone who would listen not to put anyone, or anything first, ahead of, or in place of Him.

"God saw that the wickedness of man was great in the earth, and that every imagination of the thoughts of his heart was only evil continually" (Gen. 6:5). But just notice how God showered His love on them, even though they were so very, very evil. He told Noah to preach to those wicked people for 120 years. God gave them a huge second chance. Truly, our days on this earth are our second chance too.

Grace offers the person who is sinning time to repent and time to learn to love God. Yes, time to figure out what this life is all about.

That chance comes to us only because God is totally gracious and fair to everyone. Grace is the special kind of love God has just for sinners. He gave those sinful people mega-time to repent, and He has done that for each succeeding generation since then. Sinners are the only ones who need God's grace. Grace is love that is given to someone who has spurned God's love and disobeyed His law. Noah knew what God was doing! Yes, Noah knew God! He looked into God's eyes, and what does the Bible say he saw? "Noah found grace in the eyes of the Lord." (Gen. 6:8). That's right! Noah saw love in God's eyes. Noah knew God could not stand to allow man to be doomed to die without giving him a chance to repent. Noah knew God's grace would provide a way for everyone to be saved. That is if they wanted to be saved. Noah knew God well enough that he knew God could not stand to be unfair. Noah had this knowledge because he had built up a trust relationship with God. He found God to be trustworthy, and he knew God would continue to be that way. Noah trusted God! That's why he loved Him.

Grace offers the person who is sinning time to repent and time to learn to love God.

If we haven't sinned, we don't need a grace period—a time in which we can learn to understand the difference between loving God and sinning against Him. God doesn't destroy us, on the spot, even when we continue to cherish our own selfish desires. That's grace! He gives us time to contemplate and change our minds. Then He allows us to come and ask Him for forgiveness.

Why does God give every one of us this kind of time? Because He loves us. What a God—that He would give the likes of any sinner a chance to repent. But that's just who God is! And, of course, every last one of us is a sinner. That means we all need grace. A time to contemplate the sin we have committed and make a firm choice to either repent or continue choosing to sin. In this world we all need to repent. That means we all need to choose whether we want to accept His amazing gift of forgiveness. That's an amazing offer. Each person in Noah's day made that choice. Only eight people accepted God's grace, His amazing, undeserved love. Yes! That is what grace is: Love that is undeserved.

Everyone on this planet needs God's grace. Noah needed it too! Every last one of us inherited a sinful nature from our first parents—Adam and Eve. They sinned! Then after the flood, God gave those eight people who weathered the storm a beautiful promise. And yes, God even gives that promise to each of us today. It is a huge promise! And it is an exceptional thread of His love.

Through that gift of grace, we, too, can look into God's eyes today and see that there is still grace in them. How do we access His grace? It takes place through reading our Bible, through the guidance of the Holy Spirit, and through prayer. We really can still find grace in God's eyes today! I'm so glad we can still see God's grace today.

All of this happened before God wrote His commandments down at Mount Sinai. Before that, on this planet, all of His commands were given to people orally. God gave them to Adam and Eve orally too. Those commands were in existence way before God ever wrote them in stone on that mountain in Sinai. That is why God provides grace. Since the law has been in existence forever, there has always been a need for grace. The need for grace comes when there is freedom to sin. If there's no law to obey, then there's no law to break. You can't break a law if there isn't one. But if there is a law, it can be broken. Breaking God's law is an act of sin, for the Bible says, "Sin is the transgression of the law" (1 John 3:4). It also says, "where no law is, there is no transgression." God continues by saying, "Therefore it is of faith, that it might be by grace" (Rom. 4:15–16).

Since God gives us choices, we are free to do things differently from what God wants us to do them. Even if God did not make the law known to us—there would still be sin, for God's law has always been in existence. The law is what defines what sin is. Sin is what causes us to need grace. If you are not sinning, you don't need a grace period that offers a person time to repent and turn away from sinning.

There would be no sin if there weren't a law because that's what sin is. It is called sin when we disobey God's law. Therefore, if there is no law that we can sin against—there is no sin. But we know there is sin. We know God does have a law, and when we disobey it, we know we are sinning. This special promise, saying no law/no sin that I am talking about, is something we see quite often. Seeing it gives us faith in God's grace. So, let's look at the very special promise God gave Noah and his family right after they came out of the ark. It was heartwarming for them, and it is still heartwarming for us today. It is also beautiful in a visual way. All of us enjoy it today whenever we see it. I bet you've already guessed what I am talking about. Yup! It's a gorgeous gift. It is His gift of the rainbow. God made it for every living creature. It perfectly mirrors the beauty of both His love and His law.

Our God is the Master Artist. He painted His special promise in the sky for Noah and all generations. It spans from creation clear down to when He comes in the clouds of heaven. He used the sky for His canvas. I consider the rainbow to be one of the most beautiful visual expressions of God's love in existence. Below is God's promise to all people on earth. It is a forever promise.

I realize we covered the following verses in chapter four, but let's just take a moment and place a magnifying glass over them. I am tremendously impressed that God took the time and effort to make sure we realize He has a word in the following verses that means this promise was made to every living creature. That word is **all**. And God used the word *all* when He told us all of the creatures He created come under the same loving care no matter what kind of creature they were. God loves them all. This tells us that the life God gives to each creature is very important to Him. Yes! Clear down to the angleworms and beyond. At least I think the words (every living creature of all flesh) would include angleworms. They have breath, and that breath came from God. And they are flesh.

Do you remember this verse? Jesus said, "Are not five sparrows sold for two farthings, and not one of them is forgotten before God?" (Luke 12:6). WOW! Now listen again as God Himself carefully mentions every type of creature He made, and He says they are all included in the promise He gave to us through the rainbow. "And God spake unto Noah, and to his sons with him, saying, And I, behold, I establish My covenant with you, and with your seed after you; and with every living creature that is with you, of the fowl, of the cattle, and of every beast of the earth with you; from all that go out of the ark, to every beast of the earth. And I will establish my covenant with you, neither shall all flesh be cut off any more by the waters of a flood: neither shall there any more be a flood to destroy the earth. And God said, This is the token of the covenant which I make between me and you and every living creature that is with you, for perpetual generations: I do set my bow in the cloud, and it shall be for a token of a covenant between me and the earth. And it shall come to pass, when I bring a cloud over the earth, that the bow shall be seen in the cloud: and I will remember my covenant, which is between me and you and every living creature of all flesh; and the waters shall no more become a flood to destroy all flesh. And the bow shall be in the cloud; and I will look upon it, that I may remember the everlasting covenant between God and every living creature upon the earth. And God said unto Noah, This is the token of the covenant, which I have established between me and all flesh that is upon the earth" (Gen. 9:8–17). Yes, God made this promise to all living creatures—not just mankind. His promise was to all the birds and animals too. God promised all of them that they would never be destroyed by such a massive flood ever again. That promise is made anew every time God creates a rainbow for us to see. I say, Thank You, Lord. It didn't take Satan long after the flood, to re-establish his control over the whole earth again. He incited a man named Nimrod to defy God. And Nimrod listened to Satan's lies. He decided that he could outsmart God. Nimrod's solution sounds just like what the devil would do. And why not? Satan was the one who incited Nimrod to do it. Remember! Lucifer wanted to be God. This is a violation of God's second command. Let's look at it.

2. "Thou shalt not make unto thee any graven image, or any likeness of any thing that is in heaven above, or that is in the earth beneath, or that is in the water under the earth. Thou shalt not bow down thyself to them,

nor serve them: for I the LORD thy God am a jealous God, visiting the iniquity of the fathers upon the children unto the third and fourth generation of them that hate me; And shewing mercy unto thousands of them that love me, and keep my commandments" (Exod. 20:4–6).

He thought he could take God's throne from Him. Satan thought he was very smart when it came to taking care of number one—himself. Now Nimrod was feeling just as smart as Lucifer had felt toward God. But! How wrong he was! No one can defy God and live to receive eternal life—unless, of course, they repent. But Nimrod had made his choice, and, "He began to be a mighty one in the earth. He was a mighty hunter before the LORD" (Gen. 10:8–9). "And the beginning of his kingdom was Babel" (Gen. 10:10).

The meaning of the words "before Me," in God's first commandment, mean "instead of" or "in place of." These same words, "before the Lord" are also used in other Bible verses. Nimrod was a not-too-distant relative of Noah and his three sons who weathered that storm of storms in the ark. That descendant, plus all of the people living in the city, which he built, determined in their hearts that they were not going to let God destroy people ever again by a flood. They thought they had a foolproof plan! They definitely underestimated God! They decided to build a tower so tall that God would never be able to destroy them by another flood. Do you realize what that means? They were defying God. I say, the gall, the nerve of them!

Evidently, they did not believe the promise God gave Noah and his descendants. I wonder what they thought that beautiful rainbow was all about! That promise is such a beautiful thread of God's love. Why build such a tower if there wasn't going to be another flood? Sounds like they didn't believe their own ideas, doesn't it? The truth is they didn't believe God. They thought God was lying to them. Sound familiar? This sounds like what happened in the Garden of Even. We too! Each of us today needs to think things through, and if we are making spurious preparations to save ourselves, recognize the fact that we lack faith in God, and do not trust Him. What a God He is to accept us! Thank You, Lord.

Whenever good people are in danger, God goes into action to save those who choose to love Him. Obviously, there were people in Nimrod's city who did love Him. Remember, God is not willing that any perish. So God provided a way out for those who loved and accepted Him, who did not think He was lying to them. But that does not mean we will not suffer. God will not violate the devil's freedom to disobey His law. But there is a day coming when all sinners who choose to persecute God's people will be no more. What a day it will be.

The city Nimrod built was the beginning of the ancient pagan kingdom of Babylon. We can also read about another Babylonian king in the book of Daniel. Nebuchadnezzar was its king. That original, ancient, pagan city that Nimrod built was destroyed, but Satan saw to it that there was another built to take its place. One that had the same purpose—defy God, and make a citadel for idol worship. You see, Satan still wanted to be God. And he thought he still had a chance to do just that (see Gen. 3:5; Ezek. 28:2,6,9). What he told Eve in the garden plainly shows his plan. "Ye shall be as gods, knowing good and evil." He will never give up. It is still his plan today. Nebuchadnezzar defied God too! Knowing the beginning of the history of ancient Babel helps us understand why the Babylon of Nebuchadnezzar's day was what it was. He, too, espoused paganism. It took twenty-six years for God to bring him to his knees before he would kneel before God in love. Unlike his distant relative, who refused to honor God, Nebuchadnezzar eventually gave his whole heart to the Lord. How pleased God must have been.

Whenever good people are in danger, God goes into action to save those who choose to love Him.

Isn't it amazing how quickly things disintegrated after the flood? And isn't it amazing too, that God was willing to save Noah's whole family—even though He knew things would go sour very soon? What a God! He saved Noah's children, even though He knew their close descendants would disobey Him so soon and bring about more terrible disasters. Again, I say, what a loving God. They were all God had to work with! He loved them, and He loves us so much that He was and still is willing to put up the sins of all ages—ours included.

We use the word "babble;" the same way they used it for the name of the tower they built. We say someone is just babbling when they rattle on and on, and no one can understand what they are saying. It is confusing when people say things that conflict with one another and cannot be understood. The very meaning of the word "babel" is confusion. That is what Nimrod and his people were doing when they disobeyed God. They were babbling. And the things that happened at that tower happened because of Nimrod's defiance toward God. You see, he was too wise in his own eyes!

He was boastful and proud. He thought he could outwit God. Actually, he thought he could disobey God and save himself through the work of his own hands. In his mind the tower he was building took God's place. So for him, that tower was before, and in place of God. In other words—another god, an idol. And I can just picture him idolizing it. In my mind's eye, I can see a big grin spreading across his face as he exulted that he had bested God. But no one but God can save anyone from sin or from a flood like He sent them.

Yes, Nimrod's real god was Satan—that liar, that teller of those pagan myths of old. Nimrod put Satan in place of God in his heart. Remember—Satan told his lies through a medium when he talked to Eve. And the snake Satan used was cursed for allowing Satan to use him. Nimrod invited Satan into his life when he determined in his heart to defy God. He allowed that serpent of old to use him. We, too, must be sure we are believing God and not Satan's lies. Here is the curse God placed on that snake in the Garden of Eden. Obviously, God did not create snakes to crawl on their belly, because having to crawl on its belly was part of its curse.

"And the Lord God said unto the serpent, Because thou hast done this, thou art cursed above all cattle, and above every beast of the field;

upon thy belly thou shalt go, and dust thou shalt eat all of the days of thy life" (Gen. 3:14).

And, yes, animals have freedom of choice too. Certainly, the snake did. They, too, choose to do good or evil. And the snake was punished for what he did. Our God is a God who loves all of the creatures He made. That makes me wonder if the animals who choose to obey God will go to heaven. Wouldn't that be a lovely gift—for both us and our animals! God wants to make us happy, so I wouldn't be at all surprised to see them there.

Myth says when Nimrod died, his wife followed in his footsteps. She told lies that would establish Nimrod as the sun god. She and Nimrod laid down the founding attributes of the city of Babel together. That myth is still alive today through astrology. They worshipped the planets and stars. The sun was their chief god. I guess you could say, the sun was their god of gods, in their pagan culture. The days of the weekly cycle (https://1ref.us/19r, accessed Aug. 5, 2020) that we have today were named after the pagan gods of the ancient Greeks and Romans. Sunday was named for the sun god. Monday for the moon god, etc.

According to myth, Semiramis was beautiful. But she was also very wicked. Myth claims she wanted to keep the worship of her dead husband alive. So when he died, she dumped his body into a river. Then she told people that they wouldn't see him anymore because his soul and spirit had gone to heaven.

I do not know if Semiramis realized it was Satan who was encouraging her to tell people to worship the sun. Or that Satan was the one who impressed her to tell them the sun god was her husband. Neither do I know whether she knew her tale was the beginning of something huge that Satan was planning. But she must have realized the devil might be using her. I can't imagine that God would not speak to her and try to get her to do what was right. God always tries to woo us to Himself through love. Just look at how beautiful the promise and remembrance of God's love is! "The Lord hath appeared from old unto me, saying, Yea, I have loved thee with an everlasting love: therefore with loving kindness have I drawn thee" (Jer. 31:3).

But she failed to listen, and she set the stage for the work of the antichrist power. The preposition "anti" also means "instead of, or in place of." In this case it was instead of Christ. They were worshiping the sun instead of worshipping God, our Savior. Sunday is the papal sabbath.

I find it interesting that it was the first day of God's creation week that was given the name Sunday—and that it was day of the week they worshiped the sun. Satan has always wanted to be first—so why not have the first day of the week represent his day. He wanted to be God! So why not the sun god. The sun is the largest star in our solar system that God created for the purpose of setting time—days, weeks, months, and years. Thus, it would make Satan feel very important and powerful to be worshipped on that day.

Also, she defied God by telling the people it was Nimrod's kingdom; the same lie Satan told Eve. Yes, it Satan, who convinced her of this lie, "Ye shall not surely die." (Gen. 3:4). Semiramis obeyed Satan just as Eve had done. But Semiramis deliberately lied, whereas Eve was deceived. That means she believed God was as bad as Satan told her He was. Eve distrusted God!

We are saved by faith in God. The pagans chose to have no faith in God. Therefore, they could not be saved. Not unless they recognized their need for God and turned to Him for help. Adam trusted God. He did not think God was bad. Rather, he chose to eat the fruit and disobey God, so he would not lose Eve. He, too, put his wants ahead of God's will.

The Bible tells us Adam was not deceived. He didn't think God had done anything bad. Eve believed what the serpent said. She thought God was trying to withhold something good from her. She wanted what she thought God wouldn't give her. "And Adam was not deceived, but the woman being deceived was in the transgression" (1 Tim. 2:14).

Semiramis, like the serpent, told the people of Babel they should worship Nimrod as the sun god. Thus, she instituted sun worship. And it is still well and alive today. According to the A. R. Fausset, Bible Dictionary (https://1ref.us/19s, accessed Aug. 5, 2020)—"Sun worship was the earliest idolatry." That means Nimrod was the first idol worshiper. I can't help but wonder if it is significant the page number in the dictionary happens to be the number of the antichrist? I don't know. But it seems very unusual.

The myth continues by saying when Semiramis died, she ascended into heaven and became the moon goddess. Satan wanted Semiramis and Nimrod to be worshipped. It suited his plans for destroying God's credibility. The myth continues by saying she ascended up to the moon. Thus, they worshiped her too. Jeremiah tells us what happened to Israel when they worshipped the "queen of heaven." It is one of the names given to the moon goddess. Just look at what God had to say about it. "Learn *not* the way of the heathen, and be not dismayed at the signs of heaven; for the heathen are dismayed at them" (Jer. 10:2, italics supplied).

When God sent the prophet Jeremiah to the people to bring them back to Himself, they, too, defied God. They said to Jeremiah, "As for the word that thou hast spoken unto us in the name of the Lord, we will not hearken unto thee. But will certainly do whatsoever thing goeth forth out of our own mouth, to burn incense unto the queen of heaven, and to pour out drink offerings unto her, as we have done … for then had we plenty of victuals, and were well, and saw no evil" (Jer. 44:16–17). I am sure Satan was whispering in their ears. Again, he must have blamed God for what was happening to them. It looks like he rewarded them for following him. See if you agree. For they said, "But since we left off to burn incense to the queen of heaven, and to pour out drink offerings unto her, we have wanted all things, and have been consumed by the sword and the famine" (Jer. 44:18).

These were God's children doing this. The ones who were supposed to be witnessing to the pagans. How it must have hurt God. His people were worshiping the sun god instead of worshipping Him. It wasn't God who brought the trouble—it was Satan and they themselves. Satan brought them trouble just as he brought Job trouble. Look at Jeremiah's reply. "Because of the evil of your doings, and because of the abominations which ye have committed; Therefore is your land a desolation, and an astonishment, and a curse, without an inhabitant, as at this day. Because ye have burned incense, and because ye have sinned against the Lord, and have not obeyed the voice of the LORD, nor walked in His law, nor in His statutes, nor in His testimonies; therefore this evil has happened to you, as at this day" (Jer. 44:22–23). Their God of love did not leave them in the dark. He told them exactly whose fault it was that they were having so much trouble. It was their own. Yes, it was their choice to believe Satan rather than believing God.

The same false gods were worshipped in all of the countries. Yes! They were the same gods, but in each country, they were given a different name. Here are some of the names. "Because that they have forsaken me, and have worshipped Ashtoreth the goddess of the Zidonians, Chemosh the god of the Moabites, and Milcom the god of the children of Ammon, and have not walked in my ways, to do that which is right in mine eyes, and to keep my statutes and my judgments, as did David his father" (1 Kings 11:33).

Then God proceeded to tell them what would happen to them, because of their rejection of Him. (Read Jer. 44:24–30) The gods spoken of here are the planetary gods from Nimrod's day. The queen of heaven is Semiramis—the moon god. It, too, is from Nimrod's day.

> *Anything we honor, instead of honoring God, becomes our idol.*

"And he put down the idolatrous priests, whom the kings of Judah had ordained to burn incense in the high places in the cities of Judah, and in the places round about Jerusalem; them also that burned incense unto Baal, to the sun, and to the moon, and to the planets, and to all the host of heaven" (2 Kings 23:5).

Let's think about God's first commandment again. It tells us how to love Him. God says one way to love Him is by not putting other people or things ahead of or in place of Him. Anything we honor, instead of honoring God, becomes our idol. It certainly was not an act of love toward God when Nimrod refused to obey Him. But let's take a look at God's simple solution. It was brilliant. And it worked out marvelously well! It brings to my mind this beautiful verse concerning God's wisdom. *"The foolishness of*

God is wiser than men; and the weakness of God is stronger than men. For ye see your calling, brethren, how that not many wise men after the flesh, not many mighty, not many noble, are called: But God hath chosen the foolish things of the world to confound the wise; and God hath chosen the weak things of the world to confound the things which are mighty; and the base things of the world, and things which are despised, hath God chosen, yea, and things which are not, to bring to nought things that are: that no flesh should glory in His presence," (1 Cor. 1:25–29, italics supplied).

God wove a thread of His love into the lives of the inhabitants of Babel. See if you agree with me! Instead of destroying them, He confounded their language. Truly, God's solution to the problem was very simple. Yet, it took care of the situation almost immediately, and it extinguished their present problem for the time being. The Bible says the language barrier instantly put an end to the tower of Babel they were building.

It is almost impossible for people to work together if they do not speak the same language. So each group, who could speak alike, moved to a new location. God used tough love on those people in Babel. Through His loving action, He thwarted their plans and removed the wicked from the vicinity of the righteous. What a beautiful thread of love that was—it allowed God to end the evil worship that took place there. Each group found a new place in which to live. God has such simple solutions to such difficult problems.

I believe God placed these stories in the Bible so we could see the threads of His love for the people in each age. When we see how much He loved them, we can also see how much He loves us. His actions also teach us that we are not loving Him when we put other things or other people ahead of our love for Him. We are not to make anyone or anything first in our affections. Only God must be first! So how do we show God we love Him? We put Him first, last, and best in everything we do. He is the only One we are counseled to worship. He alone is our God. He alone will someday give us our hearts' desires. I am looking forward to seeing Him someday. How about you? And that great event is well worth any trouble we go through to receive it.

By the way! God chooses each of us. He is not willing that even one person be lost. The problem is, often, we do not choose Him. A lot of times, it is because of a lack of understanding on our part. It is so simple! All we have to do is love Him by obeying His commandments—then we are His chosen children. He is just waiting for us to learn this and choose to obey Him—no matter what happens to us for doing so. Oh, yes! Satan is still as busy as he was in Job's day. That does not mean we have not been chosen. God chooses all who obey Him—whether it looks like we are chosen or not. In time, He will help us understand. I'm so glad. Just look at Paul, Nebuchadnezzar, and John the Baptist, for example.

CHAPTER NINE

The Next Two Commands

---•••---

When obeyed, the third and fourth commands in God's ten-commandment law, also show God we love Him. The third commandment says,

3. "Thou shalt not take the name of the L{ORD} thy God in vain; for the L{ORD} will not hold him guiltless that taketh his name in vain." (Exod. 20:7)

The words "in vain" mean "falsely, lying about God." He is our holy God. To defame Him or take His name lightly and not hold it in high regard is a sin. We don't like to be made fun of, or lied about, or called names, and neither does God. It certainly wouldn't be out of love if we defamed God by not trusting Him. In so doing, we would be telling Him we think He is not being truthful with us—like Eve did. That same old serpent is doing everything in his power to deceive us today too. It is happening on a daily basis—right now. Actually, we must be on our guard second by second!

When Satan told Eve God was lying to her, he was ruining and running down God's name. She believed Satan instead of believing God. It's hard to understand why she would believe the serpent because God had such a close relationship with her—walking and talking with her in the cool of the evening! Those were special threads of His love. Yet she, a perfect human, fell under Satan's obvious deceit and lies. If she could fall to his lies so easily, even though she was a perfect being, certainly, we are apt to fall even more easily. The years have taken their toll on the human race. Also, keep in mind that we have the same privileges as those two people in the garden had—a close relationship with our Creator.

Now, let's also look at the last command in the first section of God's law. It, too, showed Eve that God loved her. It shows God we love Him too when we agree to keep His date with us. Yes, He asks us out for a date every single week! It provides us with time when He has our full attention, and we have His. It is about us loving Him and Him loving us. God says,

Remember! Don't forget! What does He want us to not forget? Here it is!

4. "Remember the Sabbath day to keep it holy. Six days shalt thou labour, and do all thy work: But the *seventh* day …" What seventh day? Why! It's the seventh day of the week that God doesn't want us to forget! It's called Saturday on calendars all over the world. Saturday—the Sabbath:

"… is the sabbath of the Lord thy God: in it thou shalt not do any work, thou, nor thy son, nor thy daughter, thy manservant, thy maidservant, nor thy cattle, nor thy stranger that is within thy gates: For in six days the Lord made heaven and earth, the sea, and all that in them is, and rested the seventh day: wherefore the Lord blessed the sabbath day, and hallowed it" (Exod. 20:8–11).

God's Sabbath is the most special day there is. God wants us to spend it with Him. In His fourth commandment, He turns our thoughts back to the day He created us. He doesn't want us to forget that He is our Creator. When we keep the seventh day of the week holy, it shows God we know He is the One who created us. It is God Himself, who set us apart for a holy use—and He wants us to know He has sanctified both us and His day, and that He claims us as His child. When we worship on that day, it shows others that we belong to Him. Just look at how beautiful these words are. They tell us what He gave us to let us know how to love. We love Him when we live in accordance with His law. Praise God! What the Father did for us by allowing His Son to die for our sins at the cross—plus much, much more, and what the Holy Spirit is now doing for us, makes all of this possible. "And I gave them my statutes, and shewed them my judgments, which if a man do, he shall even live in them" (Ezek. 20:11).

If we do these things, we will be in harmony with God! All we have to do is give the Holy Spirit permission to help us give our all to God. I am so glad God is willing to do this and change our hearts into loving hearts like His. What a huge gift it is!

As I have said before, and I don't think it can be stressed too much, God leaves us free to make our own choices in life. Freedom of choice is a precious gift. It's the gift that caused God to have to go the long, extra miles He went to save sinners. Yes, it is freedom of choice that gives us the freedom to sin.

Love does not control—control is the devil's tactic. But because God is love, He wouldn't think of denying us the freedom to choose to serve Him, or instead, choose to serve someone or something else. If God had withheld freedom of choice from us, He would have ceased to be LOVE! For love does not control.

Love does not turn its back on someone who is hurting, either. Love upholds and supports those who are believing a lie. It opens people's eyes to what is going on in their life and helps them remain true to God. Love does no ill to his neighbor. I'm so glad God gives us freedom to make our own choices in life. But, with that freedom comes a huge responsibility.

These are the first four commandments in His law. Matthew draws our attention to the fact that Jesus answered the canon lawyer's question by asking him a question in return—(a canon lawyer is a lawyer who works with biblical laws). The lawyer asked Jesus, "Which is the great commandment in the law? Jesus said unto him, Thou shalt love the Lord thy God with all thy heart, and with all thy soul, and with all thy mind. This is the first and great commandment" (Matt. 22:36–38).

Yes, these first four commands are the commands that, if obeyed, specifically show God we love Him. Why in the world would we want to disobey one of those laws—the laws that are specifically aimed at our personal love for God. They provide us with the privilege of giving God a hug of obedience. He waits for that hug, with His arms open wide. He wants to hug us back. I can hardly wait for the day He gives me that great, big, bear hug of love in person. How about you?

The other six laws, when obeyed, also show God that we love Him. God tells us to love our neighbor. So, when we love our neighbor, we are loving God too because we are doing what He has asked us to do. Therefore, we are also doing His will when we keep those last six commands. I agree with Matthew. Truly, the first four commandments are the greatest commandments in the law because God should always be first in our hearts. Without Him, we wouldn't know anything about love, neither love for God, nor love for anyone else. For we only love Him because He loves us. That sounds kind of selfish at first glance. But it really isn't because we learn through show and tell. God is the greatest shower and teller there is. Please excuse the slang! "We love Him, because He first loved us" (1 John 4:19).

But, if these first four commands, make up the first and greatest command, what are the other six? They can't be greater! So, what does God call them? We'll talk about it in the next chapter. See you there!

CHAPTER TEN

Love Thy Neighbor As Thyself

We've looked at what Jesus said concerning the first four commands in His law, and found that He divided the ten-commandment law into two sections. Then He gave each section a title. Section one is a summarization of the first four commands in His law, and we found those four laws show us how to love God supremely.

> *God's whole law is about love.*

The second section consists of the last six commands. That section is about loving other people. Thus, God's whole law is about love. Here is what Jesus said, concerning the second half of His law. He considers all of His commandments as being only two commands because He said, "And the second is like unto it, Thou shalt love thy neighbor as thyself. On these two commandments hang all the law and the prophets" (Matt. 22:39–40).

Did you notice what Jesus said hangs on those two commands? He said, all of the law and everything the prophets had to say hang on them. In other words, God says everything the prophets wrote is part of

His law. That means we are to keep all ten of His commands, plus all of the other laws God told the prophets to write. That's why God gave us the prophets—they bring our attention to what God is telling us to do in each phase of history. The prophets were sent to help us understand all of God's commands—yes, clear down to the very day He comes to take us home with Him.

The explanation of God's laws by the prophets can be trusted. Why? Because those prophets wrote what God told them to write; therefore, their words are inspired by God Himself. If we carefully listen to Jesus' words, they will teach us the same things He taught His disciples. Just before Jesus went back to heaven, He got after them for not listening to what the prophets had told them. He said, "'Oh foolish ones, and slow of heart to believe in all that the prophets have spoken! Ought not the Christ to have suffered these things and to enter into His glory?' And beginning at Moses and all the Prophets, He expounded to them in all the Scriptures, the things concerning Himself" (Luke 24:25–27).

Besides that, God lets us know whether a law is only for a specific occasion, or whether it is for a longer period of time. He specifies in His Word and places a difference between His eternal ten-commandment law and others that are just for some specific, shorter-lived period of time. He tells us why that extra law was given, and tells us the specific time period for its use. Yes, God provides us with laws written to meet special needs and special occasions. But, the majority of His laws come under the umbrella of the Ten Commandments; and they are not for just one special event or specific period of time.

Let's look at those last six commands and see what else God wants us to do! But first, allow me to share a verse with you the Holy Spirit just impressed me with. It answers a question I have about myself. What does God mean when He tells us to love our neighbor as we love ourselves? Maybe that's where I need to begin! I have a hard time loving myself. I don't think I am attractive! But the Bible tells me I was created in His image. So, I guess I am putting God down when I dislike myself. I should love my looks since I was made in His image! I guess that's a real problem for me. So! I have a way to go! That means these commands definitely are for me. Do you realize I am not alone with my problem; we all have our own personal hangups. You see, I don't think God is just talking about my bodily features. I believe He is basically talking about my mental and psychological characteristics. Or better said, my character. Those changed when Eve sinned.

But when I say I am unattractive, I am talking about my bodily features. God will change those physical attributes when He recreates me at His coming. He will remove all of the imperfections sin has caused. But the features of my character change as I accept His love into my heart. God tells us how this comes about, and it, too, involves freedom of choice. He says, "But we all, with open face beholding as in a glass the glory of the Lord, are changed into the same image from glory to glory, even as by the Spirit of the Lord" (2 Cor. 3:18). Hallelujah! It's looking at Jesus that changes me. Therefore, there is no need for me to feel that I look ugly. I can change that through my own choices to become like Jesus! Now back to those commandments.

5. "Honor thy father and thy mother: that thy days may be long upon the land which the Lord thy God giveth thee" (Exod. 20:12).

God has a way of saying things simply! So everyone can understand! His simple yet rich words produce love in the human heart. Such care! Such understanding! and such grace! His commands show us, true, pure love, undefiled. What a unique picture of God His commands are.

6. "Thou shalt not kill" (Exod. 20:13).

Jesus said, "Ye have heard that it was said by them of old time, Thou shalt not kill; and whosoever shall kill shall be in danger of the judgment: But I say unto you, That whosoever is angry with his brother without a cause shall be in danger of the judgment: and whosoever shall say to his brother, Raca, shall be in danger of the council: but whosoever shall say, Thou fool, shall be in danger of hell fire" (Matt. 5:21–22).

It is a sin to make fun of someone. A simple little ditty just came to my mind. It goes like this: "Sticks and stones will break my bones, but words will never harm me." That's not true! The words of this ditty are a lie.

Lies are very damaging. Words can be very psychologically damaging. Words kill a person's spirit. Words can cause a person to commit suicide. We commit all kinds of sins with our words.

Those kinds of actions do not come from God. That is why we will be burned up in hell if we are unloving to our brother or sister. And here is what happens to those who make fun of others. Yes, it is God who says those who do such things are in danger of being burned up in hell. Wouldn't you say that's extremely serious? That's why God says, "Therefore if thou bring thy gift to the altar, and there rememberest that thy brother hath ought against thee; Leave there thy gift before the altar, and go thy way; first be reconciled to thy brother, and then come and offer thy gift. Agree with thine adversary quickly, whiles thou art in the way with him; lest at any time the adversary deliver thee to the judge, and the judge deliver thee to the officer, and thou be cast into prison. Verily I say unto thee, Thou shalt by no means come out thence, till thou hast paid the uttermost farthing" (Matt. 5:23–26).

7. "Thou shalt not commit adultery" (Exod. 20:14).

Just listen to what Jesus says about this! Again, He tells us to go the extra mile. We are even to refuse to think about committing the sexual acts God has told us not to do. You see, when we think a thought, it won't be long until we reap an act. Those thoughts are placed in our minds by Satan. It's him tempting us to disobey God. It's him out to destroy us. He hates us. God made us in His image and didn't do so the same for Lucifer. Satan is jealous of the gift God gave us.

"Ye have heard that it was said by them of old time, Thou shall not commit adultery: But I say unto you, That whosoever looketh on a woman to lust after her hath committed adultery with her already in his heart. And if thy right eye offend thee, pluck it out, and cast it from thee: for it is profitable for thee that one of thy members should perish, and not that thy whole body should be cast into hell. And if thy right hand offend thee, cut it off, and cast it from thee: for it is profitable for thee that one of thy members should perish, and not that thy whole body should be cast into hell" (Matt. 5:27–30). By the way! I don't believe Jesus was speaking literally, and telling us to actually cut off a body part, such as a hand if it was used for committing a sin. Cutting one's hand off would not help the person to discontinue his sin. It would only encumber his or her life more. Jesus only wanted to show us how drastically important it is to stop sinning. He was using a figure of speech. Now let's continue.

"It hath been said, Whosoever shall put away his wife, let him give her a writing of divorcement: But I say unto you, That whosoever shall put away his wife, saving for the cause of fornication, causeth her to commit adultery: and whosoever shall marry her that is divorced committeth adultery" (Matt. 5:31–32). Instead of making the laws weaker, Jesus told them to make His commands stricter. He didn't tell people to just keep the letter of the law; He laid a magnifying glass over His law. Read the rest of chapter 5 of Matthew, for more instruction Jesus gave concerning loving your brother.

8. "Thou shalt not steal" (Exod. 20:15).

9. "Thou shalt not bear false witness against thy neighbor" (Exod. 20:16).

10. "Thou shalt not covet thy neighbor's house, thou shalt not covet thy neighbor's wife, nor his manservant, nor his maidservant, nor his ox, nor his ass, nor any thing that is thy neighbor's" (Exod. 20:17).

So! Do you love yourself enough? Do you desire to be like Jesus? Each of us can only emulate God through God's power. I must believe He made me in His image. It is the image of a perfect God. That image has been drastically marred by sin, but praise God, our marred image can be changed by Him. All we have to do is choose to let Him change us through His love. It will turn us back to the perfect image of His love mankind had in the beginning. All I have to do is ask him to forgive me for my unbelief and my sin. All God needs is my permission to change me.

How simple is that! But, I can only believe and obey Him through the help of the Holy Spirit. Remember, the Bible says, "With God, all things are possible" (Matt. 19:26). That means, I too, can love myself, love God, and love my neighbor. God, help me! I must accept it, because God said it, and because I believe He is telling me the truth. But I can only accept it through faith in Him. Read Luke 10:29–37 to discover who your neighbor is. I am sure you already know!

I find it very comforting to know that the law of God is a picture of my Savior. I am also glad God's law shows us the close ties between the three of Them—the Father, Son, and Holy Spirit. That is where the law concerning the prophets comes in. Those laws, when obeyed, tie us to God,—yes, they are another connection between God and us. Actually, we find that all three of the Beings who are our One God had a role in being our Savior! It takes all Three of Them to accomplish our salvation. It's that big of a deal! Together, They are saving us. The individual love we receive from each of them gives us a complete picture of Their combined love and shows us the unique, loving connection between Them and us. In this way, the story of Their love is enhanced. It takes all of the threads of God's love to provide a total picture of our God. Our salvation could not happen if one thread were missing.

Jesus not only knows our feelings, He experienced them because He became human like us

Did you understand the extra special thread between God and us, which makes a very special cord of love between Him and us? That thread will shine brighter with everything we learn about Them. It helps us see how everything Jesus did weaves us together with Them. It erases any doubt concerning Their great love for us. You know which thread I am talking about, don't you? It's about worship.

Yes, it is the fourth commandment in His law. It tells us how to worship Him. It has to do with our weekly date with Him. It shows us that we are connected to God in many more ways than just reading the Bible through. We must become emotionally attached to our Savior through His bonds of love. Jesus not only knows our feelings, He experienced them because He became human like us—and thus, He is "God with us" (Matt. 1:23). Jesus' human ties bind Him to us and us to Him.

God's worship command is one of the most beautiful threads of the entire fabric of His love. It is able to weave our life and His together. When we worship Him, our act of worship brings understanding and love. In the next chapter, we will see how God keeps trying to bring mankind back into harmony with Himself through His worship law.

CHAPTER ELEVEN

A Lesson on Obedience (The background which led up to the giving of the manna)

This lesson was for God's chosen people. Soon after God confused the language of the people at the tower of Babel, He chose Abraham to be a missionary to all who choose to love and serve God. This happened before many centuries went by, and Abram was living at Ur of the Chaldeans. God spoke to Abram and told him to leave that place. He did not want Abram to live among those wicked people, so He said to him, "Get thee out of thy country, and from thy kindred, and from thy father's house, unto a land that I will shew thee: And I will make of thee a great nation, and I will bless thee, and make thy name great; and thou shalt be a blessing: and I will bless them that bless thee, and curse him that curseth thee: and in thee shall all families of the earth be blessed. So Abram departed, as the Lord had spoken unto him" (Gen. 12:1–4).

He was seventy-five when he left his country and moved away from his relatives. He ended up stopping and dwelling at Haran for a while. That is where Abram's father died. It could be the trip was too much for him at his age. But this trip was made because God told Abram to move away from his family. Abram obeyed God. After he took care of his father's needs, he resumed the journey God told him to take, "and they went forth to go into the land of Canaan" (Gen. 12:5).

"And the Lord appeared unto Abram, and said, Unto thy seed will I give this land: and there built he an altar unto the LORD" (Gen. 12:7). Then God encouraged him, saying, "Fear not, Abram: I am thy shield, and thy exceeding great reward" (Gen. 15:1).

And Abram asked, "Lord God, what wilt thou give me, seeing I go childless?" (Gen. 15:2). "And he brought him forth abroad, and said, Look now toward heaven, and tell the stars, if thou art able to number them: and he said unto him, So shall thy seed be. And he believed in the LORD; and he counted it to him for righteousness" (Gen. 15:5–6). But Sarai just did not get pregnant! So, she took things into her own hands. That's always a dangerous thing to do! God let her learn from that experience. How patient God is—to think that He would allow her to flub as bad as she did. Man cannot improve God's plans! But she tried to! She distrusted God and suggested to her husband that he should help God out. How? By having a child through her maidservant.

Oh, what grief it is causing still today! But our wonderful God helped her see her error. What a picture of God's love this is! To allow her to do this wrong and still let her become the mother of the Jewish nation. Listen to her regrets! "And Sarai said unto Abram, My wrong be upon thee: I have given my maid into thy bosom; and when she saw that she conceived, I was despised in her eyes: the LORD judge between me and thee" (Gen. 16:5).

Then God restated His covenant to Abram. "When Abram was ninety years old and nine, the LORD appeared to Abram, and said unto him, I am the Almighty God; walk before me, and be thou perfect. And I will make my covenant between me and thee, and will multiply thee exceedingly.

And Abram fell on his face: and God talked with him, saying, As for me, behold, my covenant is with thee, and thou shalt be a father of many nations. Neither shall thy name any more be called Abram, but thy name shall be Abraham, for a father of many nations have I made thee. And I will make thee exceedingly fruitful, and I will make nations of thee, and kings shall come out of thee. And I will establish my covenant between me and thee and thy seed after thee in their generations for an everlasting covenant, to be a God unto thee, and to thy seed after thee. And I will give unto thee, and to thy seed after thee, the land wherein thou art a stranger, all the land of Canaan, for an everlasting possession; and I will be their God" (Gen. 17:1–8).

But! God also gave him a vision showing future events! After seeing it, Abraham became frightened and engaged in lying to save his neck. But God still came to him again. Wow! What a forgiving God our God is. If God was to save mankind, He had to work with the people who were on the earth, and Abraham was the best He had. All of them were sinners. All of them made mistakes, but Abraham was more righteous than anyone else. At least he was trying to obey God.

Have you noticed when God promises something He often waits, and waits, and waits some more before He fulfills His promise? I may be wrong, but it looks to me like God gives us time—time to flub—yes, time to sin, and then time to grow and time to learn from our sin. Yes, and time to build our faith. Faith can't grow if we feel God has given us all of the answers. How patient He is. He gives us time to learn from our mistakes. I believe that is what God was doing for both Sarah and Abraham!

It was after they flubbed that God told Abraham that Sarah would be the one who would give birth to the promised child. Yes, it was after all of their trying to come up with a solution that God told them she would be the one to bring forth the promised baby. God alone has the solution for our woes. What a shame they didn't wait on the Lord and believe His promise. Look what God told Abraham about Sarah becoming pregnant. "As for Sarai thy wife, thou shalt not call her name Sarai, but Sarah shall her name be. And I will bless her, and give you a son also of her: yea, I will bless her, and she shall be a mother of nations; kings of people shall be of her" (Gen. 17:15–19). What a shock that must have been. And just look at the unbelief Sarah still had—even after all the things which had taken place. She knew she had done wrong! Now, look at what else she did. I'm amazed.

"Sarah laughed within herself, saying, After I am waxed old shall I have pleasure, my lord being old also? And the Lord said unto Abraham, Wherefore did Sarah laugh, saying, Shall I of a surety bear a child, which am old?" And God said, "Is anything too hard for the Lord? At the time appointed I will return unto thee, according to the time of life, and Sarah shall have a son" (Gen. 18:12–14).

I am awed over how tenacious God was by still honoring Sarah. Especially when I look at what Sarah's reaction was when God told her husband she would have a baby. Consider this! Since God knows everything, He knew that Sarah would lie. But God still held to His plan. I am sorry! You are probably getting tired of hearing this expression from me, but I just have to say—WOW! What a wonderful, longsuffering God we have. Now, just look at what she did. "Then Sarah denied, saying, I laughed not; for she was afraid. And he said, Nay; but thou didst laugh" (Gen. 18:15).

What a God we serve! She had the gall to lie to God, and He still worked with her. What a God—that He continued to love the human race. But then, that's just who God is—a lover of all. Not accepting the lie, but accepting the person who lied, even though they have broken His law. Are you aware of who this is talking to Sarah and Abraham? We will look into who this God is a little more later on—when we talk about God forming His church on earth. But I am going to tell you right now too—up front—it was Jesus. He was the "Lord" who was talking to her. Isn't that beautiful? He was the One who created her that she was communing with. All I can say is, WOW AGAIN! God truly does wow us still today. Not too long after this, Sarah did get pregnant, just as Jesus promised. But notice, it didn't happen until after both of them were beyond childbearing age—yes, after it was humanly too late for her to get pregnant. This makes it all the more miraculous—and helps firmly cement and verify in our minds that the conception of that baby truly was an act of God. I think God must have done this for all of the doubters in our day. He wants to save every last one of them. It gives us hope when we doubt—something we need to steer clear from doing. Read the twentieth chapter of Genesis to see what else she did before God gave her the seed He promised. It, too, shows what an amazing God we serve.

Now fast forward—and look at some lessons God gave His chosen people after their nation had grown considerably. The giving of the manna in the wilderness is important because it lets us know God still expected them to keep His Sabbath day holy at that time in earth's history. It also gave God another chance to show and tell His people how much He loved them. It was huge! Oh, how He yearned for them to love Him back!

God sent them to Egypt to save them from a huge famine. And now, He had just removed them from Egyptian bondage. He had miraculously held back the Red Sea so they could cross through it on dry ground to safety. The water swept back over the path they had just crossed through the sea. It had destroyed their enemies right before their eyes! That is mind-boggling! It certainly was a mighty display of God's power. It's good to keep these blessings of God's people nestled in our minds. They were and are marvelous manifestations of His protective love. He has loved all of His people throughout their stay on this earth, and He will do so until the very day He takes them home.

God gave the Egyptians chance after chance to repent and begin treating His chosen people right. Time and time again, the Egyptians refused to let God's people leave Egypt. God bent over backward to get this heathen nation to do what was right. He wanted to save them. But every time they let their greed get in the way. Yes, their greed won out. It is sad, but for most of us, it will be the same way. Just before Jesus comes back, greed and distrust will win out. It will be each person's free choice. We see it rapidly building up all over the world today.

The Israelite people God had chosen as His missionaries were not loyal to Him. Can you believe that! After all the love and miracles God had just performed to save them, they were soon grumbling about not having what they considered to be the goodies of Egypt. Yes, it was all about selfishness and not getting the favorite food they craved. Instead of being thankful for not being beaten with whips by their taskmasters, they were angry with God for instructing Moses to lead them out into the desert where they could not have everything they wanted to eat. Listen to their grumbling! Notice who they blamed for their lack of food! "Would to God we had died by the hand of the LORD in the land of Egypt, when we sat by the flesh pots, and when we did eat bread to the full" (Exod. 16:3).

Can you believe it! They were actually saying food was more important to them than being alive and more important than not being beaten. They wanted rich food, not just plain fare. They wanted to make pigs of themselves by overeating and stuffing themselves with the foods they considered special. They lived to eat rather than eating to live. They decided they would rather die or be beaten rather than go without their favorite food. I find it utterly amazing! But I am not so sure we are any different today—myself included. It is easy to criticize others—but, if it came right down to it, would I complain too—if I was placed under certain circumstances. Scary, huh! Do I live to eat? Would I rather die than give up certain foods? I personally find those to be serious thoughts.

They decided they would rather die or be beaten rather than go without their favorite food.

Right now, I am suffering from GIRD—and I, too, am having a hard time staying on the very meager diet I must be on to get well. They put their stomachs first—in place of and instead of God. At this point in time, food was their idol. They idolized and worshipped it. They loved those foods more than they loved God. At least they thought they did! Was food really their god? Sadly, for some, the answer is probably, yes. That's pretty bad! To think that food was more important to them than God. What a slap in God's face that was. But wasn't it the same with Eve? Food seems to be one of Satan's favorite temptations for getting us to sin.

Notice also, who it was that started that siege of murmuring. It appears that some of the Egyptians who fled from Egypt with the Israelites were not truly dedicated to God. Over and over, this happened to God's people. They would choose to chum with those so-called friends, and those friends led them away from God. That, too, has been a common tool that Satan has continued to use for destroying God's people throughout the ages. Often, family members are used by Satan too! "And the mixt multitude that was among them fell a lusting: and the children of Israel also wept again, and said, Who shall give us flesh to eat?" (Num. 11:4).

Here are some verses in the book of Numbers, which give us a more picturesque description of what they were dreaming about. They said, "We remember the fish, which we did eat in Egypt freely; the cucumbers, and the melons, and the leeks, and the onions, and the garlick" (Num. 11:5). These were not bad foods. In fact, some of them are the very ones I must give up to get well and perhaps stay well. It comes pretty close to home, doesn't it! What was bad was the importance they placed on them. Just look at the words they used to explain how they felt. I find those words shocking! "But now our soul is dried away: there is nothing at all, beside this manna, before our eyes" (Num. 11:6). They got so upset with Moses that they said to him, "Ye have brought us forth into this wilderness, to kill this whole assembly with hunger" (Exod. 16:3).

But God was feeding them very special food. And notice that again, it wasn't really Moses they were finding fault with; it was God! And Moses told them so. You see, it was God who told Moses to bring the Israelites out of Egypt. God knew their grumbling came from the selfishness in their own hearts. He saw their unwillingness to obey Him.

That's why God had led them into the wilderness in the first place. It was so He could show them just how selfish they were. They couldn't be saved from their sins if they didn't know they were sinning. They must know what sin is and what their own personal sins were. Only then would they have a desire to ask God to forgive them. Only then could God prepare them for the job He had for them to do. Only then could they choose between God and their own selfish desires.

God has a job for each of us, too. No one else can do our job for us. God has a handpicked, special task for every single person on earth, just as He did for them. The story of Job gives us a good example of that, and that story tells us exactly who it is that caused the trouble—it was Satan himself. He is always in the mix! And Job came to understand that God was testing him. "He knoweth the way that I take: when He hath tried me, I shall come forth as gold" (Job 23:10). Isn't that beautiful? Job thought so too, and he recognized that this was what God had just done for him. "He performeth the thing that is appointed for me" (Job 23:14).

It was God's choice to have the children of Israel witness for Him. During their captivity, they were not able to obey on pain of death. So God needed to let them see that they would not obey Him and that they would not lead others to love Him, even if they were not in dire straits anymore than they would when they were being tormented by people who were controlling them and keeping them captive.

God is in the business of saving people through love. The simple lessons He was about to give them, on obedience, and self-sacrifice were for their good—lessons their stubborn hearts needed. Because of their resistance to obeying Him, God had to administer tough love! God didn't make it tough. They made it tough through their continued decisions to disobey Him. God would not lose them to His enemy, Satan, without a fight. They had been in captivity so long that they lost sight of how to honor God's holy Sabbath day. So God had a talk with Moses, saying, "Behold, I will rain bread from heaven for you; And the people shall go out and gather a certain rate every day, that I may prove them, whether they will walk in my law, or no. And it shall come to pass, that on the sixth day they shall prepare that which they bring in; and it shall be twice as much as they gather daily" (Exod. 16:4–5).

God was testing them so they could see how far they had slipped from obeying Him during their captivity. This also shows us that God's law had been given to them before it was written at Mount Sinai. For how could God test them to see if they would obey His law if He hadn't already given it to them. Up until that time, God's law had been passed down, mouth to mouth, from when the people had been saved in the ark. Some of the younger Israelites probably didn't even know they were being rebellious toward God, so this was God's opportunity to instruct them and bring them into a better understanding on how to keep His Sabbath day holy. It also showed them how they could tell God that they loved Him. What a privilege—a privilege we, too, have. For God says, "He who has My commandments and keeps them, it is he who loves Me" (John 14:21, NKJV).

These verses show us that God still expected them to rest from their work on the seventh day of the week—His holy Sabbath day. When the people complained, Moses said to them, "Your murmurings are not against us, but against the Lord" (Exod. 16:8). Those words should have been very sobering to them. They should have caused them to think twice about how they were acting.

They should make us think twice too when we murmur about how God treats us. Sometimes God has to get between Satan and us—just as He did in Job's day. That isn't a pretty picture. So God informed Moses He had heard the peoples' grumbling and complaining. Then He continued to share His plan for their redemption. What a plan it was. He would show them His love by allowing them to go their own selfish way. He would not remove their freedom of choice. He said to Moses, "Speak unto them, saying, At even ye shall eat flesh, and in the morning ye shall be filled with bread" (Exod. 16:12). Did you hear that? Did you notice God's reason for doing this? Here it is! He said, "And ye shall know that I am the Lord your God" (Exod. 16:12).

God's whole purpose in giving them what they clamored for was so they would "*know Him.*" That's an astounding example of God's tough love. He was tough on them because He didn't want them to be lost. He wanted to save them. What a God to be willing to save those who grumbled, complained, and blamed Him for refusing to give them what they wanted. God was giving them something better than what they wanted! It was called "manna"—bread from heaven. But they weren't satisfied. They had their eyes fixed on the present rather than on the future. They failed to consider the miracles God was performing for them.

So God instructed Moses to have each man gather the amount He knew they would need. Yes, God personalized it. This made it a personal test for each person. Each one was only responsible for what God told him to do. God said, "Gather of it every man according to his eating, an omer for every man, according to the number of your persons; take ye every man for them which are in his tents. And the children of Israel did so, and gathered, some more, some less.... He that gathered much had nothing over, and he that gathered little had no lack;" (Exod. 16:16–18). Wouldn't you call that a miracle? I would!

"And Moses said, Let no man leave it till the morning" (Exod. 16:19). They must believe and have faith that God would keep His promise and give them more manna the next morning. They must obey, even if they felt like it was a waste to throw away what was left over. They must place God in control of their life. They must have faith that He would continue to supply their needs. Those who did not have faith were afraid because they had noticed "when the sun became hot, it melted" (Exod. 16:21, NKJV).

God was endeavoring to teach them to trust totally in Him. We need to have that kind of trust too. If we don't, we won't make it either, just as Eve didn't. But Eve had a second chance. The whole human race is getting its second chance now. There will be no third chance. Now, look at what some of them did! They disobeyed and "left of it until morning, and it bred worms and stank" (Exod. 16:20). They flunked the test.

Those who disobeyed lacked faith, even though they knew God was talking to Moses and instructing him face to face on what they were supposed to do. They chose to disobey God. They chose to distrust their Creator! Instead, they trusted their own deceitful hearts. Isn't that something! They trusted themselves more than they trusted God. Instead of leaning on God, they leaned on their own understanding. Sound familiar? God tells us not to do that, too.

Lest we get proud, we need to realize we do the same types of things today as they did. How do I know? God says, "Therefore thou art inexcusable, O man, whosoever thou art that judgest: for wherein thou judgest another, thou condemnest thyself; for thou that judgest doest the same things. But we are sure that the judgment of God is according to truth against them which commit such things. And thinkest thou this, O man, that judgest them which do such things, and doest the same, that thou shall escape the judgment of God? Or despisest thou the riches of His goodness and forbearance and longsuffering; not knowing that the goodness of God leadeth thee to repentance? But after thy hardness and impenitent heart treasurest up unto thyself wrath against the day of wrath and revelation of the righteous judgment of God; Who will render to every man according to his deeds: To them who by patient continuance in well doing seek for glory and honour and immortality, eternal life: But unto them that are contentious, and do not obey the truth, but obey unrighteousness, indignation and wrath, tribulation and anguish, upon every soul of man that doeth evil, of the Jew first, and also of the Gentile; But glory, honour, and peace, to every man that worketh good, to the Jew first, and also to the Gentile: For there is no respect of persons with God. For as many as have sinned without law shall also perish without law: and as many as have sinned in the law shall be judged by the law; (For not the hearers of the law are just before God, but the doers of the law shall be justified. For when the Gentiles, which have not the law, do by nature the things contained in the law, these, having not the law, are a law unto themselves: Which shew the work of the law written in their hearts, their conscience also bearing witness, and their thoughts the mean while accusing or else excusing one another;) In the day when God shall judge the secrets of men by Jesus Christ according to my gospel" (Rom. 2:1–16).

The Bible says, "Trust in the LORD with all thine heart; and lean not unto thine own understanding. In all thy ways acknowledge Him, and He shall direct thy paths" (Prov. 3:5–6). On Friday, the sixth day of the week, Moses said to them, "This is that which the LORD hath said, To morrow is the rest of the holy sabbath unto the LORD: bake that which ye will bake to day, and seethe that ye will seethe; and that which remaineth over lay up for you to be kept until the morning. And they laid it up till the morning, as Moses bade; and it did not stink, neither was there any worm therein" (Exod. 16:23–24). Again! God performed a miracle! For those who obeyed the Lord, their food was not allowed to spoil or to be eaten by worms. Because of their belief in Him, God performed a miracle for them.

Then Moses instructed them further. "Six days ye shall gather it; but on the seventh day, which is the sabbath, in it there will be none" (Exod. 16:26). Even after all of those miracles, there were still people who failed to trust God. How do we know? The Bible says, "There went out some of the people on the seventh day for to gather, and they found none. And the Lord said unto Moses, *How long refuse ye to keep my commandments and my laws?* See, for the Lord hath given you the sabbath, therefore he giveth you on the sixth day the bread of two days; abide ye every man in his place, let no man go out of his place on the seventh day. So the people rested on the seventh day" (Exod. 16:27–30, italics supplied).

God still says to us today, "My son, despise not the chastening of the Lord; neither be weary of his correction; For whom the Lord loves he correcteth: even as a father the son of whom he delighteth" (Prov. 3:11–12). Six weeks later, God gave them the Ten Commandments cut into stone. This also shows us that the seventh-day Sabbath was still holy and that they were aware of His ten-commandment law, before their manna experience. Yes, they really did know which day of the week was God's Sabbath. Otherwise, God wouldn't have said, "Remember" (Exod. 20:8).

God was giving them further coaching on how to be His special people—his missionaries. He had covenanted with Abraham years before, and now He was training them to do the job He had always had in mind for them. What a miserable lot they were—but they were the best God had. I, too, am a miserable lot sometimes. Read Deut. 6–9. They contain more instructions that God gave them at the time He wrote the Ten Commandments for them. Yes, at that time in history, they were still His people. They had not yet been cast off by God as a nation. Their nation had not yet rejected Jesus as its Savior. Just look at the words God chose to tell them when He first chose them to be His people. He said, "Thou art an holy people unto the Lord thy God: the Lord thy God hath chosen thee to be a special people unto himself, above all people that are upon the face of the earth. The Lord did not set his love upon you, nor choose you, because ye were more in number than any people; for ye were the fewest of all people: But because the LORD loved you, and because he would keep the oath which He swore unto your fathers, hath the Lord brought you out with a mighty hand, and redeemed you out of the house of bondmen, from the hand of Pharaoh king of Egypt" (Deut. 7:6–8).

Read the rest of the chapter, plus chapter 8, to know all of the blessings God was willing to bestow on them and how He would fight for them, plus instructions of what they should do with their idols. God was keeping His promise to Abraham. God always keeps His promises. But then He gave them this warning:

"If thou do at all forget the LORD thy God, and walk after other gods, and serve them, and worship them, I testify against you this day that ye shall surely perish. As the nations which the LORD destroyeth before your face, so shall ye perish; because ye would not be obedient unto the voice of the Lord your God" (Deut. 8:19–20). When they worshipped idols, they were disowning their God. How sad! We do that sometimes too. Praise the Lord, He corrects us, just like He did them. He loves us. What a wonderful God He is!

> *God always keeps His promises.*

CHAPTER TWELVE

The Sabbath in Nehemiah's Day

―――•••―――

In Nehemiah's day, many of the people of God had strayed far from Him again. Remember, these are the descendants of the people who led the children of Israel astray when they were in the wilderness. Nehemiah was the cup bearer for king Artaxerxes at the palace in Shushan (see Neh. 1:1, 11). Because of the Israelites' rejection of God—their God—yes, the God who is the King of the universe allowed this Babylonian king to destroy the city of Jerusalem. His people caused it through their dishonor to Him.

He allowed this pagan king to aid Him by showing His people, the Jews, the result of their unfaithful actions. When Nehemiah asked his brethren about the Jews who had escaped the siege, he found they "were in great affliction and reproach: the wall of Jerusalem also is broken down, and the gates thereof are burned with fire" (Neh. 1:3).

The Bible says when Nehemiah "heard these words, that I sat down and wept, and mourned certain days, and fasted, and prayed before the God of heaven" (Neh. 1:4). Then he asked the king to give him permission to go and rebuild the gates of the city, the wall, and the temple. God was good to Nehemiah. He let him go and check things out.

When Nehemiah went and saw how bad it was, he was very shocked and grieved. In fact, he felt so bad about it that he wept for days. He was horrified that it had happened right under his nose! So, he prayed for them. You can read it in Neh. 1:5–8. Then he reminded God that He had told His people "If ye transgress, I will scatter you abroad among the nations: but if ye turn unto me, and keep my commandments, and do them; though there were of you cast out unto the uttermost part of the heaven, yet will I gather them from thence, and will bring them unto the place that I have chosen to set my name there" (Neh. 1:8–9). God does not let go of us; we let go of Him.

Oh, how strong God's longsuffering is toward His people. It should put tears of gratitude in our eyes today, too, when we stop and think how much God really does love us. This promise is open to us today, who are living in the days just before Jesus' second coming. Throughout all ages, God has gathered His people—those who love and obey Him. If we truly love Him, forsake our sins, and place His wants first ahead of our own, every single one of us can be in that number who go to heaven.

Nehemiah read the book of Moses and discovered how atrocious their sins were. Then he read it to the people. And they took action! Praise the Lord! May we do the same! "Now it came to pass, when they had heard the law, that they separated from Israel all the mixed multitude" (Neh. 13:3). Even these men could have been among those who obeyed God. They could have had God's grace shining on them, but listen to this, "it grieved them exceedingly that there was come a man to seek the welfare of the children of Israel" (Neh. 2:10).

Just listen to his evil feelings. The thirteenth chapter of Nehemiah begins by telling us what happened when God's people again began reading the book of Moses. What an eye-opener it was for them! "On that day they read in the book of Moses in the audience of the people; and therein was found written, that the Ammonite and the Moabite should not come into the congregation of God for ever; because they met not the children of Israel with bread and water, but hired Balaam against them, that he would curse them: howbeit our God turned the curse into a blessing...."

when they heard the law, they separated from Israel all the mixed multitude" (Neh. 13:1–3). They listened and acted the way God wanted them to act. What a God! What a lover of His people.

Nehemiah really had the goods on them. He knew they had disobeyed God. He also knew they had allowed those bad people to come into God's holy temple and desecrate it. They had done this even after God told them not to allow those people to come into it. Isn't it amazing this disobedient priest, Eliashib, had the gall to even prepare a great chamber in the house of the Lord for this heathen Ammonite man? A man who wasn't even supposed to be allowed to come into God's house at all. Not because God did not love him; but because he refused to love God. And here he was living there. Nehemiah realized how far they had strayed and how disobedient they were. No wonder he was grieved! That's why we, too, must read our Bibles and find out what God expects from us.

Thus, a prophet of God had again opened the eyes of God's people and guided them back to a correct relationship with their Creator. They had veered off into false worship. Yes, they were worshiping heathen gods, and they were worshiping on days not sanctified by God. And, yes again! They were even worshiping God on heathen worship days—instead of worshipping on the seventh day of the week—His holy day—and they were doing it—*right in God's own church.*

What about today? Are God's people innocently doing those same things today? Here is a poignant question one could ask: Is the devil still deceiving God's people today? Of course, he is. But does the Bible say that? Yes, it does! Here it is. "Woe to the inhabiters of the earth and of the sea! For the devil is come down unto you, having great wrath, because he knoweth that he hath but a short time" (Rev. 12:12). Many people today are disobeying God's command concerning the Sabbath—the day which has always been His holy day, but they don't realize they are disobeying Him.

The Jewish people in Nehemiah's day knew they were disobeying God. They were doing just what God said they would do. He had warned them if they associated with pagans who refused to love and accept Him, they would be in danger of disobeying Him. It is a dangerous thing to continue to do what God says not to do in the Bible. That's a picture of all of us. Satan convinces us that it is more fun to do the things he temps us to do than obey God. But stop and contemplate where it takes us. Can you see the tears in Jesus' eyes and hear his broken sobs.

These examples of their behavior help us realize what a longsuffering God we serve. In every day and age, God calls His people back to Him. Yes! Now! Today! He is calling us, you and me, to come back to a loving relationship with Him. He calls everyone. He's had a tailor-made message for the backsliders of every day and age. Many of those people were not aware of their problems, either, just like they aren't in our day. They did not know they were being disobedient to God's Sabbath command. Nehemiah's words complete the picture of how God felt at that time in history, concerning worshiping other gods and the desecration of His holy Sabbath. God never changes. He is "the same yesterday, to day, and for ever" (Heb. 13:8). I am so glad He is a consistently loving and unchangeable God.

Here is what Nehemiah saw and did about it. "In those days I saw in Judah some treading wine presses on the sabbath, and bringing in sheaves, and lading asses; as also wine, grapes, and figs, and all manner of burdens, which they brought into Jerusalem on the sabbath day" (Neh. 13:15). He was upset with their desecration of God's holy law. He was also grieved about how the pagans were marring His people. He was concerned about their lost condition. He wasn't afraid to obey his conscience. Just look at what he did: "And I testified against them in the day wherein they sold victuals" (Neh. 13:15).

God bless him. He took care of the situation as soon as he realized what was going on. He didn't let the grass grow under his feet. Right away, he let them know he knew what they were doing. Forcefully, he told them how wrong it was. Since he saw them doing it, and let them know he saw them, they could not deny they were guilty of wrongdoing. He wanted them to be saved. His words were to help them see their need of God in their life, so they could repent and come back to Him.

Again, there were non-Jews entering the city and dwelling there. They, too, were desecrating God's holy day—the Sabbath. They, too, needed to know they were doing wrong. The Jews were not teaching them about God. They, too, would be lost without this knowledge. They needed to be taught how to honor God. "There dwelt men of Tyre also therein, which brought fish, and all manner of ware, and sold on the sabbath unto the children of Judah, and in Jerusalem" (Neh. 13:16).

But the Bible does not say Nehemiah had words with the non-Jews. No, his words were for the religious leaders of the Jews. They were the ones he considered responsible for causing God's people to sin. His correction of the leaders would cause changes to come about for both groups—Jew and Gentile. Nehemiah was putting the axe to the root of the problem. Listen to what he told those wicked leaders who were leading both God's people and the Gentiles away from honoring God. "Then I contended with the nobles of Ju'-dah, and said unto them, What evil thing is this that ye do, and profane the sabbath day? Did not your fathers thus, and did not our God bring all this evil upon us, and upon this city? Yet ye bring more wrath upon Israel by profaning the sabbath" (Neh. 13:17–18).

> *Nehemiah was putting the axe to the root of the problem.*

Nehemiah didn't only talk his words. He acted on them and put teeth into them. He did not shy away from the violence and trouble that could have happened to him. He obeyed God. He did not allow fear to get in his way. Only God could have given him such courage and bravery. "And it came to pass, that when the gates of Jerusalem began to be dark before the sabbath, I commanded that the gates should be shut, and charged that they should not be opened till after the sabbath: and some of my servants set I at the gates, that there should no burden be brought in on the sabbath day" (Neh. 13:19).

Look what the merchants tried to do! They were scheming bullies! They were just waiting for him to leave so they could sneak in and sell their wares. Luckily, Nehemiah had anticipated this and had already taken care of it. "So the merchants and sellers of all kinds of ware lodged without Jerusalem once or twice" (Neh. 13:20). No! Nehemiah didn't just shrug his shoulders and say, I guess I can't stop them from hanging around the gates. He felt he needed to personally speak to them. He didn't just leave the hard part for his helper to do!

Listen to what he told those who were lingering around those closed gates. He was very forceful for the Lord. Nehemiah was no weak-kneed wimp. He tells us, "Then I testified against them, and said unto them, Why lodge ye about the wall? If ye do so again, I will lay hands on you" (Neh. 13:21).

It worked. "From that time forth came they no more on the sabbath" (Neh. 13:21). Praise God! He had called their bluff! He knew what wimps they were! Yes, they were scared of their own shadow! Just preying on people who were afraid to stand up to them. Again, one of God's servants had opened His people's eyes and let them know He still wanted them to keep His Sabbath day holy. God was still saying through Nehemiah, the same thing Jesus said when He came to this earth: "Thou shalt worship the Lord thy God, and him only shalt thou serve" (Matt. 4:10).

What a wonderful, precious, long-suffering God we serve. He doesn't just stand idly by and watch us be deceived. He does something about it. He places within the heart of one of His children the desire to make the truth known. His Word, the Bible, is available for each of us to read today, but it's our choice to accept its promises and laws or reject them. He will work with us as long as we will listen. Oh, how I love Him! I'm sure you do too! But, do we love Him enough? So much that we obey Him?

CHAPTER THIRTEEN

It's Everybody's Sabbath

While the Jewish people and the Egyptian people who fled with them were in the wilderness, God the Son, reminded, coached, and tested them. God wrote the Ten Commandments on stone tablets for all of His children to see, we included, not just the Jews. God wants all of His children to know what His ten commandments say. Every last one of us! From the day He created Adam and Eve to when He comes to take us home with Him. He wants all of us to know His law still stands. He wants us to know it is still His law! He wants us to know that He still loves everyone! Jew and Gentile Alike! The only difference between the Jews and us is that they were chosen to teach the Gentiles about God. But as a nation, they rejected Jesus as their Savior. So now each one of them comes singly just as we do. But that's really no different than it always was from the get-go! From Adam to us! Each person accepts Jesus as their Savior singly. And it's the same today. God wants all of us to be able to know His law has not been tampered with. That is why He chiseled and ground His commands into a set of rocks. And there is another reason too, but we'll study that later!

It's about Jesus being the Rock. And that's why He wrote the commandments Himself instead of having Moses or someone else write them. He wanted to make it crystal clear that He was the one who wrote them.

That's why it's called God's law—not the law of Moses. And that's why someone else's name was not attached to it. How blessed all of us are that God let us know all about His laws. Here are the words which verify their authenticity. "The tablets were written on both sides; on the one side and on the other they were written." He did it so we can know the "the tablets were the work of God, and the writing was the writing of God engraved on the tablets" (Exod. 32:15–16). So! Now we know we can be sure. It truly is God's law!

God told the Jewish people how to keep the Sabbath, the seventh day of the week, holy just as He told Adam and Eve. He also included, right in the command itself, what would happen to them if they disobeyed it. He told Eve she would die if she ate the forbidden fruit. Likewise, God told the children of Israel they would be put to death if they failed to keep His special day holy.

God was not threatening them! He was preparing them for the future temptations Satan would thrust upon them. God was fortifying them, so they would know the truth and realize how important His holy day was. You see, if they knew the truth before Satan lied to them, they would be able to see through his lies and see that he was disagreeing with God. They would know without a doubt that Satan was lying. What a stronghold Satan had on Eve; and what a stronghold Eve had on Adam.

Notice that the word "whoever" is used to designate who the people were that came under the jurisdiction of His law. If the Sabbath had only been made for the Jews, God wouldn't have commanded Adam and Eve to keep it. They were not Jews! Notice also, that the Ten Commandments were not written down for us on earth until God wrote them at Mount Sinai. When God gave the ten-commandment law to Israel at that time, He said; "Six days may work be done; but in the seventh is the sabbath of rest, holy to the Lord: Whosoever doeth any work in the sabbath day, he shall surely be put to death" (Exod. 31:15).

Did you catch that? God was telling the Jews to keep the Sabbath holy, and all through it, He says, *"whosoever."* Why did He tell them to keep it? He was pointing them back to Creation. He wanted them to worship on

Sabbath, just as He wanted Adam and Eve to keep it. It wasn't anything new or a law just for them! Rather, it was a continuation of what God had always wanted every single person to do—even the angels in heaven—like we read earlier. It not only includes everyone on earth but it also includes the beings on all the other worlds who have mankind (created beings) living on them. That means all the whoevers who were ever created were to keep it, so they could believe they were created by God too.

Yes, and have you noticed right in the command itself, God included people who were not Jewish! Among those present at Mount Sinai, there were non-Jews. That's right! He included them in His command. God does not want anyone to have any cause for doubt whatsoever concerning who His law is written for! Since the Jews were not the only ones mentioned in His ten-commandment law, "**whosoever**" includes everyone and anyone! God would have said the same thing if He had been talking to us in the United States or anywhere else on earth. But God was talking to Israel, so He mentioned their name. And then He said, "Whosoever doeth any work in the sabbath day, he shall surely be put to death. Wherefore the children of Israel shall keep the sabbath, to observe the sabbath throughout their generations, for a perpetual covenant" (Exod. 31:15–16).

God was saying, since I want everyone—including all of the whosoevers—to keep it, certainly, I would want you Jews to keep it. Then He said to the Jews He was talking to, I want all of you to keep it forever. "It is a sign between me and the children of Israel for ever: for in six days the Lord made heaven and earth, and on the seventh day he rested, and was refreshed" (Exod. 31:17).

No! God wasn't saying it was only a sign between Him and the children of Israel. God wasn't even intimating that. Instead, He was saying that the obedience of the Jewish people was supposed to be an example for all people. They were supposed to tell everyone about their wonderful God. So whenever they obey God's law, they are showing all of the "whoevers," how they, too, can show others that they also are God's children. And the law tells everyone—all of the "whoevers" that they were also created by God.

Isn't that beautiful? I'm not a Jew, but I am His child! IF I love Him. That is, if I choose to be His child. I'm so glad God gave me that privilege. And isn't it grand that I can know for sure that His commandments were really written by Him? We can be sure of this because the Bible tells us so. "He gave unto Moses two tablets of the Testimony, tablets of stone, written with the finger of God" (Exod. 31:18, NKJV). Thus, the Ten Commandments are a covenant or agreement between God and us. I'm so glad God wrote His law Himself. And I'm so glad He wrote it for all mankind! The reason Jesus said it was a sign between Himself and the children of Israel is because that is who Jesus was talking to. The Bible is for all people. That means each person who reads the Bible can put their name in that slot in the sentence where it says "whosoever." Look at this beautiful verse. "And the Spirit and the bride say, Come. And let him that heareth say, Come. And whosoever will, let him take the water of life freely" (Rev. 22:17). This is why I can say, "whosoever means me"! I love that song that says whosoever means me. God wants all of us to be righteous. Those who disobey His law are unrighteous, and that includes all of us. For all of us are unrighteous. We are only righteous through the shed blood of Jesus. God says through Paul, "There is none righteous, no, not one: There is none that understandeth, there is none that seeketh after God. They are all gone out of the way, they are altogether become unprofitable; there is none that doeth good, no, not one" (Rom. 3:10–12).

It has been that way since Lucifer's disobedience in heaven. But the blessed truth is that God seeks after us. No one but God would take on such a discouraging job. What a privilege He hands us. That He would call us to obey His laws of love. It is only those who listen to the voice of God and obey His commandments that will be saved. He gives us much hope through His promise of forgiveness! Just listen to this! God says through Timothy that it's good for us to pray for each other. "For this is good and acceptable in the sight of God our Savior; Who will have all men to be saved, and to come unto the knowledge of truth" (1 Tim. 2:3–4).

God's ten-commandment law is a universal law. It includes all of the people God has ever been created. No matter what country, or who God is speaking to, He commands us to obey His Sabbath command and all of His other commands as well. He wants all of us to realize that He is the One who created us. You see, God has other worlds, where other men live. Remember! God called the angel named Lucifer—a man (Ezek. 28:9). Notice also that the word "worlds" is in the plural tense. "God, who at sundry times and in divers manner spake in times past unto the fathers by the prophets, Hath in these last days spoken unto us by his Son, whom he hath appointed heir of all things," now the clincher: "by whom also he made the worlds" (Heb. 1:1–2).

Isn't that exciting? They, too, are guided by God's ten-commandment law. God expounded to Moses in the book of Numbers on other laws and on what the prophets wrote, and He says that those laws and writings are important too. He said, "On these two commandments hang all the law and the prophets" (Matt. 22:40).

> *In God's community of unselfish love, we have a responsibility not only to God but to everyone else.*

This means that on these two commandments hang the Ten Commandments. And on the Ten Commandments hang all of the other laws and whatever the prophets wrote in principle. They all agree with each other. The same punishment is given to all who disobey His ten-commandment law. God is fair, and God tells the truth. Without trust in God, we cannot live. He is the source of our life. But in God's community of unselfish love, we have a responsibility not only to God but to everyone else. If we violate their freedom by disobeying His law, then there are consequences. This agrees with God's statement concerning those who do not obey His Laws: "Because he hath despised the word of the Lord, and hath broken his commandment, that soul shall utterly be cut off; his iniquity shall be upon him" (Num. 15:31).

Yes, God's laws are for the whole human race. The Jews were just His conduit. It doesn't matter who you are. God requires obedience from you. Notice that this verse does not say whether the disobedient person it was talking about was a Jew or not. All that mattered was whether they were obedient. Anyone who is disobedient and refuses to repent or will not ask God to forgive them will receive their punishment. We are each punished for our own sins in the end if we do not accept God's payment on our behalf. And, yes, Satan will be punished for his part in deceiving and enticing the sinner to disobey God. And while the children of Israel were in the wilderness under the direct rulership of God, they found a man violating the Sabbath by gathering sticks upon the Sabbath day. God had just given them His ten commandments. They were told what the penalty was for disobedience. They were given manna six days a week but not on the Sabbath. In the hot desert, they were told explicitly not to build a fire. This man was openly and defiantly breaking God's law. To allow this go unpunished would be to negate the entire Ten Commandments. To negate the Ten Commandments would undo the nation. It was on this covenant that the nation was founded. It was the ground of their existence. "And they that found him gathering sticks brought him unto Moses and Aaron, and unto all the congregation. And they put him in ward, because it was not declared what should be done to him. And the LORD said unto Moses, The man shall be surely put to death: all the congregation shall stone him with stones without the camp." (Num. 15:32–35).

The words "all the congregation" includes all of the Jews and non-Jews. Therefore, this statement is also true: "One law and one manner shall be for you, and for the stranger that sojourneth with you" (Num. 15:16). What a God! How fair He is. You don't have to be a Jew physically to receive His blessings. All you have to do is love Him to receive eternal life. God is only doing what He has to do so He can bring heaven and earth and the people in each place into harmony with Him. He hates it more than we do. It breaks God's heart to see all the sinfulness of mankind. He does not want to destroy anyone—not even Lucifer—but He has to destroy sin—and that makes the sinner involved in this destructive force. The sinner is sinful, i.e., sin. The following verses in the book of Exodus, concerning the strangers in their land, also agree with God's fourth commandment, which says,

"Remember the sabbath day, to keep it holy. Six days shalt thou labour, and do all thy work: but the seventh day is the sabbath of the LORD thy God: In it thou shalt not do any work, thou, nor thy son, nor thy daughter, thy manservant, nor thy maidservant, nor thy cattle, nor thy stranger that is within thy gates: For in six days the LORD made heaven and earth, the sea, and all that in them is, and rested the seventh day: wherefore the LORD blessed the sabbath day, and hallowed it" (Exod. 20:8–11). God points us back to what He did on the six days of creation, and the prophet Isaiah adds his voice to the conclusion, by saying, "Also the sons of the stranger, that join themselves to the LORD, to serve him, and to love the name of the LORD, to be his servants, every one that keepeth the sabbath from polluting it, and taketh hold of my covenant; Even them will I bring to my holy mountain, and make them joyful in my house of prayer: their burnt offerings and their sacrifices shall be accepted upon mine altar; for my house shall be called an house of prayer for all people" (Isa. 56:6–7).

What a promise! And God is giving it to all mankind! And why not? The thing that was special about the Jews was that they were to teach other people about Jesus. Allow me to repeat—they failed to do their God-given work. But remember! To do this work, they had been given great advantages. They had Abraham, Isaac, and Jacob as their fathers. Great men of faith. They saw God's mighty hand deliver them from Egypt. They were at Mt. Sinai and saw the glory of God. They had the Ten Commandments written with the finger of God. They had the rest of the oracles of God given to them by Moses. Still, they rejected their Savior, Jesus, the One God had commissioned them to tell everyone about. God wants all to know that Jesus can save them from their sins—and He wants all to know about His Sabbath command. Especially now, at this time in earth's history, we need to be showing people that God still loves them and that He still wants them to keep His special day holy. God still wants His people to let everyone know that His Sabbath is the seventh day of the week. He says, "The LORD God, which gathered the outcasts of Israel saith, Yet I will gather others to him, beside those that are gathered unto him" (Isa. 56:8).

Sin is a very serious thing. Sin is what caused our world to be thrown into chaos. Sin kills. All of us are sinners. A sinner can't pay for or correct his own sins. That's why God wrote down His laws of love for all to see. His laws are a safety net, so we will know to stay away from sin. It wasn't written just for the Israelites. It was written for all people everywhere. God says disobedience to His law is sin. Lawlessness is a failure to obey God's law, and that is what sin is—failure to obey God. "Whosoever committeth sin transgresseth also the law: and sin is the transgression of the law" (1 John 3:4). Yes, sin is disobedience to God's laws—yesterday, today, and forever. And God says that "All have sinned, and come short of the glory of God" (Rom. 3:23).

Jesus is the only sinless human who has ever lived. The payment we receive for doing the works of sin is death. Not that God brings death, but that we bring it on ourselves because we do the things which cause death. Sin is what causes death. We sin! And it is work—let me tell you! And the paycheck I will receive for my sinful work will be death. That is if—and I like that "if"—if I study my Bible, read His law, and discover I am sinning, and then go to Him and ask Him to forgive me, and then accept His forgiveness, and obey Him. He will forgive all of my sins.

But if I don't ask Him to forgive me, and I don't stop committing those sins, I won't be forgiven. *I must ask, repent, and then follow Jesus.* Here's what God says my payment for those sins will be. "The wages of sin is death." But, praise God! The bottom line says, "the gift of God is eternal life through Jesus Christ our Lord" (Rom. 6:23). The Lord wants everyone to repent. Nothing would make Him happier.

If you carefully read each one of the ten rules in God's law, you will find that each one is a command to love God and/or love our fellowmen. God's commandments are not just arbitrary rules written down, so God can show us who is boss. No! God loves us, and our obedience to those laws show Him that we love Him. They also show other people we love

God, and they will show God that they love Him too. Those laws show us eternal life can surely be ours!

We do not know how to love God on our own because we are born in sin. But when we see God's example, He shows us how to love Him. His biggest show of love was when He sent His Son, Jesus, to save us from our sins. It is John who tells us we only love God because He loved us first (see 1 John 4:19). I'm so glad God showed all of mankind how to love Him by sending Jesus to live here and demonstrate His Father's love to us. Wow! What a thread of love that was and still is. Yes, it is everybody's Sabbath—not just a Sabbath for the Jews. It couldn't be just the Jewish Sabbath! Because it has been in existence forever. Remember! God has no beginning or end. His law is forever, just as He is forever.

Jesus had a work for the Jews to do because He wanted all of us to become Jews through loving Him. That was God's plan. He wants all of us to become His children. Legally, all children are heirs and belong to their father and mother. Each child receives the portion their parents decide to give them after they die.

When God created Adam and Eve, they were His children through creation. When they sinned, they lost that status. Jesus bought back that privileged family tie when He died on the cross for us. Now, through Jesus, you and I are not only His created children but we are also His adopted children as well. That is if we agree to the adoption! Jesus is the one who makes it possible for us to be reunited into the family of God. Through Jesus' shed blood, it is possible for the Father "to redeem those who were under the law, that we might receive the adoption as sons" (Gal. 4:5, NKJV).

Jesus' payment on the cross really did pay for our sins, and that makes us legally God's children again—with all of the privileges and requirements. Paul says, "For he is not a Jew who is one outwardly, nor is that circumcision which is outward in the flesh; but he is a Jew who is one inwardly; and circumcision is that of the heart, in the Spirit, and not in the letter; whose praise is not from men but from God" (Rom. 2:28–29, NKJV).

God makes it crystal clear that anyone who loves and honors Him is His child. He says, "You are all sons of God through faith in Christ Jesus.

For as many of you who were baptized into Christ have put on Christ. There is neither Jew nor Greek, there is neither slave nor free, there is neither male nor female; for you are all one in Christ Jesus. And if you are Christ's, then you are Abraham's seed, and heirs according to the promise" (Gal. 3:26–29, NKJV).

We who love and obey God are some of those descendants He was talking to Abraham about. Not only did the promise come to us through Jesus, but it also came to Abraham through Jesus too. When Jesus came as a baby to Bethlehem, God's promise He made to Abraham was fulfilled. Paul says so. "When the fullness of the time had come, God sent forth His Son, born of a woman, born under the law, to redeem those who were under the law, that we might receive the adoption as sons. And because you are sons, God has sent forth the Spirit of His Son into your hearts, crying out, 'Abba Father!' Therefore you are no longer a slave but a son, and if a son, then an heir of God through Christ" (Gal. 4:4–7, NKJV).

Paul exclaims, "As many as are led by the Spirit of God, these are sons of God. For you did not receive the spirit of bondage again to fear, but you received the Spirit of adoption by whom we cry out, 'Abba Father.' The Spirit Himself witnesses with our spirit that we are children of God, and if children, then heirs—heirs of God and joint heirs with Christ, … that we may be glorified together" (Rom. 8:14–17, NKJV). That makes Jesus our big brother and His Father—our Father. What a priceless heritage! The angels in heaven were in existence before the Jews. Adam and Eve were in existence before the Jews. The people in Noah's day were in existence before the Jews. Those who built the Tower of Babel were in existence before the Jews. Then God chose Abraham and his descendants to spread the good word of the gospel. Abraham is the father of the Jewish nation. Then, there were Jews.

> It's <u>not</u> the Jews' Sabbath! It's everybody's Sabbath!!!
> God says so! And the truth is—this commandment
> is the Lost Thread of God's Love ! ! !

CHAPTER FOURTEEN

Change of the Julian Calendar

The Julian calendar, of the Roman Empire, was instituted by Julius Caesar about forty years before Jesus was born. It was like our present calendar. It had the same seven-day cycle that God created when He formed the earth and us. The week began with Sunday and ended with Saturday, the seventh day of the week.

The solar year, the one God made at Creation, was eleven minutes and a few seconds less than the year the Julian calendar espoused. Thus, the calendar mankind constructed was not in exact harmony with God's calendar. Consequently, each year there was a little time lost. To help synchronize man's timing with God's celestial bodies, they introduced what we call leap year. It takes care of that discrepancy. It is

> *The Julian calendar, of the Roman Empire, was instituted by Julius Caesar about forty years before Jesus was born.*

important to know this because it makes it so we can know for sure that we are keeping the same day of the week that God, Adam, and Eve kept on that first Sabbath of creation week. God made the Sabbath, and He made the celestial bodies and their circuits. The only way we can know our calendar is correct is if it matches God's celestial time clock. Yes, that is the only way we can know for certain that we are really keeping God's true Sabbath. As long as no one changes our calendar so causes it to become out of sync with God's celestial bodies or changes God's weekly cycle, we can use our present calendar.

But if someone does change the weekly cycle and makes a law saying we must follow it, that law will be in opposition to God's Law. It will not change which day God tells us to keep holy. Saturday, the seventh day of the week which God created, will still be God's Sabbath—not the one mankind calls the sabbath. It would be very confusing, and out of sync with God's will and His clock—the solar system. Man would be putting his day in place of and instead of God's holy day.

CHAPTER FIFTEEN

Jesus' Parents Taught Him to Keep the Seventh-day Sabbath Holy

---

Jesus was born into a Jewish family. His heavenly Father placed Him with Jewish parents because He knew they would faithfully keep all His commands. Also, God knew Joseph and Mary would teach His Son, Jesus, to obey His heavenly Father. The Bible verifies this by saying, "Jesus increased in wisdom and stature, and in favor with God and man" (Luke 2:52).

For Jesus to be in favor with God, He would have to be keeping His commandments. Keeping the seventh day of the week holy was just one of the ways Jesus was in favor with His heavenly Father. When we obey God, we are truly in favor with Him too. God gave us the Bible, too—so we would have a way of knowing for sure, without a doubt, that we are loving and obeying Him, and also so we would know we were showing love to each other.

Jesus came to this earth to give us an example of how He and His Father want us to live and honor Them. Jesus did everything we must do. Our doing doesn't save us! It is Jesus' doing and His death on the cross that saves us. He paid for our sins. If we love God, we will have faith in what the Father, Son, and Holy Spirit have done and are still doing for us. We will trust Them explicitly! Grace—the unmerited love that God gives to sinners—is God's part in the salvation equation, and faith is our part. Let's look at that equation again as it is stated in the Bible. "By grace are ye saved through faith; and that not of yourselves: it is the gift of God: Not of works, lest any man should boast" (Eph. 2:8–9).

So! If my works don't save me, what good are they? I puzzled over that for a long time. Then it finally dawned on me! Works are those hugs and kisses I have been talking about. Every time I say "no" to Satan, I am saying "yes" to God and telling Him I love Him. That's why God says, "if you love Me," obey Me, "keep my commandments." It is my works of obedience that show Him I love Him. I like that! It makes whatever I am doing more tangible when I picture myself giving God a hug. And God likes to give us hugs back. To me, hugs from God are so much better than the things Satan is tempting me with.

Do you know, not only is grace a gift, but faith is a gift too. Everything we have is a gift from God. There isn't anything we can do on our own without His help. We are totally dependent on Him. I'm so glad our God is so trustworthy—aren't you? God is the one who tells us faith is a gift from Him. He tells me so I can trust Him and know He really is the One who gives it to me. God isn't secretive about His gifts. He tells us plainly who gives us this gift. He says, "God hath dealt to every man the measure of faith" (Rom. 12:3).

Did you catch that! He says He gives *every single person* a measure of faith! Have you taken time to think seriously about it? The Father actually sent His Son, Jesus, to fulfill all righteousness. Isn't that wonderful? We can't do righteous things or be righteous without His help. So, the Father actually sent His Son, Jesus, to do the impossible for us. He did do the impossible while inhabiting a human body. What a gift! That's amazing. Thank You, Father. Thank You, Jesus.

Keeping the Sabbath day holy is one of the extra-special ways we can be right with God. It's the most special way we can love Him. It's the commandment Satan works the hardest to get us to disobey. Why do I think it is more special than the others? It is because it has to do with our worship of Him and our special time to spend with Him. When you spend time with someone, you get to know them better. It's special! It is through God's Word, the Bible, that we learn how and what God wants us to do. Jesus Himself learned how He should act by reading the Old Testament. Jesus is the living Word—He lived God's Word every day of His life while He was here on earth.

Through Jesus' actions, the Father has left us a trail of obedience. A perfect example—if you please. So today, yes, this very day, we can know how to walk in Jesus' footsteps and do what Jesus did. If we walk in His footsteps, we will know for sure we are doing God's will. Sabbath observance was, still is, and will continue to be an extremely important issue with God. Keeping the Sabbath holy reminds us that Jesus is the one who created us. Keeping the Sabbath holy is just one way we spend time with God. You can't have a relationship with someone if you don't spend quality time together.

After Satan tested Jesus in the wilderness, the Bible says that Jesus "returned in the power of the Spirit into Galilee: and there went out a fame of him through all the region round about. And he taught in their synagogues, being glorified by all. And he came to Nazareth, where he had been brought up: and as his custom was, he went into the synagogue on the sabbath day, and stood up for to read" (Luke 4:14–16).

There are many verses that say Jesus kept the Sabbath holy. Look at this one! He left Nazareth and "came down to Capernaum, a city of Galilee, and taught them on the sabbath days. And they were astonished at His doctrine: for his word was with power" (Luke 4:31–32). Every chance they got, the Jewish religious leaders criticized Jesus on how He kept the Sabbath. Jesus upheld what He did and tried to help them see they were wrong. When they chided Him for healing people on the Sabbath, He said to them, "If a man on the sabbath day receive circumcision," (in other words, is circumcised on that day) "that the law of Moses should not be broken; are ye angry at me, because I have made a man every whit whole on the sabbath day?" (John 7:23).

It was His custom to keep the Sabbath by going to church and by healing people. The Jews were circumcising their babies on the Sabbath in order to obey Moses' law of circumcision, yet they condemned Jesus for healing on the Sabbath. Sounds like a double standard to me. They were making the Sabbath a burden for people with their many rules—rules God did not sanction. Please allow me to share a personal insight. We are Seventh-day Adventists, and we do not believe in attending school on Sabbath. My husband had graduated from law school. And he was granted the privilege of taking the exams to get his legal license, but the exam was scheduled to take place on Sabbath. So he talked to the teachers about it, and they were very co-operative. They arranged for him to stay at an apartment that weekend while the other students took their exam. There was also a Jewish student whose convictions wouldn't allow him to take his exam on Sabbath either. They placed both of them in the same apartment and had someone stay with them. This was done to make sure they did not make any contact with the other students before they took their exams. They did not want them getting answers to questions.

That Sabbath, my husband's eyes were opened concerning the strict rules of the Jewish faith. When it became lunchtime, the Jewish fellow asked my husband to open the refrigerator door for him, so he could get his lunch out. He thought he couldn't open it because it would be breaking God's law. Why did he think it would be breaking God's law? It was because He would be lighting a fire on Sabbath. The refrigerator light would come on when he opened the door, and the Jews considered this to be like lighting a fire! The Jewish religious leaders made many such rules in Jesus' day. So many, in fact, that it was difficult for people to remember all of them and keep them. Indeed, their many rules were a burden. Jesus was trying to correct this error.

Those same leaders accused Jesus many, many times, of breaking the Sabbath. But Jesus and His Father were the ones who created the Sabbath. They wrote the laws that governed how the Sabbath was to be kept. They were the very ones who made the Sabbath and declared it to be holy. They alone had the authority and right to decide how they wanted it kept.

According to the law of circumcision, babies were to be circumcised eight days after birth. This meant some babies would be circumcised on Sabbath in obedience to that law. Being circumcised the eighth day after birth caused the surgery to fall on every day in the week. Thus, many babies were circumcised on Sabbath. Jesus did not condemn them for that. Since Jesus allowed it, that means it was not a sin for them to circumcise their babies on Sabbath. After all, Moses would never have made a law that was contrary to God's will. He was a man of God, and if he had misunderstood what God wanted done, God would have corrected him.

The apostle Paul was circumcised the eighth day after his birth. We learn this from a sermon he preached to the Philippian people. Here is Paul's boast to those people. It shows that He was proud of his heritage and that he never felt any parent who circumcised their baby on Sabbath had done wrong. Here is what Paul said, "Circumcised the eighth day, of the stock of Israel, of the tribe of Benjamin, an Hebrew of the Hebrews; as touching the law, a Pharisee;" (Phil. 3:5).

> *Moses would never have made a law that was contrary to God's will.*

Also, Isaac was circumcised eight days after he was born. "And he gave him the covenant of circumcision: so Abraham begat Isaac, and circumcised him the eighth day" (Acts 7:8). Likewise, John the Baptist's parents did the same. "And it came to pass, that on the eighth day they came to circumcise the child; and they called him Zacharias, after the name of his father" (Luke 1:59). Even our Savior's parents obeyed the law on circumcision. "And when eight days were accomplished for the circumcising of the child, his name was called JESUS, which was so named of the angel before He was conceived in the womb" (Luke 2:21).

Jesus didn't see any difference between circumcising their babies on Sabbath and believing it was OK to make a man completely well on the Sabbath. It appears that Jesus did not consider either service to be an act of disobedience to His law. And why would He? The Father Himself had decreed it and told an angel to give His message to Joseph, even before he and Mary had come together. "Now the birth of Jesus Christ was on this wise: When as his mother Mary was espoused to Joseph, she was found with child of the Holy Ghost. Then Joseph her husband, being a just man, and not willing to make her a public example, was minded to put her away privily. But while he thought on these things, behold the angel of the LORD appeared unto him in a dream, saying, Joseph, thou son of David, fear not to take unto thee Mary thy wife: for that which is conceived in her is of the Holy Ghost. And she shall bring forth a son, and thou shalt call his name JESUS: for he shall save his people from their sins" (Matt. 1:18–21).

These people were not working to make their living by circumcising babies. If the doctors had opened their offices and made it a point to go into the business of making money by doing circumcisions, and if they had decided to make circumcising babies on the Sabbath part of their work-week, then it would have been wrong. It would have been treating the Sabbath like any other working day of the week. I am sure since they were complaining about Jesus healing on the Sabbath, none of them opened their medical practices on the Sabbath day. They wouldn't have wanted to give Jesus an opportunity to tell them they were doing wrong. Then, they really would have been hypocrites!

Notice what else these religious leaders did to cause people to have unbelief in Jesus! They were bent on causing Him trouble. What a shame they went down that path and were blinded by Satan. They verbally attacked Him, too, for healing people on the Sabbath. Look at these cases. "They brought to the Pharisees him that aforetime was blind. And it was the sabbath day when Jesus made the clay, and opened his eyes" (John 9:13–14). They said, "This man is not of God, because he keepeth not the sabbath day. Others said, how can a man that is a sinner do such miracles? And there was a division among them" (John 9:16). They couldn't even agree among themselves whether Jesus was wrong.

"Now it happened on another Sabbath, also, that He entered the synagogue and taught. And a man was there whose right hand was withered. So the scribes and Pharisees watched Him closely, whether He would heal on the Sabbath, that they might find an accusation against Him." (Notice their evil intentions! They were not showing love or trying to help Jesus become aware of His supposed sin. They were trying to catch Him doing something they thought was wrong).

"But He knew their thoughts, and said to the man who had the withered hand, 'Arise and stand here.' And he arose and stood. Then Jesus said to them, 'I will ask you one thing: Is it lawful on the Sabbath to do good, or to do evil? to save life, or to destroy?' And when He had looked around at them all, He said unto the man, 'Stretch out your hand.' And he did so, and his hand was restored as whole as the other." (Notice their angry reaction!) "But they were filled with rage, and discussed with one with another what they might do to Jesus" (Luke 6:6–11, NKJV). They were not acting from love; they were reacting from selfish hatred.

They did not see Jesus' act of healing as a miracle of love. Jesus used the man with the withered hand to teach them it is always right to alleviate suffering on the Sabbath. Just as it was right to heal on other days of the week. Healing was not Jesus' occupation. He did not make His living by healing people. When He healed people, He was not working. He was showing love to those who were sick. He was showing them what His Father is like.

We do not know why Jesus chose to heal this particular man. But it seems very likely, that He healed him because it would help Him make His point. The man had been sick for a long time. In this way, Jesus showed them He had the authority to decide what was lawful for Him, the Son of God, to do on the Sabbath. To them, His actions came across as extreme. Jesus could read their thoughts.

They probably reasoned, "This man could have waited until after the Sabbath to have his hand healed." Therefore, he was a prime candidate for Jesus to show both His authority and His love. God does not want people or animals to suffer on Sabbath nor on any other day of the week, for that matter. But healing was not the only issue about which the religious leaders heckled Jesus. Just look at what else they questioned Him on! The real issue was whether He was God and whether He had the authority to tell them how to keep the Sabbath day holy.

Jesus' Parents Taught Him to Keep the Seventh-day Sabbath Holy

"And it came to pass on the second sabbath after the first, that He went through the corn fields; And His disciples plucked the heads of corn, and did eat, rubbing them in their hands. And certain of the Pharisees said unto them, 'Why do ye that which is not lawful to do on the sabbath days?' And Jesus answering them said, Have ye not read so much as this, what David did, when himself was an hungered, and they which were with him; How he went into the house of God, and did take and eat the shewbread, and gave also to them that were with him; which is not lawful for to eat but for the priests alone? And he said unto them, That the Son of man is Lord also of the sabbath" (Luke 6:1–5).

That's huge! Did you get that? Jesus actually and outright told them He had the authority to decide what was right or wrong to do on the Sabbath. That He was the Lord of it! That He was GOD if you please! Jesus was very open concerning who had the authority to decide what the rules were concerning His special day. Also, Jesus had just shown them there are exceptions to all rules, by telling them how David ate the shewbread when he was starving to death. Jesus acknowledged it was unlawful for them to eat it. Jesus considered it all right for them to eat the shewbread because there was nothing else available—and no way to get anything else. They would have starved! Jesus was asking them to realize that eating something unlawful because they were starving was necessary to save their life.

You have listened to the accusations they hurled at His disciples. Jesus did not consider His disciples disobedient to the Sabbath command when they picked the grain and rolled it between their hands to remove the husk. But the Pharisees did! They called it harvesting. The disciples were not doing their daily work on Sabbath. Picking a little grain to eat, and rubbing it in their hands to get the husk off was not the same as harvesting a field of grain to earn their living. They were merely picking some grain to eat because they were hungry. They weren't even picking it to make a meal.

The Jewish leaders were constantly heckling Jesus and putting Him down. Here is another instance when they were looking for some way to condemn Him for healing on Sabbath! "Now it happened, as He went into the house of one of the rulers of the Pharisees to eat bread on the Sabbath, that they watched Him closely. And behold, there was a certain man before Him who had dropsy. And Jesus, answering, spoke to the lawyers and Pharisees," (it was the lawyers of canon law, i.e., biblical law, who were causing Him trouble. They were the lawyers who prided themselves in being experts at knowing how the laws in the Bible should be kept) "saying, 'Is it lawful to heal on the Sabbath?' but they kept silent. And He took him and healed him, and let him go."

Notice what Jesus did next! He knew what made those religious men tick. Jesus knew all about their greedy thoughts. "Then He answered them, saying, 'Which of you, having a donkey or an ox that has fallen into a pit, will not immediately pull him out on the Sabbath day?' And they could not answer Him regarding these things" (Luke 14:1–6, NKJV). The reason they were unwilling to answer Jesus' question was huge. They knew they would not allow one of their animals to die for lack of care on the Sabbath. They wouldn't want to lose the money they had invested in the animal should it die. Jesus knew their hearts. Jesus did not want people or animals who were sick to die for lack of care on the Sabbath. They knew that too! They were just angry with Him.

God is not unreasonable! He wants us to take care of people's needs even if it means they require care on His holy day, such as cows being milked. Milk cows are in severe pain if they are left unmilked for a whole day. If it is something that can be taken care of ahead of time, such as cooking or going to a doctor for a non-emergency appointment, it is not to be done on Sabbath. But you don't stop loving someone to obey a law of love. So, Jesus used this means to let the people know God's laws were being misinterpreted. He used the man with a withered hand because He wanted them to know He, the one who made the Sabbath in the first place, is the One who determines what is right to do on that day.

Those canon lawyers were treating Jesus just like the men did who led Mary Magdalene into sin and then accused her of sinning. They went and told Jesus about her sin, just so they could cause Jesus trouble. So Jesus wrote in the sand to show them their sins. They didn't want to own up to them; neither did they care about her welfare. They wanted to condemn Jesus more than they wanted to obey God. We, too, must guard against our selfish desires. We must always make God first, last, and best, above what anyone else says or thinks. Jesus said to His disciples, "If ye keep My commandments, ye shall abide in my love; even as I have kept My Father's commandments, and abide in His love" (John 15:10).

Again, Jesus was telling them He was equal to His Father; that He, too, was God. And that this gave Him the right to tell them how the Sabbath should be kept. Jesus never taught that the commandments should not be kept. Rather, He pointed out that even one jot, the smallest letter of the Greek alphabet, or one tittle, the least stroke of a pen, which is the smallest portion of one of the letters of the alphabet, would not be changed in His law. Not even a very tiny portion of the law may be altered. He asked them and then proceeded to tell them, "Think not that I am come to destroy the law, or the prophets: I am not come to destroy, but to fulfill. For verily I say unto you, Till heaven and earth pass, one jot or one title shall in no means wise pass from the law, till all be fulfilled" (Matt. 5:17–18).

That will never happen! God's law will never be done away with. Our heaven and earth, as we know it, will pass away after the righteous are taken to heaven. It will be burned up when God plans to burn it up. But God is going to replace it after He has judged the wicked. No, Jesus did not come to do away with the Ten Commandments. He came to show us how to keep them. When you fulfill a command—you do what it tells you to do. Jesus came and did what the commandments told Him to do.

These are only a few examples of what Jesus taught about keeping the Sabbath day holy. Each one of these experiences was a teaching moment for His disciples. He daily taught them how to deal with people who criticized Him and His law. Jesus did not tell them He was preparing them to be witnesses for Him, but that is part of what He was doing was preparing them for the job He was going to give them once He went back to heaven.

Read all of one of the gospels to find out other things Jesus taught about His holy day. Make Jesus your teacher. Listen to the Holy Spirit as

He guides you into all truth. The Sabbath was set apart for us so that we could come closer to God and lead others closer to Him too. Not only that—we must forsake all of our sins. In Isaiah chapters 58 and 59, the prophet Isaiah informs us of many ways the people thought they were pleasing God. But they were wrong! They were doing things God did not want them to do, and Isaiah told them how they should change. Yes, they needed to change!

It is no different in our day. All of us need to spend time alone with God, so His Spirit can speak to our hearts and teach us what is right. We need to read God's Word and make sure He would approve of what we are doing. It's all there in the Bible. We need to choose to have God be our teacher. We need to listen to the Holy Spirit and do what He tells us to do. The Holy Spirit will never tell us to disobey what God says in His Word. If it disagrees with God's Word, it is not coming from the Holy Spirit. We need to spend time with God every day—not just on Sabbath. He says, "If thou turn away thy foot from the sabbath, from doing thy pleasure on my holy day; and call the sabbath a delight, the holy of the Lord, honourable; and shalt honour him, not doing thine own ways, nor finding thine own pleasure, nor speaking thine own words: Then shalt thou delight thyself in the LORD; and I will cause thee to ride upon the high places of the earth, and feed thee with the heritage of Jacob thy father: for the mouth of the Lord hath spoken it" (Isa. 58:13–14).

I am so glad the Father sent Jesus to us to demonstrate how loving and just He is. Our obedience does not save us, but it shows God we love Him. It's Jesus' obedience and His payment for our sins on the cross that saves us. It is Jesus' payment for our sins that makes salvation possible for

> *The Holy Spirit will never tell us to disobey what God says in His Word. If it disagrees with God's Word, it is not coming from the Holy Spirit.*

each one of us! That is *if* we also obey Him and accept His precious gift of forgiveness. Whenever we do what He asks us to do, it is like throwing our arms around Him, and giving Him a great big bear hug. Have you given Him one today? Every time we obey Him we are saying, Yes, God, I am willing, and I will do whatever you ask me to do. It is when we obey Him that we say,

"I love You, God."

CHAPTER SIXTEEN

Jesus Even Kept it Holy in His Death

Jesus and His disciples honored God in a very special way the weekend He was crucified. How did they honor God? They were obedient to His law of love. Their obedience caused them to keep God's Sabbath holy even during the crisis of the crucifixion of Jesus. A time when they could have said, "What's the use." "Evil is winning," etc. They could have gone the easy route, the route with less fear for their own safety. But praise God, they didn't! Instead, they clung to their faith and obeyed God. And Jesus rested in the tomb over the Sabbath too. Yes! Jesus rested in the tomb and kept the Sabbath holy even in His death.

There were secret followers who honored that Sabbath too. One was Joseph of Arimathaea (see Mark 15:43). Let's look at him first. The Bible pinpoints exactly which Joseph it is talking about. He was a man of great importance in more ways than one. First in importance is the way he treated Jesus. We should always put Jesus first in our lives and hearts, just as Joseph ended up doing. He played a major role in seeing that Jesus rested from His work of redemption on the Sabbath day.

Jesus Even Kept it Holy in His Death   155

Let's set the stage! Jesus was crucified on the sixth day of the week—the day before the Sabbath. That's Friday! In the Bible, the sixth day of the week is called the preparation day. That's because they always used Friday to prepare for the Sabbath. Jesus died that Friday. "And now when the even was come, because it was the preparation, that is, the day before the sabbath" (Mark 15:42). Notice this verse refers back to Creation. It reminds us that each day begins and ends at sunset. How loyal Jesus was to God's law. He rested on the Sabbath even in this crisis. He was making it possible for us to spend eternity with Him in heaven. It was a rest from sin and every bad thing.

He died the same day He was crucified. People who were secret followers took Jesus' body down from the cross that same day and laid it in a tomb. There were women who professed to love Jesus too. The men and the women worked together to honor Him. But they were unable to finish embalming Jesus that day because the Sabbath arrived before they had finished preparing Him for burial. They, too, honored God's holy Sabbath day even in the face of this crisis. I think God made this possible. It would help to permanently impress its importance on all humanity forever.

About now, you may be thinking. Duh! Of course, Jesus died the day He was crucified! Well, that's exactly how I felt, too, the first time I read it! But I found out that what usually happens when a person is crucified is totally opposite of what I thought. Rather, it is usually a long, drawn-out, very painful, slow process. Typically, people who are crucified don't die the same day. Sometimes it would take days for them to die. It blows my mind just thinking about it. It's a terrible way to die.

We know Jesus died the same day, because the Bible says so! Joseph went and asked Pilate if he could take Jesus' body down from the cross so He could rest in the tomb over the Sabbath. Listen to Pilate's conversation with him. When he talked with Pilate, he found that *Pilate was amazed that Jesus was already dead Friday afternoon!* So Pilate checked to see if Joseph was telling the truth. He wanted to know if Joseph knew what he was talking about.

Mark tells us the centurion was a follower of Jesus, too, but he followed Jesus at an even greater distance. He was more secretive about it. Nicodemus, too, was a secret follower of Jesus! All three followed Jesus at a distance. "And Pilate marvelled if He were already dead: and calling unto him the centurion, he asked him whether He had been any while dead. And when he knew it of the centurion, he gave the body to Joseph" (Mark 15:44–45).

All three were witnessing for God when they upheld Jesus. They witnessed Jesus' divinity while He was on the cross too. It took guts for Joseph to go and ask Pilate if he could take Jesus' body down from the cross and thus expose his allegiance to Him. But his desire to keep the Sabbath holy, and also his desire to honor his Lord, outweighed his fear. He wanted to get Jesus' body down from the cross before the Sabbath arrived. That desire was stronger than his fear! And it won out. He was a Sabbath-keeper and a very good man. Also, the Bible tells us he was a counselor. According to *Strong's Concordance*, this indicates he was a "member of a council" (that means he was a member of an advisory or legislative body). This means he was a very important person legally.

The legislative body was wise to have him on their council, for the Bible says, "And, behold, there was a man named Joseph, a counsellor; and he was a good man, and a just: (the same had not consented to the counsel and deed of them;) he was of Arimathaea, a city of the Jews: who also himself waited for the kingdom of God" (Luke 23:50–51). In other words, even before Jesus' crucifixion, Joseph did not go along with what those evil men were planning to do to Him. Isn't that amazing? I especially find this surprising because he lived in one of the cities of the Jews! It would be hard to live there and do what he did. This shows us he really loved Jesus.

The next verses really show us his loving deeds toward his Savior. For the Bible goes on to say; "This man went unto Pilate, and begged the body of Jesus. Then he took it down, and wrapped it in linen, and laid it in a sepulchre that was hewn in stone, wherein never man before was laid" (Luke 23:52–53). He was really sticking his neck out when he did this—he could have been killed. It was a brand-new tomb. Tombs were probably very expensive.

Luke adds this information. He tells us, "And that day was the preparation, and the sabbath drew on. And the women also, which came with him from Galilee, followed after, and beheld the sepulchre, and how His body was laid. Then they returned, and prepared spices and ointments; And rested the sabbath day according to the commandment" (Luke 23:54–56).

The centurion had just witnessed all that had taken place during Jesus' crucifixion. No wonder he came out in the open. No wonder he no longer kept his belief in Jesus a secret. What he saw that day caused him to believe Jesus truly was the Son of God. Listen to Luke's testimony. "And it was about the sixth hour, and there was darkness over all the earth until the ninth hour. And the sun was darkened, and the veil of the temple was rent in the midst. And when Jesus had cried with a loud voice, he said, Father, into Thy hands I commend my spirit: and having said thus, He gave up the ghost. Now when the centurion saw what was done, he glorified God, saying, Certainly this was a righteous man" (Luke 23:44–47). Those were catastrophic occurrences.

But Mark's rendition, concerning the centurion, was even more accepting of Jesus. It was very heartwarming. He witnessed the same things Luke did, but just look at what he said. He didn't say the centurion called Jesus a righteous man. Here is Mark's rendition of the centurion's words. He went further. "And when the centurion, which stood over against Him, saw that He so cried out, and gave up the ghost, he said, Truly this man was the Son of God" (Mark 15:39).

John also talks about two men who were secret disciples of Jesus. Both of them were very influential. John adds Nicodemus to the mix. This is why the women were working with those men to get Jesus ready for burial. All of them were followers of Jesus. The women were very open about their allegiance, whereas the men kept their association with Jesus fairly secret. Just look at what John said about it. "After this Joseph of Arimathaea, being a disciple of Jesus, but secretly for fear of the Jews, besought Pilate that he might take away the body of Jesus: and Pilate gave him leave.... And there came also Nicodemus, which at the first came to Jesus by night, and brought a mixture of myrrh and aloes, about an hundred pound weight. Then took they the body of Jesus, and wound it in linen clothes with the spices, as the manner of the Jews is to bury" (John 19:38–40).

Mark's rendition. He makes it very clear what day of the week it was when all of this took place. "Now when the even was come, because it was the preparation, that is, the day before the sabbath" (Mark 15:42). What an important piece of information this is! These verses verify Jesus was crucified on Friday, and that on that same sixth day of the week, His disciples prepared spices and ointments for embalming Him. Why? To anoint Jesus' body for burial!

The women had spices they wanted to anoint him with too, and they weren't able to get all of them ready for use before the Sabbath arrived. Jesus had taught them not to work on the Sabbath. So, on Friday, their normal day to prepare for the Sabbath, they got everything ready for His burial. That took some doing! They also helped place Him in the tomb that day—just before the Sabbath arrived. But they did not finish embalming Him because the time had slipped away from them. It was getting too close to sundown. The women had more spices they wanted to put on Jesus. But it was evening—almost Sabbath. So they honored Jesus after He died by waiting until after the Sabbath was over to finish embalming Him.

> *They honored Jesus after He died by waiting until after the Sabbath was over to finish embalming Him.*

There were some other astounding things which happened that Friday. Things that were very different from anything that had ever happened before. They were extremely significant! First of all, the veil in the temple, which kept human eyes from seeing into the Most Holy Place, was ripped open for all to see. That was the place in the temple where God met with His earthly priests. Anyone who looked into the Most Holy Place in God's temple without permission died.

That is why the veil was there. It protected people from accidentally looking in and being destroyed. Why did looking at God kill them? Because sinful man cannot look on a holy God and live. God's holiness and brightness kills them, just like it will when Jesus comes back to earth. "And then shall that Wicked be revealed, whom the Lord shall consume with the spirit of his mouth, and shall destroy with the brightness of his coming" (2 Thess.2:8). That veil was a safety measure. It kept human eyes from seeing into the Most Holy Place in God's Temple. The temple was occupied by God Himself. Isn't that marvelous and just like our loving God to place a protecting veil around His dwelling place to keep people from being killed, just in case they accidentally looked in that direction, and saw God?

But that Friday, the day Jesus died, was different. The special curtain that shielded people from accidentally seeing God was ripped open with unseen hands and left glaringly open to all eyes. But since God was no longer there, no one died as they looked into the room dedicated to God's Most Holy Place. Their temple was no longer holy! They had rejected and killed their Savior! It was no longer the place where He met with His people on this earth. But God had not rejected them. They had rejected Him.

It is true. As a nation, the Jews had totally deserted the Son of God. They were no longer His special people when it came to witnessing to others and telling them Jesus was their Savior. Why? Well, it had nothing to do with God's choice. He had chosen them. No! It was their own choice to reject Jesus! Because of their failure to obey God, they became confused and believed the lies of the devil. They were deceived because they chose to be deceived—just like Eve did in the Garden of Eden. It was because she wanted what Satan offered her. It is sad, but the majority of them chose to follow Satan and reject their Savior. They did not believe Jesus was the Messiah. They did not believe He was God's Son or that He was God.

At that point in time, the law that required them to slay a lamb, the one that typified that Jesus would die for our sins, became instantly obsolete. Why is this true? Because when Jesus was sacrificed for their sins, it was no longer necessary to slay a lamb to indicate they believed the Lamb of God would die for them. That ceremony had just been fulfilled. It was a done deal! Therefore, they no longer needed to kill a lamb to point forward to Jesus, the Lamb of God, dying on the cross. It was outdated! The moment Jesus died, all of those ceremonial laws and requirements were obsolete. They were never more than symbols of Jesus and His plan of salvation. In fact, the whole earthly Jewish temple was just that! It was temporary until Christ would come. All of the ceremonial laws pointing forward to His payment for their sins were no longer needed. The Jewish temple had been made obsolete by the reality of the Messiah. It was now outdated and no longer needed. The true Lamb of God had been slain. So, they did not need to slay a lamb to show that they believed God would send His Son to die for their sins. Now instead of looking forward to the cross, we look back at the cross.

Praise God! Jesus has paid for our sins! It's a done deal! He has done His work of saving mankind. I am so glad Jesus no longer has to think about dying on the cross for us. Now our anticipation is to see Him face to face. What a glorious day that will be. After Joseph and Nicodemus took Jesus down from the cross, He continued to rest in the tomb until the Sabbath was past. This signified that Jesus still wanted them, and us, to keep it holy. The Father allowed Jesus to rest according to the commandment, even in His death. The Father left no room for doubt concerning His holy day. Keeping Sabbath holy was so important to God that He saw to it His Son was able to rest on it even in His death. Thus, God verified that His Sabbath day was still holy and still the day to be kept after Jesus paid for our sins.

The Pharisees got nervous on Friday because of something Jesus told them He would do on that day. So, on Sabbath, "The next day, that followed the day of the preparation, the chief priests and Pharisees came together unto Pilate, Saying," (notice their disrespect) "Sir, we remember that that deceiver said, while he was yet alive, After three days I will rise again. Command therefore that the sepulchre be made sure until the third day, lest his disciples come by night, and steal him away, and say unto the people, He is risen from the dead: so the last error shall be worse than the first" (Matt. 27:64).

Sounds to me like they weren't sure He wouldn't come back to life. They were concerned that Jesus just might do what He said He would do. So this is why they asked Pilate to make it safe. So, "Pilate said unto them, 'Ye have a watch: go your way, make it as sure as you can.' So they went, and made the sepulchre sure, sealing the stone, and setting a watch" (Matt. 27:65–66).

What a shame it is that Pilate went along with their request. But just as nothing could alter the Father's plan concerning what happened to Jesus on Friday, nothing could alter what happened to Him on the Sabbath day, either. Praise God! Evil men could not change God's plans. Jesus would die and pay for our sins. Neither could any actions of man keep Jesus in the tomb. No, sir! Jesus could not be kept in the tomb. I say again, now we can live with certainty that Jesus has paid for our sins. We know we have been saved. Now we must show our belief by doing our part. The day Jesus rose from the tomb was the most spectacular day of all. Without the victory of the third day, the victory of the other two days would not have been complete. Jesus must come forth from the grave. Hallelujah! He had conquered death! Death could no longer keep Him in the grave! Listen to this dramatic account of His resurrection. Close your eyes and envision yourself there. "In the end of the sabbath, as it began to dawn toward the first day of the week, came Mary Magdalene and the other Mary to see the sepulchre. And, behold, there was a great earthquake: for the angel of the Lord descended from heaven, and came and rolled back the stone from the door, and sat on it. His countenance was like lightning, and his raiment white as snow" (Matt. 28:1–3). Notice how small and feeble the guards were feeling! All bravery and pride had fled. Their pride and bravery were totally gone.

Just look at how it affected the guards and keepers of the tombs! "And for fear of him the keepers did shake, and became as dead men"

(Matt. 28:4). But for the women, it was a day of rejoicing—a glorious surprise! "The angel answered and said unto the women, Fear not ye: for I know that ye seek Jesus, which was crucified. He is not here: for he is risen, as he said. Come, see the place where the Lord lay" (Matt. 28:5–6).

Wow! What excitement! What encouragement! They must have been elated. Jesus had actually risen from the dead on the first day of the week as He said He would. Yes, Sunday followed Sabbath. And what a teaching moment the whole ordeal of Jesus' death, burial, and resurrection was. Great examples of keeping the Sabbath holy was displayed at each phase.

These experiences were rich with knowledge the disciples needed. They needed confirmation of the truth so that they could bring people into the new baby church Jesus would ask them to form. Time had almost run out for Jesus to teach them what they needed to know to form His church. There were issues they would face, which Jesus needed to teach them about before He went back to heaven. They faced the same false ideas people are being bombarded with today.

You've heard those ideas! You know what they are! People say you can't really know which day of the week is the Sabbath. But they claim to know which day is Sunday. God calls Sunday the first day of the week, and so it is on our calendar—still today. If a person knows which day of the week is Sunday, then they also know which day is Sabbath. God says there are seven days in a week. He says Sabbath is the seventh day of the week. This, too, verifies that Sunday is the first day of the week.

The biblical records of Jesus' death, burial, and resurrection pinpoint the days that were kept holy at that time in history. They explicitly tell us which day was the first day of the week, and which day was the Sabbath, the seventh day of the week. The record of Jesus' death also shows the Sabbath has been kept holy ever since Creation up to the time of His death. If the records at the time of Jesus' death are correct, then all of the records after His death are correct too. Bible records give us assurance of the Bible's accuracy. The Bible also verifies that "Abraham obeyed my voice, and kept my charge, my commandments, my statutes, and my laws" (Gen. 26:5), and those laws included the Sabbath command. Sabbath is still the seventh day of the week. It is the same day of the week Jesus kept the Sabbath on. I like that! I can visualize Him keeping it in heaven right now and looking down on us with love in His eyes as we keep it holy with Him. Every time we keep it holy, we are giving Him a hug. I can just feel Him hugging me back. That puts a smile on my face. How about you?

CHAPTER SEVENTEEN

Your Debt of Sin— Nailed to the Cross

What was nailed to the cross? Certainly not the eternal law of God! Jesus talked to His disciples about that very issue in their day. People were teaching erroneous things based on error concerning God's ten commandments even back then. Matthew tells us about it. He quoted Jesus as saying, "And seeing the multitudes, he [Jesus] went up into a mountain: and when He was set, His disciples came unto Him" (Matt. 5:1–2). He taught them the beatitudes and many other things, and then He said, "Think not that I am come to destroy the law, or the prophets: I am not come to destroy, but to fulfil" (Matt. 5:17).

He assured His disciples that He would not change the Ten Commandments or what the prophets wrote. He said He came to fulfill them. Disobedience was rampant, as we have seen. Why else would Jesus take the time to tell them He didn't come to destroy the law? If it hadn't been an issue, He wouldn't have been coaching them on that subject. He came to obey all the laws of God. The Holy Spirit is convicting us on those same issues today. He is our teacher and guide. Jesus did what the law told Him to do, and He also obeyed the instructions of the prophets. Jesus considered what the prophets said and what the Ten Commandments said to be equally important. That's because everything God's prophets said and talked about agreed with God's holy law. They uphold each other.

The prophets wrote about Jesus. They prophesied His coming, His death, and everything else concerning Him. God has always taught that what the prophets wrote was true. He has always said His ten-commandment law would last forever. And why not? The prophets wrote and said what God told them to write and say. It's just that Satan was and still is doing his dirty work—trying to confuse people just like He confused Eve in the Garden of Eden. Nothing is new. We still live in the same wicked world—but not for long!

So, what did Jesus mean when He said He came to fulfill the law? Let's use a simple law to help us grasp what He meant. When you fulfill the law that says, "Stop on red," what do you do to fulfill it? Do you drive right through the intersection while the light is still red? Silly question, huh! Of course, you don't. You do what the law tells you to do. You stop and wait for the light to turn green before you go through it. Obedience to that law fulfills it. You do what it tells you to do.

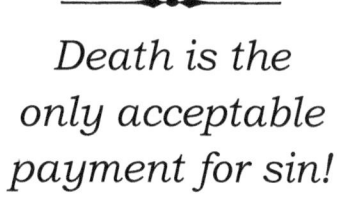

Death is the only acceptable payment for sin!

When Jesus obeyed the law, He fulfilled it. Actually, He came to show us how to fulfill the law of God. Jesus both showed, and told us how to obey all of His laws; the Ten Commandments included.

Every person who has lived on Planet Earth has broken it. When we break it, we commit sin. For God says, "Sin is the transgression of the law"—i.e., the act of breaking it (see 1 John 3:4). You break it when you disobey and fail to do what it tells you to do. Jesus came to keep the law to show us it can be kept. Then, He died on the cross and paid for those sins. Sin is very serious. It causes death! To pay for those sins, someone who had not broken them had to die. Death is the only acceptable payment for sin! Jesus made that payment for us. We will die because we have sinned. But if we love Jesus and accept His payment on our behalf, we will never have to die the type of death which is permanent—the second death. When Jesus died on the cross, He died the second death.

Jesus did what we failed to do. Dying on the cross wouldn't have done man any good if Jesus had broken only one of God's commands. To break it, God would have had to sin. Jesus wouldn't think of doing that! He could not break God's law and still be our Savior. To save us, Jesus had to be sinless, and breaking God's law would have made Him a sinner.

The Pharisees asked Jesus a question about His law—just to tempt Him. Listen to what Jesus told those who were hassling Him. They asked, "Which is the great commandment in the law?" (Matt. 22:36). To make it simple to understand, Jesus divided God's ten laws into two groups. Then He told them keeping the first four commands showed them how to love God. Here is the summary of that first set of commands, just as Jesus summarized it. "Thou shalt love the Lord thy God with all thy heart, and with all thy soul, and with all thy mind. This is the first and great commandment" (Matt. 22:37–38).

God's law teaches our love for God is paramount. But God wants us to love our neighbor too. When we love our neighbor, we are also loving God. One of the ways we can tell God we love Him is by loving our neighbor. How can that be? It is because we are obeying God when we love our neighbor. God says, "Owe no man anything, but to love one another: For he that loveth another hath fulfilled the law" (Rom. 13:8). Pretty simple, isn't it? God is not a hard taskmaster—the devil is!

Jesus says the second section of His commandments shows us how to love other people. Jesus told His disciples the second set of commands was just like the first set—they tell us how to love. But it's telling us how to love others instead of how to love God. Here it is! "And the second is like unto it, Thou shalt love thy neighbour as thyself. On these two commandments hang all the law and the prophets" (Matt. 22:39–40). Jesus says, loving our neighbor is the second greatest commandment in His law. It consists of the last six commands. They tell us how to love others.

The Pharisees were trying to break down the peoples' trust in Jesus. We need to open our eyes and realize there are people in our day doing that very same thing, but a good majority of them don't realize they are teaching error. They were brought up believing them. They do not realize the Ten Commandments were *not* nailed to the cross. They don't know they are teaching the opposite of what Jesus taught. That is why we must read our Bibles and know what it says. I choose to believe what Jesus said! His words echo loud and clear down to our time. Do you remember what Jesus told the Pharisees who questioned Him? He said, "For verily I say unto you, Till heaven and earth pass, one jot or one tittle shall in no wise pass from the law, till all be fulfilled" (Matt. 5:18). Jesus was telling us that God's law will never change.

Jesus has not come back to earth to take us home to heaven with Him *yet*. We have not been in heaven for a thousand years *yet*. The great judgment scene has not taken place *yet*. The earth has not been cleansed from sin or burned up *yet*. Furthermore, God has not done away with His law. He never will do away with it! Back in those far-off days, through Solomon, God said, "Let us hear the conclusion of the whole matter: Fear God, and keep his commandments: for this is the whole duty of man. For God shall bring every work into judgment, with every secret thing, whether it be good, or whether it be evil" (Eccl. 12:13–14).

The Ten Commandments are the law God will judge mankind with at the end of time. Jesus told His disciples, "Heaven and earth shall pass away, but my words shall not pass away" (Matt. 24:35). None of God's words have been done away with. God's total law is still in effect today. Jesus verified that not even the dotting of an i would be removed from His law. So why would one whole command be nailed to His cross!

Jesus' disciples desperately needed to hear these words; otherwise, they wouldn't be able to confidently share this valuable truth with us. It's marvelous how He taught them what they needed to know so that they could successfully bring the Christian Church into existence. It's been many years, and it may be many years yet till He comes back again to get us. How tedious the wait sometimes seems. Yet, how necessary it is for us today. What's the hold-up? God is waiting until every person who will come to Him has come. Oh, how much He loves us. He is probably more anxious for that time to come than we are. Thank You, Father, for sending Jesus to teach us what You want us to know!

In heaven, we will no longer need God's law to tell us what sin is. We, of all the beings God has made, will know through our own disobedience and experience of living through the hell disobeying them have caused, they will be indelibly impressed on our minds for all eternity. We will never forget His great love for us. Do you think He will do away with His law? I hope you can say with affirmation—certainly not! There is no reason to do away with a law that shows us God's character of love. A law that tells us how to love God and each other. Here is the reason I can say this so boldly: God says, "And it shall come to pass, that from one new moon to another, and from one sabbath to another, shall all flesh come to worship before me, saith the LORD" (Isa. 66:23). We will be gladly living out His laws.

We will come and worship Him in heaven, and later on, on the earth made new. Remember, God's law is a perpetual covenant. That means its lasting ability is without end. The law has never been changed by God, and it never will be changed by anyone else, either. Faith is believing and trusting that God will do what He says He will do. If we could see it, then it wouldn't take faith to believe. Faith is our part. We must have faith that God will do what He says He will do, or we will not be saved. Faith and grace must clasp hands. Faith is simply believing something even though we can't see it with our eyes.

"But God, who is rich in mercy, for his great love wherewith he loved us, Even when we were dead in sins, hath quickened us together with Christ, (by grace ye are saved;) And hath raised us up together, and made us sit together in heavenly places in Christ Jesus: That in the ages to come he might shew the exceeding riches of his grace in his kindness toward us through Christ Jesus. For by grace are ye saved through faith; and that not of yourselves: it is the gift of God: Not of works, lest any man should boast" (Eph. 2:4–9).

That sounds wonderful! He will show us the exceeding riches of His grace! God will still rule the universe with love. The difference between now and then is that no one will want to sin again. Nahum brings us to our senses. He says, "What do ye imagine against the LORD? he will make an utter end: affliction shall not rise up the second time" (Nah. 1:9). What a marvelous promise that is.

God will still be the ruler. He will still rule with His laws that teach us how to love. We will love those laws! God says, "I change not" (Mal. 3:6). That, too, assures us He will still rule with those same laws. Heaven and earth, as we know it, has not passed away yet. It did not pass away when Jesus died on the cross, either. But our heaven and earth, as we know them, *will* pass away sometime in the near future, just as Jesus says it will. Therefore, Peter said, "Nevertheless we, according to His promise, look for new heavens and a new earth, wherein dwelleth righteousness" (2 Peter 3:13).

We are looking forward to that day. That is the period of time when all flesh will come and worship before Him. That very special worship service will take place in the earth made new. Won't that be wonderful? I can just see in my mind's eye all of us kneeling together, worshiping our Creator in awe and love. This is what Jesus was talking about when He said He didn't come to destroy the law or the prophets. He was just saying His law would not be done away with. Since man cannot do away with God's law. What was nailed to that old rugged cross? Jesus was nailed to the cross. And since He was the real fulfillment of the ceremonial law that had pointed forward to His sacrificial death, that, too, was nailed to the cross. The fulfillment of the ceremonial laws in Christ on the cross is how our sins are forgiven.

Paul says our sins were nailed to it. "And you, being dead in your sins" (on death row because of our sins), "and the uncircumcision of your flesh," (our lack of love), "hath he quickened together with Him" (made alive) "having forgiven you all trespasses" (sins) (Col. 2:13). In the margin in my Bible, it says, it is "our certificate of debt" that was blotted out. Isn't that wonderful? Our debt of sin is gone! Jesus has already paid for it. Jesus did away with the debt that "was against us, which was contrary to us, and took it out of the way, nailing it to His cross" (Col. 2:14). Praise

God, that debt has been paid! It was paid for at the cross. Jesus paid it. That's what was nailed to the cross! But the Ten Commandments, including the Sabbath commandment, was the broken law for which Jesus paid the penalty. It is nonsensical to say that paying the penalty of a broken law means that the law is now done away with. No, the law still stands because the penalty has been paid. If the penalty is not paid, then the law is meaningless because no law stands without enforcement. The Ten Commandments hang together. You cannot break one, according to James, without breaking the whole. If the Ten Commandments matter, then the Sabbath matters. If the Ten Commandments don't matter, the Sabbath doesn't matter. But all ten matter because Jesus paid the penalty for the whole human race that broke them.

That fills my heart with gratitude and love. Paul says the handwriting of requirements were wiped out and nailed to the cross. The words, "wiped out," signify they came to their death when Jesus died. They are no longer in existence or necessary. Once Jesus died for our sins, we were no longer in debt. So we no longer needed to slay a lamb to show we believed the lamb of God will be slain. Why? Because Jesus, the Lamb of God, has already been slain. What tremendous news this is. Your debt and mine have been paid.

All we have to do is gratefully accept God's gift of grace. We do that by loving Him and thanking Him for the greatest gift of love that was ever given. How do we love Him? He says, "And this is love, that we walk after his commandments" (2 John 1:6). In other words, obey them. It wasn't just anyone who paid my debt. It was the great, loving God of every living creature—the Creator of everything. He is the one who paid my debt and yours—The Son of God. Yes, He's the one who paid for every last one of my sins and yours. What a marvelous, matchless God! They each did their part! Together, the Father, Son, and Holy Spirit took care of ALL SIN! Thank You, Jesus, for going through so much pain to save us! Thank You, Father, for allowing Your Son to die in our place! That means we really are your little girls or your boys! Thank you for allowing Your Son to be killed to pay for my deliberate sins. This would be extremely difficult for any father to endure. Thank You, Holy Spirit, for teaching me daily how to follow in Jesus' footsteps. Thank You for helping me be Your child.

It's not just those written requirements that were wiped out, but most importantly, it was our sins that were wiped out (see Col. 2:14). It included all of the ordinances or rules that became necessary when mankind first committed sin. Those laws told people what they needed to do so they could show people they believed Jesus would come and pay for their sins. Yes, it's those outdated rules and instructions that were nailed to the cross. Those laws were not called God's law. Some of them were called "the handwriting of ordinances" (Col. 2:14), another set of rules was called "the laws of Moses" (*see Luke 2:22; John 7:23; 1 Cor. 9:9*).

Jesus' death blotted out all of those laws—and all of the handwriting of ordinances that were against us. All of the ones that had to do with the animal sacrifices. They pointed forward to Jesus' death on the cross. They died when they were no longer needed. Not the Ten Commandments. Jesus spoiled the principalities and powers of evil and the principalities and powers of Satan. Yes, Satan's powers are the powers Jesus spoiled. Jesus did not come to blot out the Ten Commandments. He came to save us and defeat Satan! May our hearts overflow with joy and appreciation for Their wonderful gift.

> *Jesus did not come to blot out the Ten Commandments. He came to save us and defeat Satan!*

CHAPTER EIGHTEEN

Jesus Said He Would be Crucified

The disciples didn't have a clue that Jesus would be killed. Yet He was very vocal about it. He told them what was going to happen! In fact, it has been God's message from the very beginning of time on this earth. God told Abraham, "Behold, I am with thee, and will keep thee in all places whither thou goest, and will bring thee again into this land; for I will not leave thee, until I have done that which I have spoken to thee of" (Gen. 28:15). What else did God tell him? "Thy seed shall be as the dust of the earth, and thou shalt spread abroad to the west, and to the east, and to the north, and to the south: and in thee and in thy seed shall all the families of the earth be blessed" (Gen. 28:14).

The disciples knew the history of God's people. They were aware of the plan of salvation. Yet they didn't talk with Jesus about His death that loomed so near. Jesus said to them, "Behold, we go up to Jerusalem; and the Son of man shall be betrayed unto the chief priests and unto the scribes, and shall condemn him to death, And shall deliver him to the Gentiles to mock, and to scourge, and to crucify him: and the third day

He shall rise again" (Matt. 20:18–19). He told them exactly what was going to happen to Him.

The next day, Jesus healed a child who was being hassled by the devil. "And it came to pass, that on the next day, when they were come down from the hill, much people met Him. And, behold, a man of the company cried out, saying, Master, I beseech thee, look upon my son: for he is mine only child. And, lo, a spirit taketh him, and he suddenly crieth out; and it teareth him that he foameth again, and bruising him hardly departeth from him. And I besought thy disciples to cast him out; and they could not. And Jesus answering said, O faithless and perverse generation, how long shall I be with you, and suffer you? Bring thy son hither. And as he was yet a coming, the devil threw him down, and tare him. And Jesus rebuked the unclean spirit, and healed the child, and delivered him again to his father" (Luke 9:37–42).

What a marvelous display of God's power and love this was. But take note of his disciples' fear. Jesus tells us why the disciples did not understand the things He was telling them. "And they were all amazed at the mighty power of God. But while they wondered every one at all things which Jesus did, he said unto His disciples, Let these sayings sink down into your ears: for the Son of man shall be delivered into the hands of men. But they understood not this saying, and it was hid from them, that they perceived it not: and they feared to ask Him of that saying" (Luke 9:43–45).

That's right! The truth about what was going to happen to Jesus was hidden from them even though Jesus told them everything. What a lover God is. He will do this for us, too, concerning last day events if we need Him to. He knows what we can and cannot take. Look at this beautiful verse that tells us why God gives us fear. "Like as a father pitieth his children, so the Lord pitieth them that fear him. For he knoweth our frame; he remembereth that we are dust" (Ps. 103:13–14). Now that's really tender love. Read Luke 18:31–34.

The same thing happened again and again, and they were kept from understanding what Jesus was telling them. So when we are unable to understand something, maybe it is because God knows it would be too hard on us. Notice that after Jesus had risen from the dead, an angel brought His words back to their memory! I will not speculate as to why this happened to them. We will be able to ask Jesus about it when we talk with Him in heaven! Won't that be an exciting conversation? God had a very good reason. He's a lover—not a controller. He knows what each person can and cannot take. He is in the business of securing our salvation. It is good for us to know these things, so we don't become too critical of ourselves or others. We, too, just like the disciples, probably will not be able to understand everything that takes place just before Jesus comes back to get those who love Him.

Listen to this! Here is a conversation between some of His disciples and an angel. It took place when they went to the sepulchre Sunday morning to finish anointing Jesus with their spices: "And they found the stone rolled away from the sepulchre. And they entered in, and found not the body of the Lord Jesus. And it came to pass, as they were much perplexed thereabout, behold, two men stood by them in shining garments: And as they were afraid, and bowed their faces to the earth, they said unto them, Why seek ye the living among the dead?" What a happy shock that must have been! And how enlightening it was. "He is not here, but is risen: remember how He spake unto you when He was yet in Galilee, Saying, The Son of man must be delivered into the hands of sinful men, and be crucified, and the third day rise again. And they remembered His words" (Luke 24:2–8).

They had lived daily in very close connection with Jesus. In fact, they had communed with Him for more than three years. I would find this information rather upsetting if God had not shared the above verses with us. It makes me wonder how many times I don't understand what Jesus is telling me today. But it's true! Even though they walked and talked with Jesus every day, even though they were His friends and His disciples, they didn't understand!

Perhaps, this is going to be our experience only over something different—over something concerning Jesus' second coming! Perhaps there will be many things we will not remember when we are going through the final weeks just before His return. I believe Jesus did it for the disciples' benefit. Perhaps it will be the same for us so that the Holy Spirit can work on our hearts, and Satan can do his dirty work. Only God can answer those questions. But this I do know! When it is over, we will be glad it happened just the way it did.

We claim to be Jesus' friends too! Could it be that sometimes we are just as blind? Could it be that when He tells us something in His Word, He shields us because it would be too hard on us right then? No one desires painful experiences! Jesus didn't, either! But He was willing to go through them and die so He could save us. God, help us leave those things in Your hands.

This helps us understand why Mary was crying, too, early that Sunday morning. And why she was grieved when she went to the tomb, and why things weren't the way she expected them to be. There were tears in her eyes! Oh, how she missed Jesus! She felt as if her whole world had fallen apart. And it had! And so had ours! But not the way she thought. It was wonderful rather than bad. If she had truly understood, she would have been ecstatic! But she was very distraught. We do well to remember this when we fail to understand things that happen to us in these last days. We must read our Bibles and try to understand what God is telling us. We must realize that we, too, will face confusing circumstances.

Jesus wants to walk with us too. And He will walk with us if we invite Him to. We must believe what God tells us in His Word. We must believe the Holy Spirit when He shares something that is totally opposite of what we have previously believed. We must realize God may purposely guard us against knowing things that might cause us trouble.

The Holy Spirit will never tell us to do anything He does not agree with. I keep repeating this statement because it is a life and death matter. The litmus test is—whatever the Holy Spirit convicts us of must agree with the Bible. If it doesn't agree with the Bible, then it's not the Holy Spirit who is speaking to us. It is our own imagination or our enemy, the devil, whispering in our ear. Remember! Never forget! God says, "To the law and to the testimony: if they speak not according to this word, it is because there is no light in them" (Isa. 8:20). Our Bible confirms whether something is true! For it says, "Thy word is truth" (John 17:17).

You can't always trust what you see, either. You must trust what God says more than your own senses. That's what the disciples hadn't done. Satan will tempt us to believe our own senses when good or bad things come to us in these last days. We, too, must trust God's Word more than anything or anyone else, even ourselves. Look at this! "For as yet they knew not the scripture, that he must rise again from the dead" (John 20:9).

After they left, "Mary stood without at the sepulchre weeping: and as she wept, she stooped down, *and* looked into the sepulchre, And seeth two angels in white sitting, the one at the head, the other at the feet, where the body of Jesus had lain. And they say unto her, Woman, why weepest thou? She saith unto them, Because they have taken away my LORD, and I know not where they have laid Him" (John 20:11–13).

This was a natural human reaction. After all, she knew how the Pharisees had treated Jesus. So, of course, she thought the Jews had come that Sunday morning and stolen His body. She thought she was talking to the gardener. But it was Jesus. See how easy it is to trust ourselves! Then, "She saw Jesus standing, and knew not that it was Jesus" (John 20:14). Then Jesus talked to her, but she didn't know who she was talking to. "Jesus saith unto her, 'Woman, why weepest thou? whom seekest thou?' She, supposing him to be the gardener, saith unto him, Sir, if thou have borne him hence, tell me where thou hast laid him, and I will take him away" (John 20:15).

Up to this point, she had not recognized His voice. But just look at the electrifying transformation which took place when Jesus spoke her name! "Jesus saith unto her, Mary. She turned herself, and saith unto him, Rabboni; which is to say, Master. Jesus saith unto her, Touch me not; for I am not yet ascended to my Father: but go to my brethren, and say unto them, I ascend unto my Father, and your Father; and to my God, and your God" (John 20:16–17).

"Then the same day at evening, being the first day of the week, when the doors were shut where the disciples were assembled for fear of the Jews, came Jesus and stood in the midst, and saith unto them, Peace be unto you" (John 20:19). Notice that His disciples were not there for a Sunday worship service. They were hiding because they were afraid the Jews would kill them. After all, they were Jesus' disciples. The Jews did not like Jesus. It was Peter who had been questioned while the Jews were persecuting Jesus, and he had lied and said he didn't know Jesus. But Peter had made some drastic changes since that day. Now, on the eve of Jesus' resurrection, notice what was frightening them as Jesus appeared in their midst. Because of Jesus' sudden appearance, and their failure to notice the nail prints in His hands and His pierced side, they were afraid. They thought He was a ghost.

"And when he had so said, he shewed unto them his hands and his side. Then were the disciples glad, when they saw the LORD. Then said Jesus to them again, Peace be unto you: as my Father hath sent me, even so send I you. And when he had said this, he breathed on them, and saith unto them, Receive ye the Holy Ghost" (John 20:20–22). Did you hear that? What a commission. If we truly love Jesus, this is our commission too. Later on that same day, two of the disciples went to Emmaus, a village some distance from Jerusalem. As they walked along, they talked about everything that had happened. Unbeknown to them, Jesus was the man who was drawing close to them. He caught up with them and began walking beside them. But He kept them from knowing who He was because He wanted to teach them why He had to die. Of course, His crucifixion was the talk of the area. It was a horrible thing that had happened—much like when we talk about the most devastating hurricanes or other catastrophes that happen or the gun incidents that have killed a lot of innocent people recently.

They were amazed that this man didn't know anything about what had just taken place. So the disciples told Him all about what had happened to Jesus—not knowing it was Jesus they were talking to! "Then He said unto them, O fools, and slow of heart to believe all that the prophets have spoken: Ought not the Christ to have suffered these things, and to enter into his glory? And beginning at Moses and all the prophets, he expounded unto them in all the scriptures the things concerning himself" (Luke 24:25–27).

When they got to their destination, they invited Jesus in to stay the night with them because it was dusk. They wanted Him to stay, so they could hear more. Jesus accepted their invitation, but they still didn't recognize Him. Then Jesus did something He had often done in their presence. They invited Him to eat, and "as He sat at meat with them, He took bread, and blessed it, and brake, and gave to them. And their eyes were opened, and they knew Him; and He vanished out of their sight" (Luke 24:30–31).

Oh, how surprised and excited they were. "And they said one to another, Did not our heart burn within us, while he talked with us by the way, and while He opened to us the scriptures?" (Luke 24:32). Then they rushed back to the upper room just to tell the others what had happened and to let them know Jesus really had risen from the dead. And suddenly, Jesus was standing there in the midst of them! WOW! But how sad that they didn't believe Him earlier when he told them what was going to happen.

Jesus came to let all of them know He was alive and was ready to tell them what they should do after He went to heaven. Let's look at the instructions Jesus gave them. He told them, "All power is given to me in heaven and in earth (Matt. 28:18)." Look at the New King James Version. It says, "All authority has been given unto Me in heaven and in earth"

(Matt. 28:18). What a confirmation this is. Jesus' Father authorized Him to have the same authority He had. And Jesus told them, "repentance and remission of sins should be preached in His name among all nations, beginning at Jerusalem" (Luke 24:47, NJKV).

They were told to give the good news of salvation to the Jews first. And why not? They were the ones God chose to do that work in the first place. They already believed in God and knew Him—they just did not know Jesus was their Savior. But they should have known. Then Jesus told the disciples they were to tell all people about everything they had just witnessed. The Old Testament was the only part of the Bible in existence at that time. Jesus said to them, "Go ye therefore, and teach all nations" (Matt. 28:19). "Teaching them to observe all things whatsoever I have commanded you: and, lo, I am with you always, even unto the end of the world. Amen" (Matt. 28:20).

Jesus never said one word about the Sabbath being done away with when He left to go to heaven. He had already told them His ten-commandment law would remain forever! The Sabbath had always been kept from eternity. So why would He say such a thing? Neither did He command them to keep Sunday in honor of His resurrection. Jesus never instructed anyone, anywhere, to honor Sunday. Instead, He told them they were to do the same work He had been doing. What was that work? It was teaching people about God, healing the sick, and keeping God's commandments. And that included Sabbath worship. The commandment itself specifies which day of the week is God's Sabbath day.

Luke recorded the final meeting Jesus had with His disciples too. Jesus made no mention of the Sabbath command being nailed to the cross. Neither did Jesus give them a command to change their worship day to Sunday instead of Sabbath in honor of His resurrection. They knew better than to do that. That is something God's enemy, the devil, concocted. It's one of His lies. I will talk about it in my book titled *The Devil Made Me Do It!*

Listen to Mark's account of this meeting. He said unto them, "Go ye into all the world, and preach the gospel to every creature. He that believeth and is baptized shall be saved; but he that believeth not shall be damned. And these signs shall follow them that believe; In my name shall they cast out devils; they shall speak with new tongues; They shall take up serpents; and if they drink any deadly thing, it shall not hurt them; they shall lay hands on the sick, and they shall recover" (Mark 16:15–18).

Then "they asked Him, saying, Lord, wilt thou at this time restore again the kingdom to Israel? And He said unto them. It is not for you to know the times or the seasons, which the Father hath put in his own power. But ye shall receive power, after that the Holy Ghost has come upon you: and ye shall be witnesses unto me both in Jerusalem, and in all Judaea, and in Samaria, and unto the uttermost part of the earth" (Acts 1:6–8).

What kind of power would they receive? They would receive the power to obey God, so their life could be a witness of the truth. Think how discouraged they would have been if they had been told how long it would be before Jesus would come back to get them. Our all-wise God shielded them from such disappointing news. He does that for us today, too. As the disciples watched Jesus rise into the air, the Father sent angels to comfort them. How special that is. "And when he had spoken these things, while they beheld, he was taken up; and a cloud received him out of their sight. And while they looked stedfastly toward heaven as he went up, behold, two men stood by them in white apparel; Which also said, Ye men of Galilee, why stand ye gazing up into heaven? this same Jesus, which is taken up from you into heaven, shall so come in like manner as ye have seen him go into heaven. Then returned they unto Jerusalem from the mount called Olivet, which is from Jerusalem," (notice it says) "a sabbath day's journey" (Acts 1:9–11).

Jesus' instructions were crystal clear. He hadn't changed the Sabbath. And His disciples obeyed His commands. Isn't it a blessing that the angel told them how Jesus would come back to get them someday! They said He would come back the same way He left. I believe the clouds that hid Him from their sight were clouds of angels because, in the book of Revelation, John repeats some of those same words. He says, "Behold, he cometh with clouds; and every eye shall see him, and they also which pierced Him" (Rev. 1:7).

The reason I think it was clouds of angels is because Matthew gives us this graphic picture of Jesus' second coming. He says, "When the Son of Man shall come in his glory, and all the holy angels with Him, then He shall sit upon the throne of His glory" (Matt. 25:31). And in another place, we are told that there are so many angels in heaven that they can't be counted. "But ye are come unto mount Sion, and unto the city of the living God, the heavenly Jerusalem, and to an innumerable company of angels" (Heb. 12:22). What a wonderful day that will be! Well worth going through all the pain. Words fail to express the splendor of it all. Then Jesus will walk with us, as He did with His disciples. I can't wait! How about you?

CHAPTER NINETEEN

Jesus Walked with Them

Yes, Jesus walked with them. He will walk with us too if we let Him. Like them, even though we do not always understand what is going on behind the scenes, if we hang onto the Lord and obey the pleading voice of the Holy Spirit, we will make it through everything God has planned for our life. As we yield to the voice of the Spirit, we will be changed. God is more than willing to change us. We are perfected as we choose to be true to Him. In the end, everything will turn out glorious for all who truly love Jesus. This is because God only leads us through hard situations if He needs to do it to perfect us. It is certain that we will face hardship and frustration. So it does us good to take in the disciples' experience and internalize it. It can be a help to us as we walk in Jesus' footsteps. Look at the experience Mary went through and internalize what it did for her so that it can help you too. "The first day of the week cometh Mary Magdalene early, when it was yet dark, unto the sepulchre, and seeth the stone taken away from the sepulchre" (John 20:1). What a shock! What did she do when she realized someone had moved the stone? She ran back to where the disciples were hiding in fear and told them about it. Immediately, Peter and another disciple ran back to the tomb with her. It was John. He never mentions his own name when he writes about himself; rather, he said,

"Then she runneth, and cometh to Simon Peter, and to the other disciple, whom Jesus loved" (John 20:2).

Yes, John calls himself that "other disciple." But both good old Peter and John did have some trust in Mary. Enough that it caused them to go and investigate. They rushed to the tomb to find out if what she said really was true. They had to see for themselves whether the body of Jesus was missing. "So they ran both together" (John 20:4). And John got there first. "And he stooping down, and looking in, saw the linen clothes lying" (John 20:5)! But John did not go in! Instead, He waited till Peter got there. Peter didn't just look in, he "went into the sepulchre, and seeth the linen clothes lie, And the napkin, that was about his head, not lying with the linen clothes, but wrapped together in a place by itself" (John 20:6–7). Then! After Peter had gone in, John also went in and believed. Now John believed Jesus' body really was missing. He had to see it to believe it. Kind of like Thomas, huh!

But you can't always trust what you see, either. You must trust what God says more than you trust your own senses. That's what they had not done! Satan will tempt us to believe our own senses, too, when good or bad things come to us in the last days. We, too, must trust God's Word more than anything or anyone else. What a learning experience this was for them. They definitely learned that they should trust God and God alone. "For as yet they knew not the scripture, that he must rise again from the dead. Then the disciples went away again unto their own home" (John 20:9–10).

And Mary was left there all alone! I can just hear her heartbroken sobs and feel her loneliness. But, whether she perceived it or not, God was with her. God is always right beside His children when they go through rough experiences. It is so valuable we have this knowledge when we go through traumatic things like Mary was going through. More than once, I have studied with people and seen Satan use their loneliness to get them to disobey God and, ultimately, disbelieve what God says in His Word. It is heartrending to see people lose their faith in God's Word. Just look at what God says to us, "I will never leave thee, nor forsake thee. So that we may boldly say, The Lord is my helper, and I will not fear what man shall do unto me" (Heb. 13:5–6). Yes! God never leaves us or forsakes us. Unless we ask Him to! Then it is we ourselves who turn away from Him. It's our choice. He will not try to force us to be His child. This godly trait of not forcing someone to blindly obey him strongly shows us God's real love.

Mary truly loved Jesus. She wasn't about to let anyone shake her love for God. So, she stayed at the tomb, but she wasn't alone. How blessed and honored she was! God's angels were near to help and comfort her. "And they say unto her, Woman, why weepest thou? She saith unto them, Because they have taken away my Lord, and I know not where they have laid Him" (John 20:13).

Then, "Jesus saith unto her, Woman, why weepest thou? whom seekest thou? She, supposing him to be the gardener, saith unto him, Sir, if thou have borne Him hence, tell me where thou hast laid Him, and I will take Him away" (John 20:15.) Up to this point, she had not recognized His voice. But just look at the electrifying transformation which took place when Jesus spoke her name! "Jesus saith unto her, Mary. She turned herself, and saith unto Him, Rabboni; which is to say, Master. Jesus saith unto her, Touch Me not; for I am not yet ascended to My Father: but go to my brethren, and say unto them, 'I ascended unto my Father, and your Father; and to my God, and your God'" (John 20:16–17). Did you catch that! Jesus did not go to heaven the day He died. Oh, yes, His breath did, but the rest of Him did not. Hmm. How do we know this? God says so!

> *Just look at the electrifying transformation which took place when Jesus spoke her name!*

"Thou takest away their breath, they die, and return to their dust" (Ps. 104:29). "His breath goeth forth, he returneth to his earth; in that very day his thoughts perish" (Ps. 146:4). "For that which befalleth the sons of men befalleth beasts; even one thing befalleth them: as the one dieth, so dieth the other; yea, they have all one breath; so that a man hath no preeminence above a beast: for all is vanity. All go unto one place; all are of the dust, and all turn to dust again" (Eccl. 3:19–20).

It is God, and God alone, who gives anyone or anything breath. Just listen to what Daniel said to Belshazzar. Thou "hast not humbled thine heart, though thou knewest all this; But hast lifted up thyself against the Lord of heaven; ... and the God in whose hand thy breath is, and whose are all thy ways, hast thou not glorified:" (Dan. 5:22–23). "he giveth to all life, and breath, and all things" (Acts 17:25).

Now, back to Mary! "Then the same day [Sunday] at evening, being the first day of the week, when the doors were shut where the disciples were assembled for fear of the Jews, came Jesus and stood in the midst, and said to them, 'Peace be unto you'" (John 20:19). Notice that Jesus' disciples were not gathered there for a Sunday worship service. They were hiding because they were afraid the Jews would kill them. After all, they were Jesus' disciples, and the Jews had just killed Jesus. Place yourself in their sandals and try to feel the fear that they must have felt.

And now, on the evening of Jesus' resurrection, notice what frightened them as Jesus appeared in their midst. Because of Jesus' sudden appearance and their failure to notice the nail prints in His hands or His pierced side, they were afraid that He was a ghost. They thought about ghosts just the way people think of ghosts today! Obviously, Satan's lie that the dead come back and appear to us as ghosts was alive and well even when Jesus lived on this earth. Satan just keeps re-circulating his same old fibs.

Notice that the disciples and the two on the road to Emmaus had failed to understand the prophets! Ahah! Could this be why they did not listen to Jesus when He told them He would have to die? They needed to read their Bibles more—and follow it. I'm afraid I, too, often fit into that scenario. We can never study our Bibles too much. But praise the Lord, just listen to their reaction to His words. Their hearts were thrilled. Now they were ready to listen! Could it be that their grief got in the way of their connection with Jesus at the time of His crucifixion! We, too, must be careful to accept the words of the prophets. God speaks to us through prophecy. If we follow the Biblical instructions concerning prophecy, it will give us understanding.

But how sad that they hadn't believed Him when He told them earlier what was going to happen to Him. But, perhaps I shouldn't say how sad! For look at what Jesus said to them then. It indicates that maybe He might have thought it would be better to open up their eyes later. God is always thinking and considering what would be good for us in any situation we are in. That's how love works! Look at Luke's rendition of what took place in that upper room. Jesus suddenly appeared to them, when they were together again, and He says, "They were terrified and affrighted, and supposed that they had seen a spirit" (Luke 24:37).

Then, Jesus drew their attention to the fact that He had hands and feet. Evidently, people back in those days were familiar with the idea that ghosts do not have feet or hands. For Jesus said unto them, "Why are ye troubled? and why do thoughts arise in your hearts? Behold my hands and my feet, that it is I myself: handle me, and see; for a spirit hath not flesh and bones, as you see Me have" (Luke 24:38–39). Dead people do NOT walk around as ghosts. The devil is the one who tells that lie. The fallen angels pose as ghosts who look like our loved ones.

Jesus had come to let them know He was alive, and that He was ready to begin giving them their instructions as to what they should do after He went to heaven. It appears that back in those days, people also perceived that the supposed ghosts didn't have hands and feet, just as many believe in our day. Satan was feeding them the same old lie he tells us today. Many of Satan's lies are like that first lie he told Eve in the Garden of Eden. He said to her "You shall not surely die" (Gen. 3:4, NKJV). And amazingly, Jesus' disciples were believing that lie, just like Eve did. Remember, in Ecclesiastes, Solomon tells us all return to dust; they no longer think or talk or breathe. They are sleeping in their graves until Jesus comes to wake them up. Won't that be a wonderful day? Find out what God says about that in another book.

So Jesus was trying to soothe their fears and let them know He had not died the permanent death of the sinner, the death no one wakes up from, the one God calls the second death. Praise God! No one has to die two times—it's our choice. Do you know how to keep from dying two times? Look at this promise: "He that overcometh shall not be hurt of the second death" (Rev. 2:11). Jesus proceeded to show them His hands and feet, and then He asked them for something to eat. He wanted them to see He really did need food and that He really did have body parts, just like all living people have. "And when He had thus spoken, he shewed them his hands and his feet" (Luke 24:40).

Notice what happened next. This should give us great courage when we have trouble knowing right from wrong. He said to them, "And while they yet believed not for joy, and wonder, he said unto them, Have ye here any meat? And they gave Him a piece of broiled fish, and of an honeycomb" (Luke 24:41–42). Then He proceeded to tell them all about the experience they had just gone through and why they had to go through it. What a wonderful Savior. If you wish to read about this meeting, it is in Luke 24:44–49.

We should not be down on ourselves if we are doing all in our power to obey God. And remember, God does not wag His finger at us when we are weak. Rather, He sends the Holy Spirit to help us. *"The Lord is merciful and gracious, slow to anger, and plenteous in mercy. He will not always chide: neither will he keep his anger for ever. He hath not dealt with us after our sins; nor rewarded us according to our iniquities. For as the heaven is high above the earth, so great is his mercy toward them that fear him. As far as the east is from the west, so far hath he removed our transgressions from us. Like as a father pitieth his children, so the Lord pitieth them that fear Him. For he knoweth our frame; he remembereth that we are dust" (Ps. 103:8–15).* He loves you greatly. Ask Him! He will give you the strength to love Him back!

CHAPTER TWENTY

Jesus—Worship Him—He is God

That's right! God, the everlasting God, is the only God we should worship. "Thou shalt worship the Lord thy God, and him only shalt thou serve" (Matt. 4:10). His ten-commandment law tells us how to worship Him. And the fourth commandment—the only command that is about worship—tells us to "Remember"—don't forget! "the sabbath day, to keep it holy. Six days shalt thou labour, and do all thy work: But the seventh day is the sabbath of the Lord thy God: in it thou shalt not do any work, thou, nor thy son, nor thy daughter, thy manservant, nor thy maidservant, nor thy cattle, nor thy stranger that is within thy gates." then God explains why He wants us to keep the day. He wants us to copy Him. Being a copycat is the highest form of praise and admiration there is. So I want to copy Him. I don't want to forget that He is my Creator. I don't want to forget how much He loves me. Here is the rest of His command. "For in six days the Lord made heaven and earth, the sea, and all that in them is, and rested the seventh day: wherefore the Lord blessed the sabbath day, and hallowed it" (Exod. 20:8–11).

It's such a simple request. He wants us to be happy about it. We all know how much it hurts when a family member doesn't want to spend time with us. We are His family. I'm proud to be part of the family of God. Remember! He is the One who created us. And after He created us, He rested. He wants us to copy Him. When you admire someone, you do what they do. You copy them.

As we noted earlier, Satan desires worship. He doesn't care who or what we worship, as long as we do not worship God. That is part important to worship God. If we do not worship Him, we are worshiping God's enemy, the devil. He does not want anyone to worship God! He wants us to worship some man. You see, if we are doing what Satan wants us to do, that's the same as worshiping him. That puts him in control of our lives and makes him very happy. He hates God, and he knows when we worship anyone or anything else in place of God, we hurt God tremendously. The devil is both God's enemy and our enemy. If we love God, we will worship Him.

Satan desires worship. He doesn't care who or what we worship, as long as we do not worship God.

The devil does not want us to realize when we cross the line and are worshiping him instead of God. He works diligently through deceit to keep us from comprehending the simplicity of how easy it is to worship God. If we are obeying Satan, we should run from him as fast as we can. We need to run into the arms of God, who is always there for us. His arms are always outstretched, reaching out to us. So let's take a closer, deeper look at why we should worship God. We know it is God, but some of us are puzzled about who God is. Is it the Father, the Son, or the Holy Spirit?

The Bible clearly gives us an answer. Let's look at the biblical evidence that says all three of them, Father, Son, and Holy Spirit, are One God. They worked together when They created our world and us. When God—the three of Them, who are our One God—created our world, they began showing the universe that They together are One God and that They, "God," are "love." Their characteristic of love enhances our desire to worship Them. Why wouldn't we worship someone who loves us so much!

The Bible states that all three Beings, who are our One God, were present when our earth was created. Moses used the plural form of the word "God" in that very first verse in the Bible. He said, "In the beginning God created the heaven and the earth" (Gen. 1:1). If you look up the word "God" in *The Strongest Strong's Concordance* of the Bible, you will find that the word "God" comes in varying tenses. And as we learned in chapter five, the plural word for God calls the Holy Spirit Elohim, and it also calls the other Beings who are God Elohim. This word was used in the very first verse in chapter one of Genesis. This means Moses was talking about all three of the Beings who are our One God. And that same plural form of the word "God" is used again in the second verse when it talks about the Holy Spirit. Thus, we find that both the Father and the Spirit are Elohim God. They both claim the same title—Elohim. The same is true in the Hebrew dictionary, at the back of the concordance. Allow me to refresh your memory of its definition. It was "God: plural of majesty, plural in form, but singular in meaning, with a focus on great power."

Also, when I looked up the specific word which was used for the word "God" in these two verses, I found that all three of them were #430—Elohim, in *Strong's Concordance*. Thus, whether God says us or him, the plural word for God "Elohim" is used. This shows positively that this plural word for God calls them God 430 Elohim, whether They are working singly or together. They, singularly and together, are one God. Isn't that neat? It is just one more way God is different and special. They are uniquely God. I'm so glad.

It is extremely important we know this because it shows us it was Jesus who spoke to those patriarchs of old. He actually came down and communed with humanity and helped them with their trials. I wanted to restate this because of its importance to Jesus' establishment of His church after He was born of Mary. It ties His divine existence before He was born down here with His human existence.

The first Being who was introduced—by this status—was the "Spirit." It's interesting that the Holy Spirit was the first one of the three holy Beings, who are called God, was the first one to be introduced. The Holy Spirit is the person of the Godhead who is with us every day of our lives—coaching—cheering—and teaching us God's will. He is very important to both our safety and our salvation. Maybe that is why He was mentioned first as an individual. Moses said, "And the Spirit of God moved upon the face of the waters" (Gen. 1:2). The next mention we have of God individually is in verse 26. It is one Being talking to another; "And God said, Let *us* make man in *our* image, after *our* likeness" (Gen. 1:26).

Now, notice the very next verse. It is the same God talking, and it is the same God who created the man, but Moses uses the word "His," which is definitely singular. It definitely shows us God is more than one person. No, not three Gods—but One God! In this verse one of the Beings who is God is talking with one of the other Beings, who is God. If there is only one Being who is God, then God is talking to Himself. That idea should bring a chuckle to your throat! Yes, in the above verse, God used the word "us." "So God created man in his own image, in the image of God created he him" (Gen. 1:27).

This verse truly shows us there is more than one Being talking. They are talking with each other. Each had His own special part to play in creating our world and us. All three of Them, Father, Son, and Holy Spirit, are God. Together They are God! Three Beings, but one God. For me, it makes it easier to understand if I think of the three of Them as a family—the family of God. In that family, we have the Father who is over all, and we have the Son, and we also have the Holy Spirit. Look what Jesus said about Their oneness. He, too, states both He and His Father are God Elohim. Each of Them is God. Jesus said, "I and My Father are one" (John 10:30).

Remember, Moses called the Holy Spirit, "God." He said, "the Spirit of God," in Genesis 1:2. Truly, They are not one being, but They are One

God. "The Lord our God is one Lord" (Deut. 6:4). "For there are three that bear record in heaven, the Father, the Word, and the Holy Ghost: and these three are One" (1 John 5:7). Each holy Being who is our One God has an extremely important job to do in saving us. Jesus is the one who created us. He is the one who died for us. And He is the one who followed those patriarchs of old everywhere they went, and He did it clear up until the time of His birth here.

When Jesus went to heaven, the Holy Spirit took over the job of being with each one of us. All three of Them have all of the characteristics of God. Together, the three of Them are One God, not one person, but one God. Here are two more proof texts which show us that each of them is God. These Bible references that call Jesus, "God" are unrefutable. "*The birth of Jesus Christ was on this wise*: When as his mother Mary was espoused to Joseph, before they came together, she was found with child of the Holy Ghost. Then Joseph her husband, being a just man, and not willing to make her a public example, was minded to put her away privily. But while he thought on these things, behold, the angel of the Lord appeared unto him in a dream, saying, Joseph, thou son of David, fear not to take unto thee Mary thy wife: for that which is conceived in her is of the Holy Ghost. And she shall bring forth a son, and thou shalt call his name Jesus: for he shall save his people from their sins. Now all this was done, that it might be fulfilled which was spoken of the Lord by the prophet, saying, Behold, a virgin shall be with child, and bring forth a son, and they shall call His name Emmanuel, which being interpreted is, God with us" (Matt. 1:18–23).

The Greek language works differently. They only have one word for the word "God" and another word for the word "Lord." But the definition of the word God agrees with the Hebrew definition. It is #2316—Theos—and it is also used dually with other gods. (Notice I used a small "g" meaning false gods when I said this about other gods—not our holy God! Here is the definition of the word they use in the Greek language. GOD—Theos, #2316.

God usually refers to the one true God. In a very few contexts, it refers to a (pagan) god or goddess. The "Son of God" as a title of Jesus emphasizes His unique relationship to the Father. Whereas the god of this age refers to the devil. Also, we have the word "Lord" in the Greek language. LORD—Jehovah—2962: This can be a title of address to a person of higher status, lord, or sir; a master of property or slaves; or a New Testament translation of the Hebrew #151 "Lord" or #3378 "Lord," that is YAHWEH, the proper name of God in the Old Testament.

In the book of Hebrews, the same words are used for Jesus as are used for the Father. Those words are Theos #2316 and Jehovah # 2962."God, (Theos) who at sundry times and in divers manners spake in time past unto the fathers by the prophets, hath in these last days spoken unto us by his Son, [Jesus] whom he hath appointed heir of all things, by whom also he made the worlds; Who being the brightness of his glory, and the express image of his Person, and upholding all things by the word of his power," (Jesus' power) "when he had by himself purged our sins, sat down on the right hand of the Majesty on high; Being made so much better than the angels," (it is talking about when He was born down here in human flesh) "as He hath by inheritance obtained a more excellent name than they" (Heb. 1:1–4).

I wonder if God had this placed in our Bible because He knew Lucifer would claim to be His son too. The Father certainly did not want anyone to think the angels were equal with His Son, Jesus. And especially not the devil. No! Jesus and the devil are not brothers! *"For unto which of the angels said he at any time, Thou art my Son, this day have I begotten Thee? And again, I will be to him a Father, and he shall be to me a Son?" (Heb. 10:5).* Then the Father talks about Jesus, His Son, being worshiped by the angels. No one is to be worshiped except God. So this also proves that the Father considered Jesus to be God. "And again, when he bringeth in the firstbegotten into the world, he saith, And let all the angels of God worship him [Jesus]. And of the angels he saith, Who maketh his angels spirits, and his ministers a flame of fire. But unto the Son he saith, Thy throne, O God, is for ever and ever: a sceptre of righteousness is the sceptre of thy kingdom. Thou hast loved righteousness, and hated iniquity; therefore God, even thy God, hath anointed thee with the oil of gladness above thy fellows. And, Thou, Lord, in the beginning hast laid the foundation of the earth; and the heavens are the works of thine hands: They shall perish: but thou remainest; and they all shall wax old as doth a garment; And as a vesture shalt thou fold them up, and they shall be changed: but thou art the same, and thy years shall not fail" (Hebrews 1:6–12).

That's right! Jesus has always been alive—and He always will be. Now just look at these verses in the book of John. They also confirm that Jesus is God. They sound a lot like the verses in Genesis, where the Father and Son are talking together about creating mankind in Their image. "In the beginning was the Word," Jesus is the Word. "and the Word was <u>with</u> God," (2316—Theos) "and the Word was God" (2316—Theos). "The same was in the beginning with God." (2316—Theos) "All things were made by Him; and without Him was not any thing made that was made. In him was life; and the life was the light of men.… That was the true Light, which lighteth every man that cometh unto the world. He was in the world, and the world was made by Him, and the world knew Him not.… But as many as received him, to them gave he power to become the sons of God, even to them that believe on his name:… And the Word was made flesh, and dwelt among us, (and we beheld His glory, the glory as of the only begotten of the Father,) full of grace and truth.… No man hath seen God at any time, the only begotten Son, which is in the bosom of the Father, He hath declared Him" (John 1:1–4, 9–10, 12, 14, 18).

> Yes! Jesus definitely is one of the three holy Beings
> who together are our **ONE GOD!** Worship Them.
> They greatly love you, and Their Sabbath command
> truly is the thread that got lost!

CHAPTER TWENTY-ONE

Jesus, Founder of the Christian Church

Throughout the Bible, Jesus is pictured as a Rock and the founder of the Christian Church. Let's take a short journey through the Bible to establish this truth. It is very important because it tells the story of Jesus' walk here on Planet Earth. All the things Jesus did help us know who the founder of the Christian Church really was. It also shows us who did not found God's Church. It is extremely important that we know who founded God's Church on earth—the church we are now attending. We must be very sure we are attending His church. There are so many churches out there today. There is even one called the Satanist Church.

Throughout the Bible, Jesus is pictured as a Rock and the founder of the Christian Church.

In the Garden of Eden, when Jesus slew the animal to make clothes for Adam and Eve to cover their nakedness caused by sin, Jesus gave them an object lesson of what He would do for them at the cross. It pointed forward to His death and cemented in their minds the fact that sin causes death. He told Adam and Eve how to worship Him. Then, whenever in their worship, they slew a lamb, it showed God they believed Jesus would die to pay for their sins. That was a big part of the worship God expected from them at that time in history. It was when Adam and Eve sinned, that this particular act of worship began. It was Jesus who showed them how to truly worship Him!

On the sixth day of the week, God created all of the animals and everything which creeps on the earth. And the next day was Sabbath—the very first Sabbath on earth: God spent with Adam and Eve. Here is what God's Word says: "And on the seventh day God ended his work which he had made; and he rested on the seventh day from all his work which he had made" (Gen. 2:2).

On the very first Sabbath on earth, God established His church here. He wanted all of His created beings to love and worship Him. As we have already learned, God made the seventh day of the week holy by placing His blessing on it. Then He made it extra special by setting it aside for a holy purpose. He sanctified it and made it special and holy. That holy purpose was so mankind could worship Him and know how much He loved them. Can you picture Jesus kneeling down and forming the dust of the earth with His hands? Beautiful scene, isn't it. Yes, it really was Jesus who knelt down in that soil and formed Adam out of the dust of the ground.

After Adam and Eve and our earth were created, Jesus made it known that the seventh day of the week was a special day—His Sabbath day. Wow! The Sabbath of our Creator.

Have you ever stopped to think about that? Thus, even before there was a church building, God had a church. The first mention of someone worshiping God was when Cain and Abel brought their gifts to the Lord. That was supposed to be a worship service. But Cain was not worshiping God. He did not slay a lamb to show he believed Jesus would die someday to pay for his sins. That is why God did not accept his offering. Cain gave God what he chose to give Him rather than what God had asked him to give. His gift did not show he believed Jesus, the Lamb of God, would take away his sins.

He thought an offering of fruit was just as good as the lamb God asked him to offer. But he was dead wrong! You see, he was proud of the fruit that came about from his own labor. His actions showed that he thought his own works were just as good as the work of Jesus dying on the cross for him. So he rejected the fact that Jesus had to do the work of washing away his sins. He placed his pride ahead of God's command—he literally rejected God's solution to his sin problem. Thus, he sinned and turned his back on God. He refused to accept Jesus as his Savior. How sad! We can't save ourselves by our works, either. It's Jesus' work that saves us—His shed blood and perfect life is the only thing that can save us. We know this from many Bible verses. There is one that is very straightforward and easy to understand. I just have to share it with you. It was written by Paul under the inspiration of God. Listen to his experience—He claims this message was given to him for our day. He says, "To make all men see what is the fellowship of the mystery, which from the beginning of the world hath been hid in God, who created all things by Jesus Christ" (Eph. 3:9). "For this cause I Paul, the prisoner of Jesus Christ for you Gen'-tiles …" (Eph. 3:1).

There you have it! Jesus was the One who did the actual creating. The three of them made their plans together. The Holy Spirit did His part. The three of them worked together to create us and our world. Then the government of heaven was instituted on our earth. Listen to Paul's wind-up on this. Yes, Paul went so far as to become a prisoner because of his worship of Christ. And he says he became a prisoner for our sake. So we could know all about Jesus' payment for our sins. He claims this provided him a new opportunity to let mankind know more about God. "To the intent that now unto the principalities and powers in heavenly places might be known by the church the manifold wisdom of God" (Eph. 3:10). "Which in other ages was not made known unto the sons of men, as it is now revealed unto his holy apostles and prophets by the Spirit" (Eph. 3:5).

That's right! This was revealed to Paul through the Holy Spirit. And what was God's reason for revealing it to Paul? "That the Gentiles should be fellow heirs, [that's us] and of the same body, and partakers of His promise in Christ by the gospel" (Eph. 3:6). Isn't that beautiful? How long had God purposed to let His church know all of these things? It has always been His purpose. "According to the eternal purpose which he purposed in Christ Jesus our Lord" (Eph. 3:11). Yes, it has always been Jesus' purpose to save all of mankind from their sins.

And now, Paul puts in a special plug for us in our day. For those who are living just before Jesus comes back to this earth. Look what He tells us we can have. Those will not be pretty days just before Jesus comes back to get us. Just look at the evening news. The happenings in that last church still in our day as the news screams out, concerning the wickedness happening in one particular church. It agrees with what the Bible says. It says there will be "wickedness in high places" (*Eph. 6:12*). Yes, we are hearing about great wickedness against innocent people. People who thought they were giving their life to God's service. It is being loudly splashed across the news.

Do you know what God says to do about it? He doesn't say, "clean up your church." Rather He says, "Come out of her, my people, that ye be not partakers of her sins, and that ye receive not of her plagues" (Rev. 18:4). Read your Bible. Listen to God. He will never lie or deceive you. Come to Him "In whom we have boldness and access with confidence by the faith of Him" (Eph. 3:12). Paul was so right because he was listening to God. We need to listen to God too. We need to compare what people say with what God says in His Word.

Here is Paul's encouragement to the people who knew him. "Wherefore I desire that ye faint not at my tribulations for you, which is your glory. For this cause I bow my knees unto the Father of our Lord Jesus Christ, of whom the whole family in heaven and earth is named, that he would grant you, according to the riches of his glory, to be strengthened with might by his Spirit in the inner man; That Christ may dwell in your hearts by faith; that ye, being rooted and grounded in love, May be able to comprehend with all saints what is the breadth, and length, and depth, and height; and to know the love of Christ, which passeth knowledge, that ye might be filled with all the fulness of God.... Now unto Him that is able to do exceeding abundantly above all that we ask or think, according to the power that worketh in us, Unto Him be glory in the church by Christ Jesus throughout all ages, world without end" (Eph. 3:13–21).

Yes, God has always had His church on His mind. When Adam and Eve sinned, our world became the stage for the drama of sin that began playing out on our planet. It took place when Eve first yielded to the temptations of Satan and again when Adam chose to follow in her footsteps. We, too, every last one of us, has followed in the devil's footsteps. Since then, the whole universe has been watching this horror movie that is being played out fiercely in our day. Greed and all kinds of sins, especially sexual ones, are rapidly increasing. The actions of people show the result of sin. Praise God, those who obey God will be victorious. Paul tells us how he felt about what he went through. He really felt put down by evil people, but he thought it was worth every heartache and pain he endured. Listen to his description of what he went through. It was quite a comedown from the high-handed pride he started out with, and he was glad for it. "For I think that God hath set forth us the apostles last, as it were appointed to death: for we are made a spectacle unto the world, and to angels, and to men. We are fools for Christ's sake, but ye are wise in Christ; we are weak, but ye are strong; ye are honorable, but we are despised. Even unto this present hour we both hunger, and thirst, and are naked, and are buffeted, and have no certain dwellingplace; And labour, working with our own hands: being reviled, we bless; being persecuted, we suffer it: Being defamed, we intreat: we are made the filth of the world, and are the offscouring of all things unto this day" (1 Cor. 4:9–13).

You can see that Paul thought his lot in life was very difficult, but he still chose that life because He wanted to honor God, and he loved people. That is why he got so deeply involved with their welfare. Then, He wanted to make sure we know he was not running us down. Listen to his words. He considers himself to be our father. "I write not these things to shame you, but as my beloved sons I warn you. For though ye have ten thousand instructors in Christ, yet have ye not many fathers: for in Christ

Jesus I have begotten you through the gospel" (1 Cor. 4:14–15). Yes, the prophets were rooted and grounded in Christ. They were His hands, His feet, and His spokespersons and members of His church.

Obviously, God had told Adam all about sin, and about their mutual enemy, the devil. From the day they were created, they knew what sin was. Our God of love would not withhold such vital information. God alone knows to what depths the enemy will go. God has gone to the greatest lengths possible to tell all of us about Satan in His Word. What kind of a God would He be if He hadn't told Adam and Eve how dangerous Satan was! Certainly not the loving God we serve.

The very next day—the first Sabbath on earth—Jesus founded the very first Christian Church on this earth. They had a lot to learn that day. Thank God He is the best teacher there is. It was Jesus who spoke with the patriarchs of old and guided them in their worship of God. Knowing Jesus' role on the earth makes His love more tangible for us, and it is the bridge that helps mesh humanity with divinity. Jesus knew that day He got down on the ground and formed Adam out of the dust that He would die for him someday. But He did it anyway. How much do we love Him? Enough to tell the truth? Why is it so important to know it was Jesus who created us? One reason is because it shows us who was talking to all of those great men in those far-off days before the flood. And it lets us know it was Jesus who led the children of Israel through the desert.

The very first time the word "rock" is used in the Bible is in Exodus 17:6. God told Moses to smite the rock at Horeb. Actually, when the people grumbled and accused God of leading them out into the wilderness to die of thirst, their grumbling was like socking God in the face with their fist. God was the one who was providing everything they needed. It was kind of like what people say today when they say that someone "bit the hand that fed them." Only, this was the hand that was saving their very life!

Earlier, when we read the verses about their grumbling, we found they did not trust God. They needed to develop faith in Him. We found that when they fussed and didn't think God was giving them what He had promised to give them, He was testing them. He did this to help them develop faith—something they needed direly. I find it very enlightening that God told Moses to smite the rock. For as we shall see through reading these Bible verses, the true Rock is Jesus. He is the Rock who was really smitten to save us.

Do you remember the great miracles the Lord performed at the crossing of the Red Sea? How it looked like they were all going to be destroyed by the Egyptians? Very often, God takes people right to the brink of disaster and then saves them. The crossing of the Red Sea is a prime example. They had to obey. It looked like they would be committing suicide. I am sure they were afraid the water might come and cover them before they could get across. They could not do what God told them to do without faith. Another evidence of great faith was when Daniel was thrown into the lion's den. Also, the three Hebrew boys who were thrown into a fiery furnace shows us how Satan tries to destroy God's children. God likes to save us in the thick of our trials rather than from them. He does this because if we obey the Lord when things are going bad for us, we show Him and others we have decided to follow Him all the way, no matter what. It isn't God who causes the trouble. It's His and our enemy, the devil.

> *If we could see the whole picture, we wouldn't want Him to do anything different than what He did.*

Consider Job and what he went through. You will find part of the reason God does this. I can picture in my mind's eye, Satan wagging his finger at God in all of these situations. And yes, there are those who love God who are not saved but are killed like John the Baptist. But God has good reasons. Someday He will tell John all about it. If those were cookie-cutter happenings, they would not build faith. We have to have the kind of faith that shows we really do trust God. That we believe God does what is best. If we could see the whole picture, we wouldn't want Him to do anything different than what He did. Satan would scream unfair, unfair. And we would not need faith because we would always get our own way.

The special care God gave the Israelites should have generated love in their hearts. He rescued them from an extremely severe situation. The mistreatment they went through during their captivity in Egypt was horrific, but the verse does not express any love from them toward God—the great God who had just rescued them. Instead, it says, rather than loving Him, "the whole congregation of the children of Israel murmured against God" (Exod. 16:2).

With the Israelites at the Red Sea, Jesus knew their stubborn hearts. He knew they were more interested in getting their own way than loving and obeying Him. He knew they were unwilling to obey His laws of love. How sad! That they treated their Maker so terribly. God was prepping them to be His missionaries—His church.

Unfortunately, God had to show them their true selves. He has to show us our true selves, too, so we can come to obey Him and be saved. God has had to do this all down through the ages. And did you notice God gave them exactly what they asked for? Yes, He gave them just what they wanted and clamored for. Not because He thought it was good for them, but because He wanted them to find out that their personal wants were not always good for them. Our longsuffering God was willing to offer them tough love and let them learn from their mistakes. And what was His reason for treating them the way He did? He said to them, "and ye shall know *that I am the* Lord *your God*" (Exod. 16:12).

God wanted them to know how much He loved and cared for them. A great many of them still did not have faith in Him. So, God had them move again! Since they had not learned the lesson He wanted to teach them, He gave them the same lesson over again, and just look at what they did the next time. Again, allow me to repeat these verses since they talk about the Rock, which is our God. "There was no water for the people to drink. Wherefore the people did chide with Moses, and said, Give us water that we may drink. And Moses said unto them, Why chide ye with me? wherefore do ye tempt the Lord? And the people thirsted there for water;

and the people murmured against Moses, and said, Wherefore is this that thou hast brought us up out of Egypt, to kill us and our children and our cattle with thirst? And Moses cried unto the LORD, saying, What shall I do unto this people? They be almost ready to stone me. And the LORD said unto Moses, Go on before the people, and take with thee of the elders of Israel; and thy rod, wherewith thou smotest the river, take in thine hand, and go. Behold, I will stand before thee there upon the rock in Horeb;" (This was Jesus speaking to Moses, and Jesus said,) "and thou shalt smite the rock, and there shall come water out of it, that the people may drink." This reminds me that when they stuck the spear into Jesus' side to make sure He was dead, both blood and water gushed out. "And Moses did so in the sight of the elders of Israel. And he called the name of the place Massah, and Meribah, because of the children of Israel, and because they tempted the LORD, saying, Is the LORD among us, or not?" (Exod. 17:1–7).

It is hard to have faith in someone you do not love. But faith in God = life. Jesus was their lifeline. Jesus is the lifeline of all people from creation to the end of the world. He is the water of life. Faith in Jesus Christ, the founder of our church, is the key to our salvation too! Remember, God gives every single person a measure of faith. And we increase our measure by using it. That is what God wants to do for all of His people. I am so glad God gives all of us a measure of faith. It is up to us what we do with it. As we trust Him, our faith will grow. That means we ourselves personally are in control of how much faith we have! Isn't that just like God! He never meddles with our freedom of choice! That, too, helps our faith in Him grow. God still says to us today:

"I beseech you therefore, brethren, by the mercies of God, that ye present your bodies a living sacrifice, holy, acceptable unto God, which is your reasonable service. And be not conformed to this world: but be ye transformed by the renewing of your mind, that ye may prove what is that good, and acceptable, and perfect, will of God. For I say, through the grace given unto me, to every man that is among you, not to think of himself more highly than he ought to think; but to think soberly, according as God hath dealt to every man the measure of faith" (Rom. 12:1–3).

This is exactly what God did for those grumbling Israelites. They got what they chose to get. It certainly opens my eyes! I am sure that is the way He has dealt with me at times, too. So, I shouldn't have anything to grumble about. For if I have faith in Him, I will believe there is a very good reason for everything God is allowing to come my way. I just need to trust Him as Job did. Someday, He will tell me why I had to go through whatever fiery trial I endured. I know I will be satisfied when I see Him and realize He needed to do it. And I will be satisfied with the way He did it too. Just look at what God sent to them, and notice why He sent it. These verses cap all of it off. They tell us that Jesus is the Rock. WOW! That Rock followed them everywhere they went. That Rock follows us today, via the presence of the Holy Spirit. Aren't we blessed? Just listen to and take in these beautiful words!

"Moreover, brethren, I would not have you ignorant, how that all our fathers were under the cloud, and all passed through the sea; And were all baptized unto Moses in the cloud and in the sea; And did all eat the same spiritual meat; And did all drink the same spiritual drink: for they drank of that spiritual Rock that followed them: and that Rock was Christ" (1 Cor. 10:1–4). That's right! They all had the same privileges. And this next verse is positive proof that Jesus Christ was the Rock which followed them. Its message should bring us to our knees! "But with many of them God was not well pleased: for they were overthrown in the wilderness. Now these things were our examples, to the intent we should not lust after evil things, as they also lusted. Neither be ye idolaters, as were some of them; as it is written, The people sat down to eat and drink, and rose up to play. Neither let us commit fornication, as some of them committed, and fell in one day three and twenty thousand. Neither let us tempt Christ, as some of them tempted, and were destroyed of serpents. Neither murmur ye, as some of them murmured, and were destroyed of the destroyer. Now all these things happened unto them for examples: and they are written for our admonition, upon whom the ends of the world are come. Therefore let him that thinketh he standeth take heed lest he fall" (1 Cor. 10:5–12).

Just as Paul says, it is through Jesus that, "We both have access by one Spirit unto the Father. Now therefore ye are no more strangers and foreigners, but fellow citizens with the saints, and of the household of God; And are built upon the foundation of the apostles and prophets, Jesus Christ himself being the chief corner stone; In whom all the building fitly framed together groweth unto an holy temple in the Lord: In whom ye also are builded together for an habitation of God through the Spirit" (Eph. 2:18–22). Yes, the Holy Spirit desires to set up housekeeping in our hearts. What a privilege is ours!

Listen to Peter as he talked to the Jews after Jesus had gone to heaven. "Be it known unto you all, and to all the people of Israel, that by the name of Jesus Christ of Nazareth, whom ye crucified, whom God raised from the dead, even by Him doth this man stand here before you whole. This is the stone which was set at nought of you builders, which is become the head of the corner. Neither is there salvation in any other: for there is none other name under heaven given among men, whereby we must be saved" (Acts 4:10–12).

Yes, the church was built upon the godly principles of Jesus Christ. He is the founder and leader of the Christian church. Look at the words of this beautiful song titled "The Church Has One Foundation." Samuel J. Stone wrote the lyrics in 1866. It is a beautiful hymn. He lived from 1839–1900. It tells it all.

> The church's one foundation, 'Tis Jesus Christ her Lord;
> she is His new creation, by water and the Word;
> From heaven he came and sought her to be his holy bride;
> with his own blood he bought her, and for her life he died.
>
> Elect from every nation, yet one o'er all the earth;
> her charter of salvation, one Lord, one faith, one birth;
> one holy name she blesses, partakes one holy food,
> and to one hope she presses, with every grace endued.

> Though with a scornful wonder we see her sore oppressed,
> by schisms rent asunder,
> by heresies distressed, Yet saints their faith are keeping;
> Their cry goes up, "How long?"
> And soon the night of weeping shall be the morn of song.
>
> 'Mid toil and tribulation, and tumult of her war,
> she waits the consummation of peace forevermore.
> till, with the vision glorious, her longing eyes are blest,
> and the great church victorious shall be the church at rest.

No one can ever take Jesus' place! He will always be the Rock foundation of His church. His church shall stand to the end. It is worth defending and sticking with. It will be a church that keeps all of the commandments of God. God does not change. He says, "I change not" (Mal. 3:6).

Can you hear God longing for the days when His brothers and sisters will be righteous. He calls it an offering. He says through Malachi, "Then shall the offering of Judah and Jerusalem be pleasant unto the Lord, as in the days of old, and as in former years. And I will come near to you to judgment; and I will be a swift witness against the sorcerers, and against the adulterers, and against false swearers, and against those that oppress the hireling in his wages, the widow, and the fatherless, and that turn aside the stranger from his right, and fear not me, saith the Lord of hosts" (Mal. 3:4–5). I think we should be afraid to do all of these things that are especially prevalent right now. Just look at what is taking place all over the world. My heart cries over the children and parents who were separated at the border. God bless those who are doing all in their power to find and place them with family members.

CHAPTER TWENTY-TWO

The New Baby Church

Throughout His grownup years, here on earth, Jesus spent His time training His disciples. As we look at the training He gave them, take note of the many special blessings He poured on the people through that training. Just look what happened! As I have said before, most of the training Jesus gave His disciples was done before He was crucified. Our Bible tells us through the work of His disciples, "The Lord added to the church daily" (Acts 2:47).

This could only take place because Jesus' disciples looked up to Him. They were convicted in their hearts He was the Son of God—the Messiah. And the disciples' exhortation, miracles, and words impressed the hearts of the people—the people His disciples communed with. Look at what happened! The Lord! That's right! This verse says it was the Lord who added new converts to His church every day, through the good witness and work of His disciples. They and God worked as a team.

God wants us to work with Him too. But we do not add to the church just as His first disciples didn't. It is God who convicts the heart and adds to the church. Also, His disciples were under the guidance of the Holy Spirit. It was from the Spirit working on their hearts and minds that made their words and works a witness. They had just been filled with the Holy

Spirit at Pentecost. Notice! They were congenial with each other and in agreement too. They were filled with a spirit of love. "And when the day of Pentecost was fully come, they were all with one accord in one place" (Acts 2:1). "And they were filled with the Holy Ghost" (Acts 2:4).

It is always God who convicts the heart. It is done through the working of the Holy Spirit now that Jesus is in heaven. The same Spirit helps us today as helped the people back then. He helps us understand and believe God's words are true. It bears repeating that Jesus is the "Word." What was the disciples' part? First, they had to believe. In other words, trust God. Then God gave them His Spirit. Then they went and told other people Jesus was the Messiah. God performs miracles through His disciples. The people believed the witness of the disciples' was true. "Then they that gladly received his word and were baptized: and the same day there were added unto them about three thousand souls" (Acts 2:41). "And the Word was made flesh, and dwelt among us, (and we beheld His glory, the glory as of the only begotten of the Father,) [Remember! The creation story tells us the Father and Son are alike] full of grace and truth" (John 1:14). The Bible says, "Thy word is truth" (John 17:17). It also says, "The word of our God shall stand for ever" (Isa. 40:8).

> *It is God who convicts the heart and adds to the church.*

When the people came together on the day of Pentecost, there were men from all nations at that gathering. Each one spoke in his own native tongue. The Jews thought the disciples were drunk and just talking gibberish. But Peter stood up and told them they were wrong, that these men were not drunk, but instead, they were filled with the Holy Spirit. Praise God that the Holy Spirit communicated these things to Peter, so he could continue to lead Jews and Gentiles alike to Jesus. Peter knew Jesus wanted all, yes, all who would to come into His church. So Peter said to those Jewish people who had just killed his Savior, "Let all the house of Israel know assuredly, that God hath made this same Jesus, whom ye have crucified, both Lord and Christ. Now when they heard this, they were pricked in their heart, and said unto Peter and to the rest of the apostles, Men and brethren, what shall we do? Then Peter said unto them, Repent, and be baptized every one of you in the name of Jesus Christ for the remission of sins, and ye shall receive the gift of the Holy Ghost. For the promise is unto you, and to your children, and to all that are afar off, even as many as the LORD our God shall call" (Acts 2:36–39).

The whole world was in turmoil just like it is today. Yes, this was the condition of the earth, when Jesus' disciples began calling God's people into His new baby church. They had just come through great confusion and rebellion. They had just witnessed the greatest miracle the world will ever see when they saw the God of the universe raised to life. Look what it did. "And the Word of God increased; and the number of disciples multiplied in Jerusalem greatly; and a great company of the priests were obedient to the faith" (Acts 6:7). Praise the Lord!

As I have said before, God did everything He could to save all of the people. But since He is love, He could not keep Satan from doing his dirty work, for if He had, He would have been controlling Satan and removing the devil's freedom of choice. God did not, will not, and could not do that and still be a God of love. Love always leaves one free to make their own choices in life. Even the choice to serve our holy God or serve someone else instead. God is still allowing this whole scenario to take place, so everyone, human and angelic, will know without a doubt that God is fair. This freedom screams out the message loud and clear that it is Satan who is causing all the evil that is happening in our world. All must see with their own eyes just how evil Satan is. Only God knows how truly evil he is, and only God knows how long it will be before He can bring the devil's evil to an end.

That is why Jesus' disciples continued to coach and witness to all mankind, whether the ones they witnessed to believed or not. Each person was given a chance to accept God's love and forgiveness. They built God's baby church through the help of God's Spirit. They hung onto God through thick and thin. Praise God! That is what we need to do, too. Rather than hang onto a belief when we find it is not in God's Word, we must accept God's loving correction. God is very clear in His teachings. It is always easier to keep sticking to our old ways, but God will see us through the hard times if we trust and obey Him. He wants us to change when we find we are not obeying Him. He wants to save us from our sins, for He cannot save us in them. That would be a horrific duplication of what everyone has already gone through. God has promised He will not allow that to happen. "What do ye imagine against the Lord? He will make an utter end: affliction shall not rise up the second time" (Nah. 1:9). It is one of my favorite Bible texts. It is such a beautiful promise.

God had to work on Paul's heart for a long time, but finally Paul became a Christian. He made an amazing turnaround. He even witnessed to King Agrippa about being a Christian. His words must have been quite convincing! But evidently Agrippa was arguing with the Holy Spirit! He must not have realized the Spirit doesn't argue. The Spirit convicts us of our sins. Satan was whispering in one of Agrippa's ears, while the Spirit talked to him in the other one. That's just like Satan! What a shame Agrippa listened to him and refused to say. "Get thee behind me, Satan" (Matt. 16:23). We know he did because of what he said to Paul when Paul asked him, "King Agrippa, believest thou the prophets?" Paul did not give him a chance to answer but immediately said, "I know that thou believest. Then Agrippa said unto Paul, Almost thou persuadest me to be a Christian" (Acts 26:27–28).

How very, very sad! Almost persuaded—but not quite! Yes, Satan was still hanging onto a corner of Agrippa's heart. If he didn't love God with all of his heart, he didn't love Him at all. The sin he clung onto was his idol, thus, he continued to be an idol worshipper. He was clinging to his own cherished, personal desires, which were not in line with God's law. Since every one of us is a sinner, we all have these kinds of issues.

Nevertheless, it was through those Jewish Christians, in that new baby apostolic church, that God's holy Sabbath day was kept alive at that time in earth's history. Look at this verse! It confirms that the disciples of Jesus obeyed God and continued to go to church on Sabbath, even after Jesus went to heaven. All of the recorded accounts tell us the disciples kept the Sabbath of the Lord. Paul preached to the Jews many Sabbaths. After that, Paul and some of his friends began evangelizing in other areas. Listen to this account! "And the next sabbath day came almost the whole city together to hear the word of God" (Acts 13:44).

There were many Jews who believed in Jesus. This particular meeting was many years after Jesus' final meeting on earth with His disciples. During all of their contacts with Jesus, before He finally rose and went to heaven for the last time, never once, did He tell them they no longer needed to keep the seventh-day Sabbath holy. Why did Jesus tell them to keep it holy? Because He said His Sabbath would never be done away with, and nowhere in the Bible are we told it has been abolished or ever will be abolished in the future. That is why the Bible verifies that the members of the new Christian church kept the seventh-day Sabbath holy. God wants us to know it is still His holy Sabbath! Yes, God wants us to know that the seventh-day Sabbath is His holy day—the Lord's day. The Bible records eighty-four Sabbaths Paul kept after Jesus was resurrected. That is a lot. But I'm sure it's only a drop in the bucket compared to all of the Sabbaths he kept that weren't recorded in God's Word.

Paul also spoke to the Hebrew people, telling them what those early Israelites had done. He told them what provoked Moses to anger toward the Israelites in the wilderness. He said it was because they didn't believe the message God gave them when Moses told them not to collect manna on Sabbath. Paul said that the Hebrews those Israelites back there in the wilderness, who chose to disobey the command of God and go against Him by collecting manna on Sabbath, were the ones who profaned His Sabbath day.

Yes, it was the very ones Moses was guiding and leading to Canaan, to a place of safety, who disobeyed Him. And yes again! Paul told them those people in the wilderness were the ones who caused all of the trouble. They were the ones who died there. And at the time this took place, it was God

Himself who identified the Sabbath breakers, to be those who disobeyed Him by picking up manna on the Sabbath—His holy day. The writer of the book of Hebrews strongly upheld Moses to the Hebrew people in His day. He was witnessing to them! Listen to Him: as he pleads with us now and brings it right down to our day. "And Moses indeed was faithful in all His house as a servant, for a testimony of those things which would be spoken afterward, but Christ as a Son over His own house, whose house we are [God calls our physical body, our house, and he says we are God's house, and then He uses a very small word "if"] if we hold fast the confidence and the rejoicing of the hope firm to the end" (Heb. 3:5–6, NKJV). Then the writer of Hebrews, many think it was Paul, calls for us to be faithful and obey the Spirit of God. He says, speaking for the Holy Spirit: "Wherefore (as the Holy Ghost saith, To day if ye will hear His voice, harden not your hearts, as in the provocation, in the day of temptation in the wilderness: When your fathers tempted me, proved me, and saw my works forty years. Wherefore I was grieved with that generation, and said, They do always err in their heart; and they have not known my ways. So I sware in my wrath, they shall not enter into my rest)" (Heb. 3:7–11).

God was talking to the people He wished would join His new baby church. And He is also talking to us, who live in our day. That's right! We, too, must have faith in Jesus and hold fast to what He taught our fathers. We have to hold fast to what our Bible is teaching us, so we can faithfully hold onto what the Holy Spirit has and is teaching us until Jesus comes back to get us. We, too, must obey and keep His Sabbath day holy. That is why God doesn't leave us wondering about what happened to those Jews who did not listen to the Holy Spirit's voice. Through His Word God tells everyone what those people did to Him. How they tested Him. And how persistent they were in their rebellion. God also shares with us His anger toward their unbelief and disobedience. Listen to His words. "For some, when they had heard, did provoke: howbeit not all that came out of Egypt by Moses. But with whom was he grieved forty years? was it not with them that had sinned, whose carcases fell in the wilderness? And to whom sware he that they should not enter his rest, but to them that believed not? So we see that they could not enter in because of unbelief" (Heb. 3:16–19).

Remember! Eve's problem, too, was unbelief. Her unbelief in God is what got all of us into trouble. God does not want us to join that group of unbelievers. He says, "Believe on the Lord Jesus Christ, and thou shalt be saved" (Acts 16:31). God help us!

CHAPTER TWENTY-THREE

The Original Antichrist in God's Own Church

———◆◆◆———

Remember! The beginning of the antichrist was when Lucifer thought he should be God. He thought he had as much right to be God as the Father, Son, and Holy Spirit did. Then he boldly declared that he was *"a God."* Notice that I used a capital "G" for the word "God" here. That is because Lucifer was claiming to be our holy God, not just "a god." So God told Ezekiel Lucifer is a god. Do you notice I again used a small "g" for the word God? And who did we learn antichrist is? It is anyone who places himself first, instead of placing God first. It is very important we realize Lucifer was the original antichrist. He was the instigator of evil. And he refused to place God first in his affections.

> God must always be first—last—and best in all our thoughts and actions,

But this privileged angel refused to honor the members of the Trinity. He thought he should receive just as much honor as Jesus did. But Lucifer was not God. He was not equal with Jesus. He was only a son like we are sons and daughters of God. Yes, we are sons and daughters of God, too, but only through creation and by accepting Them as God. And now, since Eve sinned, and through Jesus paying for our sins, we also are his sons and daughters through adoption. God bought us back—but we must agree to the adoption. Isn't it marvelous that God was willing to adopt us? Thank You, God. I thank all three of You—Father, Son, and Holy Spirit.

These verses are addressed to the Prince of Tyrus, and they also include anyone who places themselves in an antichrist position, claiming to be God instead of and or in place of God. This prince was following Satan, the original antichrist. And, as you have noticed, there have been many of them. He and Satan were both antichrists. They were working together. And God told Ezekiel to write about it in His Word. Just look at what God told Ezekiel to say to Tyrus. When we read the message of God's prophet, Ezekiel, we become aware that God is not only talking to Tyrus but He is also talking to Lucifer, the original antichrist. God verified this by telling the prophet what this being's position was in heaven, and by describing how He made him. Ezekiel talked a long time about Tyrus, and thus about Lucifer. But the part we want to look at is in this chapter. He begins the chapter by saying, "The word of the LORD came again unto me, saying, Son of man, say unto the prince of Tyrus, Thus saith the LORD God" (Ezek. 28:1–2).

> *God bought us back—but we must agree to the adoption. Isn't it marvelous that God was willing to adopt us?*

NOTICE! Both Tyrus and Lucifer were sons of man. Yes, God called Lucifer "man," just as He called Adam man. Then God said to him, "Because thine heart is lifted up, and hast said, I am a God, I sit in the seat of God, in the midst of the seas; yet thou art a man, and not God, though thou set thine heart as the heart of God" (Ezek. 28:2). Lucifer became proud—but he was who he was only because God conferred those gifts on him. He had nothing to be proud of. If only he had been proud of his Maker and loved Him for treating him so special.

God was very candid with Lucifer and told him there was no way He would allow him to be "God." That he was a man and always would be a man—a created being. That's right, Lucifer, and Tyrus, too, for that matter, have always been created beings—nothing more than a part of mankind. That is what mankind is—beings formed out of dust. Remember "The Lord God formed man of the dust of the ground" (Gen. 2:7.)

God would not and could not allow Lucifer to get away with this sin. So, the war was on! God went into full gear to save the angels in heaven, who were being deceived by him. God's plan also included saving all of the other beings, who were living on the other worlds He had created. That's the history of our wonderful God—always going to bat for those who love Him—those who follow in His steps—those who are abiding by His loving laws. That's because He loves all of us. Then God further identified that it was Lucifer He was talking about. He did it by telling the prophet He was talking about the being who had tempted Eve in the Garden of Eden. That clue sure does convince me.

Yes, God wanted to be sure everyone understood that this verse was talking about that serpent of old. The one which was Lucifer. The one who turned himself into the devil—Satan if you please! And how did God do that? He did it by saying, "Thou hast been in Eden the garden of God" (Ezek. 28:13).

But God didn't stop there—He wanted to be sure we would know exactly who He was talking about. So God told Ezekiel to tell us that this being had also been His covering cherub, at His holy temple in heaven. "Thou art the anointed cherub that covereth; and I have set thee so: thou wast upon the holy mountain of God" (Ezek. 28:14).

Did you notice that God spoke to Lucifer as if He were talking with him face to face? But the message was given to us through Ezekiel. God wanted to make sure we knew He was talking about Lucifer, that Lucifer had this position on the holy mountain in God's temple in heaven. Then God shares with us this conversation He had with Lucifer. God said to

Lucifer, "Thou wast perfect in thy ways from the day that thou wast created, till iniquity was found in thee" (Ezek. 28:15). God gives us ample, descriptive evidence to let us know exactly who He is talking about. It definitely was Lucifer, His covering cherub. The very first antichrist was right in God's holy temple in heaven.

That blows my mind—how about you? And, of course, we know the rest of the story. God had to kick him out of heaven. The angels took sides. Thus, we should not be surprised to find that the antichrist in our day will be embedded in a church on this earth, and it will be a church that looks like it is God's true church. Then Ezekiel tells us what the result of Lucifer's rebellion was. He says, "And there was war in heaven: Michael and his angels fought against the dragon; and the dragon fought and his angels" (Rev. 12:7). Michael is the name of our precious Savior.

One-third of the angels chose Satan as their leader. They were cast out into our world, and we have had to deal with them ever since. And we will continue to deal with that old devil until Jesus comes and rescues us. But the good news is what the voice of God said from heaven about those who choose Jesus as their leader. Here it is! "They overcame him by the blood of the lamb, and by the word of their testimony" (Rev. 12:11).

What a legacy Jesus has given us. Because of His victory over sin, if we align ourselves with Him and claim Him as our Savior—through our testimony we will overcome the devil. Thank You, precious Jesus.

CHAPTER TWENTY-FOUR

How Did Antichrist Get in God's New Baby Church

———◆◆◆———

Let's talk about some of the methods Satan uses to help the spirit of antichrist take over. Hatred comes from him. Satan's hatred plays a huge part in creating an atmosphere for antichrist to work among all people. In the new baby church, it came from an astonishing source. The Jews and Romans had been enemies for a long time. Thus, the Romans harbored hatred toward the new Christians because they worshipped God on the seventh day of the week.

In the minds of the Roman leaders, as far as they were concerned, that day was the holy day of the Jews. Since the Romans and Jews already hated each other with a vengeance, the Romans also hated the day the new Christians worshipped on. Thus, they considered these Christians to be their mortal enemies. They probably considered the new church to be just another Jewish church, with a new name attached to it.

Hatred goes hand in hand with fear and abuse. When people are afraid, Satan gets busy. Fear causes people to use every tactic they can to protect themselves. Fear causes people to go overboard in their thinking. So, they didn't even see or look for the Spirit of God, which was in this new church. Their eyes and their reasoning powers became disabled through the vengeance they harbored in their hearts toward the Jews. By using that built-up hatred, Satan was able to cause mega trouble in God's new baby church. The Romans labeled that day the Jewish Sabbath, but it wasn't just the Jewish Sabbath. It was God's Sabbath. It had always been God's Sabbath! The Lord's holy day of worship! The seventh-day Sabbath is the Christian Sabbath. In other words, it belongs to Christ, the Lord. It is the Sabbath of the Lord our God.

It's too bad God's chosen messengers—the Jews—failed to truly love Him and refused to accept Jesus as their Savior. In doing this, they placed God's day of worship in jeopardy. They were just making a pretense of honoring the day by totally refusing to honor the God of that day. They honored a day above and instead of honoring the Creator of that day. Consequently, they didn't really honor either of them. But the Jews were familiar with that day of worship, and many of them thought they were doing the right thing when they kept God's fourth commandment to a "T." But the hatred they displayed was not part of God's agenda. Yes, they needed to keep the Sabbath holy. If they had kept the day holy out of love for God, then they would have been honoring the Creator of that day.

We must make sure we are obeying God too—and make sure what we are doing is both an example of and a picture of His love. Love does not mistreat or kill. Love never uses force. But both the Jews and the pagan Roman rulers were using force. God says His final act of destroying the wicked is an act that is very strange to Him. He is a creator of good—not a destroyer, and His final act will be to destroy this wicked world plus any and all who tenaciously hold onto wicked ways foreign to him.

Take in these words from the twenty-eighth chapter of Isaiah. In verse sixteen, we are introduced to the God these verses are talking about. It is none other than Jesus Christ Himself. He is telling Isaiah about Himself, and He calls Himself our Lord and Savior, Jesus Christ, the Rock in Zion. "Therefore thus saith the Lord God, Behold, I lay in Zion for a foundation a stone, … a precious corner stone, a sure foundation" (Isa. 28:16).

Because of disobedience to God, Isaiah tells us what will happen at the end of time to our earth, because of our disobedience to God. He says, "For the LORD shall rise up as in mount Perazim, he shall be wroth as in the valley of Gibeon," Why? "that he may do his work, his strange work; and bring to pass his act, his strange act" (Isa. 28:21).

If you read down through some of these verses in Isaiah, you will find that he is prophesying about what will happen at Jesus' second coming. It shows us the fate of the wicked versus the reward of the righteous. It is very fascinating. It tells us what will happen to those who love the Lord in comparison to what will happen to all who refuse to lay aside their sins and worship Jesus.

The persecuting spirit, which the people in Rome were exhibiting, was from the antichrist power. Yes, antichrist was really flexing his muscles.

> *Satan is a pro at getting people to compromise. He's a smooth talker. A slick liar!*

Constantine, the emperor of Rome, was a sun-worshiper. In order to win the pagans to the new baby Christian church, he argued that the church should keep Sunday along with keeping the Sabbath—the seventh day of the week. His idea was to make the new members feel more comfortable. Sounds like a nice thing to do! Right? Satan is a pro at getting people to compromise. He's a smooth talker. A slick liar! His main activity is studying how he can get us to sin and then trap us in our sins.

When Constantine suggested this compromise, it probably looked innocent to a lot of the people. But there was a vast difference between the two forms of worship—Christian versus pagan. Constantine was inviting pagan practices into Christ's new baby church. A church cannot stay true to God and practice compromise at the same time. This mingling of the true with the false truly was the spirit of compromise—the spirit of Satan!

Constantine's spirit of compromise easily crept into the Christian church. It's a dirty shame this spirit of evil was accepted in. Right cannot be compromised with and still be right. Right never compromises by accepting and adopting practices into its laws things that are against God's holy commandments. When it does, there is no longer any right. Neither is there any right in those who do the compromising either. Constantine brought another sin that God hates into the church. He was walking in Satan's footprints. Lucifer worshipped a false god too. Who did Lucifer worship? He worshipped himself. Pride is a dangerous trait straight from the devil himself.

Constantine claimed he thought if he allowed the pagans to continue to be sun worshippers along with worshipping on their newly chosen holy day, it would help integrate them into the new baby church. It doesn't work that way! They needed to learn to love God supremely and obey Him. He thought if the church members accepted the pagans' way of worship, it would help convert them to Christianity, and at the same time rid the church of the hated Jewish Sabbath. How wrong he was.

This was none other than Satan himself, shoving his foot into the door of God's new church. It was Satan's entering wedge. They needed to learn to love God and His Sabbath. They needed to say "no" to Satan and shut the door in his face. Also, they needed to say "no" to Constantine, for he was inviting Satan's agenda right into their church. If only they had said "yes" to God. Yes is a word each of us can say wholeheartedly to God. God, help us!

Notice Constantine's two-fold reason for doing this. Get rid of God's true day of worship and accept sun worshipers by keeping their false day of worship intact. It was a double standard! You can't worship God and still worship on a pagan holy day. No! You can't worship antichrist, or any other false god, and still be worshiping God. Neither can you worship money, i.e., greed. The word "mammon" is talking about "wealth and assets," according to the Greek Dictionary that is at the back of *Strong's Strongest Large Print Concordance*. And the Bible says, "No man can serve two masters: for either he will hate the one, and love the other; or else he will hold to the one, and despise the other. Ye cannot serve God and mammon" (Matt. 6:24).

This sounds like one of the problems we have today, doesn't it? Not even antichrist would allow anyone to steal worship from him. But he is more than happy to steal it from God! Satan definitely wants to be worshiped instead of and in place of God. He still works and will continue to work as hard as he can to destroy anyone who continues to worship God in any way.

So the church was headed for deep trouble. And that trouble was antichrist in the Christian church. The Christian church still faces that same problem today. Once Satan thrusts his foot in the door, it is hard to get him out. When this happened, and they put a pagan day in place of God's holy worship day, they began worshiping a pagan god, and they stopped worshiping the one and only true God.

It is amazing what Satan can do to each of us through deceit. That's exactly what he did with Eve. It's as if he held his hand over those people's eyes. I am sure, at first, many of them did not see where such a breach in their worship of God would lead them. We know at least some in the church members believed Satan's lies. It only takes one believer to start an avalanche. Satan usurps authority through devious ways. Now he was right in God's face, in God's own church. Imagine that!

Satan, the original antichrist, uses people this way as often as he can. We each hold the key in our own hand, to choose who we allow to control us. God alone is our stronghold. But often we do not realize we are being used. Remember my story? As you know, I have more than once fallen into Satan's trap and not realized I was being used by this master deceiver. Each one of us needs to be much in prayer. Each of us needs to know personally what God requires of us.

Remember! Obeying God is not a hard job! It's just a matter of choice. We need to read our Bibles and do what it says. If something or someone disagrees with God's Word, then they are not worshiping God. The issue is love! Are we going to love God? or are we going to stick to our own selfish desires. That's not love! It's pure selfishness! They are antichrist actions if you please. Self instead of and in place of God. I am so glad God leaves us free to make our own choices. If we choose to ask God what He wants us to do, ask for the help of the Holy Spirit, and understand His will, then we have the tools for developing a habit to obey God. Every time we obey, it will become easier and easier to do so. Every time we say Yes to God and No to Satan, our decision to follow Jesus comes a little easier.

Am I exempt from Satan's lies now? My resounding answer is NO! Absolutely not! We will not be exempt until after we have decided to follow Jesus all the way, no matter what! We make that choice—not God. We never know when probation has closed for us. It could be today if we have an accident and get killed! Also, there is a day coming when God will have to say, "He that is unjust, let him be unjust still: and he which is filthy, let him be filthy still: and he that is righteous, let him be righteous still: and he that is holy, let him be holy still" (Rev. 22:11–12), just because time is running out. Jesus can't wait any longer because everyone else has made their decision, and He wants to come get those who love Him. Each person will make a final decision to obey or disobey God. We do not know when that final decision will take place. This shows us what a wonderful God of love He is. He is waiting for us to make our choice. IMAGINE THAT!

God wants to be our Savior, and if we choose to claim Him as such, He will save us! He saves people who are loving to all people, people who show others Jesus loves them. People who are keeping God's law of love, people who are asking the Holy Spirit to guide them, and people who are praying to God and obeying Him. But evil is not waiting! It keeps forging ahead. Satan is anxious to take over. Run into the arms of Jesus. He will save you if you let Him. Be on God's side of the controversy! Satan is on the other side. He's the first antichrist! the self-pleaser! the people-user! Plus, the people who are not staying true to God, people who are walking a tightrope high in the air without GOD as their protector. All people will know whether they are obeying God or not! God will make sure of that! God is fair! Whenever we veer, even slightly, from doing God's will, we are on enemy territory and in deep trouble of being confused by Satan.

Yes! Then we are in Satan's territory! But God will accept us back if we will listen to His Spirit. When God whispers in our ear and tells us we are straying from Him, then immediately, we need to run back home into the arms of our God as fast as we can!

Satan is always in the mix when we are having trouble knowing what is right or wrong. But what is most important, God is always right at our elbow, waiting for us to ask Him for help. That includes every last one of us! Why? Because every last one of us was created to be His child. But because Eve was deceived by Satan, every last one of us is a sinner. Yes! Every last one of us has fallen into many of Satan's traps and dishonored God. Sometimes—like Adam—we know we are sinning. Other times we don't even know! Like Eve we are deceived, we fail to trust God and believe Satan's lie instead of God's Word.

We must remember this very real truth that whenever we disobey God, we are falling into a very real trap of the devil. As soon as we realize what has happened, we must immediately go to God. He alone can get us out of the trap we are in. We need His help. We can't do it on our own. We must give Him total control of our life. He will not take control—we have to give Him control of it. Better still! Don't fall into the devil's trap. Stay away from him. Don't go where he goes. God told Eve not to go near the "Tree of the knowledge of good and evil" (Gen. 2:17). Why? Because that is where God allowed Satan to go. She failed the test. She made the wrong choice. She plugged her ears and strayed from God's safety net.

When we feel confused, we can pray and ask for guidance. Our Bibles will show us what to do. James reminds us, "Know ye not that the friendship of the world is enmity with God?" (James 4:4). This includes doing like Eve did—going to places God tells us not to go. She went where there was someone who was deliberately disobeying God. The serpent knew what was right. When we do that, Satan can easily entice us to take part in their sinful practices. That's what Eve did. God says to us, "Whosoever therefore will be a friend of the world is the enemy of God" (James 4:4). Then God gives us this cheerful advice. "Do ye think that the scripture saith in vain, The spirit that dwelleth in us lusteth to envy? But He giveth more grace. Wherefore he saith, God resisteth the proud, but giveth grace unto the humble" (James 4:4–6).

"Love not the world, neither the things that are in the world. If any man love the world, the love of the Father is not in him. For all that is in the world, the lust of the flesh, and the lust of the eyes, and the pride of life, is not of the Father, but is of the world. And the world passeth away, and the lust thereof: him that doeth the will of God abideth for ever" (1 John 2:15–17). From his own personal experience, Paul wrote these words. Take into consideration and remember that Jesus stopped Paul in his tracks from doing evil and turned him around. He wants to do that for each of us.

"Grace be to you and peace from God the Father, and from our Lord Jesus Christ, Who gave himself for our sins, that he might deliver us from this present evil world, according to the will of God and our Father: ... I marvel that ye are so soon removed from him that called you into the grace of Christ unto another gospel: which is not another; but there be some that trouble you, and would pervert the gospel of Christ. *But though we, or an angel from heaven,*"

Remember, Satan was no longer an angel from heaven!

"Preach any other gospel unto you than that which we have preached unto you, let him be accursed. As we said before, so say I now again, If any man preach any other gospel unto you than that ye have received, let him be accursed. For do I now persuade men, or God? or do I seek to please men? for if I yet pleased men, I should not be the servant of Christ. But I certify you, brethren, that the gospel which was preached of me is not after man. For I neither received it of man, neither was I taught it, but by the revelation of Jesus Christ" (Gal. 1:3–4, 6–12, italics supplied).

As Christians, if we decide to do nothing that is unpleasing to God, then God will help us. Only then can we be saved. Why can God save us then? Because we have chosen, yes, there's that word again, we have chosen to obey God. It is then that He can save us. He will never save us against our will.

Then we will be like Jesus. He will never be hard on us, and neither must we be hard on anyone, either. Just think! What if Christians had failed to work with Paul—or even worse—had joined him in his evil work of killing Christians! Just think what they would have missed. Then, he was just as ardent about saving the people he was killing as he was about destroying them. Probably more so! Because he was on God's side—part of the winning team. All of us must live to love each other—even our enemies. We must not be hard on them!

God says it is dangerous to associate with someone who decides to stick to his antichrist ways and refuses to adopt right in place of wrong. But we must witness to them and love them because we cannot read their thoughts; only God can do that. We must follow God's directions. We must even try to help those who cause us trouble, those who might be ready to kill us, as Paul was doing. But also remember that God counseled His people to work with Paul. God knew Paul's heart. Paul thought he was doing what God wanted him to do. He needed someone to open his eyes.

> *Satan trembles when we pray. Prayer is one of the most powerful sources of strength God has given us.*

How can we help open someone's eyes? We do it by how we live our lives and by loving them. We must pray for them and for ourselves. All of us have things we need to learn about God. None of us love God as we should. We must ask God to guide and help us. Satan trembles when we pray. Prayer is one of the most powerful sources of strength God has given us. It is one of the best ways to hold onto God.

Our best witness is Christ's love in our hearts and lives. If it is there, people will see it. We need to remember that none of us are perfect. All of us are growing, either farther from God or closer to Him. God is the only one who knows whether someone is like Paul and could be brought to the cross. Just love them. A godly life automatically becomes a witness for good to all who come in contact with it. Whoever we are, if we are living the way God wants us to live, we are witnessing the truth.

But unfortunately, the truth is the opposite is also true. If we are not living how God wants us to live, we are also witnessing. Each of us has witnessed in both directions. Yes, we are all on this path together. I believe everyone understands the language of love. It's truly is a universal language. Taught by God! I have a motto I have adopted. It helps keep me safe when and if I use it. It is, "If in doubt, do without!"

I believe it has saved me many times from doing something foolish or disobeying God unknowingly. What a shame that Satan, the first antichrist, spit out and still spits out the language of hatred toward God and toward everyone else. We certainly do not want to follow in his footsteps.

Never forget that the key to worshiping God is through faith in what God says in His Word—the Bible and through the help of the Holy Spirit. These three, The Father, the living Word (Jesus), and the written Word—(the Bible), and the Holy Spirit are our only true guides. Remember! Don't forget! If anything we see, hear, or read disagrees with the guidance of God, "there is no light in them." Let's not let the antichrist into our church or our hearts! And if he gets in, let's kick him out! That's what God would want us to do! How do I know? Because God tells us. He said, concerning the very people we have been talking about— *"For the heart of this people is waxed gross, and their ears are dull of hearing,"* Why did God say this? Because He says they chose to reject Him. "their eyes they have closed; lest they should see with their eyes, and hear with their ears, and understand with their heart, and should be converted, and I should heal them" (Acts 28:27). And you can bet your bottom dollar that the devil and all the antichrists have done just that. They are doing what they have chosen to do! Selfishness, i.e., me first-ism, is their God.

CHAPTER TWENTY-FIVE

The New Baby Church in Deep Trouble

The church was headed for great trouble. It was very bad that in Rome, in order to win people to Jesus, the leaders of the new Christian church that Jesus had started allowed the pagan people to bring their false practices of worship into the church. It wasn't long until the church was only meeting on Sunday, the pagan day to worship, instead of on God's holy Sabbath. This was the day when they worshiped the sun. All of this happened because of the work of antichrist. He set up housekeeping right in God's own church. Isn't that amazing? John said before he died that many antichrists had already come. "Little children, it is the last time: and as ye have heard that antichrist shall come, even now are there many antichrists; whereby we know that it is the last time" (1 John 2:18).

Many today teach that antichrist has not come yet! But John tells us who the antichrist is. He says, "They went out from us, but they were not of us; for if they had been of us, they would have no doubt continued with us" (1 John 2:19). That's right! John agrees that antichrist was in the church—the very church he attended. Then he told them one of the ways they could tell who antichrist was. The form of antichrist he talked about was very telling. He said, If they do not believe that Jesus is their Savior, they are antichrist—against Christ and in place of Christ just as Nimrod was and many since then; for this is what they did. They did not believe that Jesus is the Christ. And that includes the Father, for John quotes Jesus as saying, "I and my Father are one" (John 10:30).

Certainly, if we can believe anyone, it would be Jesus. I'm sure if you are a Christian and reading this, you agree. Then John said, "Who is a liar but He that denieth that Jesus is the Christ? He is antichrist, that denieth the Father and the Son. Whosoever denieth the Son, the same hath not the Father: but he that acknowledgeth the Son hath the Father also" (1 John 2:22–23).

The Bible teaches that anyone who does not accept Jesus as divine, in other words, believe He is God and one of the three holy Beings of the Trinity, that person is antichrist or the church who claims such things is antichrist. The Dark Ages were still ahead of them. The true Christians within the church left, so they could worship the Lord the way He had taught them to worship Him. God raised up reformers such as Martin Luther and many others who tried to bring back the pure principles Jesus had taught. These faithful Christian men left the church that Jesus and His disciples had started because they could no longer stay in that church and still obey God.

The reformers were not against their church. They were only trying to get the church to come back to its original purity. We need to go back to the example Jesus taught His disciples, but there are many leaders who still refuse to change. They continue to follow the antichrist. Yes, antichrist was still within that apostolic church—the church that Jesus had His disciples form. And he is still there in our day. How sad! He will be there until Jesus comes and removes him. What a glad day that will be when all is peace and joy again. There are churches who are following his example and do not know they are. They need to re-examine the doctrines of their faith and be sure they agree with the Bible.

All antichrists claim to be equal with God. In fact, they go a step further. They claim they are God. Remember, the Jews accused Jesus of this sin. They knew what blasphemy was. It was considered to be blasphemy when a man claimed that he was God. Here is the example from God's Word. It says, "Then the Jews took up stones again to stone Him. Jesus answered them, Many good works I have shewed you from my Father; for which of those works do ye stone me? The Jews answered him, saying, For a good work we stone thee not; but for blasphemy; and because that thou, being a man, makest thyself God" (John 10:31–33).

But as I said before, Jesus was *not* just a man. He always was, and still is, and will always be God. So Jesus was not committing blasphemy when He accepted worship from people! But anyone else who accepts worship and claims to be God is committing blasphemy, and they are antichrist!

The reason we have so many denominations today is because each reformer only brought people back in line with the one principle that was being attacked at that moment in time. What principle was it? It was the one principle in their day that the church was refusing to keep the way Jesus had commanded them to keep it. For instance, the Baptists reintroduced baptism by immersion. The antichrist power had brought in sprinkling—a false practice. A practice which God did not sanction. They practiced sprinkling in place of the pure teaching Jesus had taught them. For the church members to choose to not change and to decide to refuse to follow the guidance of the reformers was to align themselves with the antichrist.

One of the principle teachings the reformers taught was that men were to be immersed under the water when they were baptized just as Jesus had taught them. The reformers were right to bring this type of baptism back into God's church. Therefore, the new church that reformer started was called the Baptist Church. Each reformer tried to bring the church back into step with one of the precepts Christ had taught His disciples and away from one false principle that the antichrist power had brought into the church via the sun-worshipers.

There has been a long line of reformers. It's too bad that each time they brought back a truth of God, they didn't join the church of the reformer before them, who had brought another Christian principle back into existence. Then these men might have been able to hold the church together and stabilize it into one true Sabbath-keeping church. That's what Martin Luther wanted to do. He was the one who fathered the Lutheran Church.

It's sad that Satan would come right into God's church and corrupt it. But that's just who Satan is! A deceiver! A majority of God's people are in churches who are still not teaching their parishioners that God's day of worship is the seventh day if the week—Saturday. They don't know they are not doing what God wants them to do. They, just like Eve, are innocent victims of Satan's hatred toward God. God bless all of them, and God bless those men, such as Martin Luther, Zwingli, and Calvin, to name a few, who listened to God's voice and obeyed Him. So many things were wrong in that church after the antichrist took over that it would have taken more than one reformer to bring it back to its pristine beauty. There would have been too much turmoil, for just one, all by himself, to accomplish that. God bless each person today, too, who listens to the voice of the Holy Spirit and honors His guidance by putting into practice any of these changes. Remember! Never forget! That God tells us through John that all of the words of God are honest and true. They are in our Bible. That is where we must go to find out all of the truth. It's as simple as that (see John 17:17).

CHAPTER TWENTY-SIX

Last-Day Promises from God

God's Word is chock full of beautiful promises concerning the last days of earth's history. Let's review some of them. They were placed in the Bible to give us who live in these last days hope and faith. And God gives us much counsel in His Word too. He doesn't leave us in the dark about what to do to honor Him and become His child.

How do we honor and acknowledge God the Father today? We honor Him by obeying Him and by accepting His Son, Jesus, as our Savior. That's the way God's true children have always honored Him. Many today teach that Jesus was just a good teacher—God's Son, yes, but not God.

As we've seen, our Bible tells us very plainly who God is. It says the Father, His Son Jesus, and the Holy Spirit are God. And since none of those great men from ages past have brought back the true Sabbath, the Seventh-day Adventist Church considers it their mission to bring it back. The Bible clearly teaches the seventh-day Sabbath is God's only Sabbath day. Satan does not want us, the Christians of our day, to realize its great importance. He does not want us to know it is imperative to our salvation that we worship God on His true, holy day of worship.

We at the Seventh-day Adventist Church are interested in the salvation of all of our Christian brothers and sisters in Christ. The seventh-day Sabbath is the law that is paramount for our day. That's because it is the one command of God that has not been brought back to His church, by one of the earlier reformers. In fact, desecration of this command is one of the main reasons the new baby church started on its downhill ride to apostasy in the first place.

Many people in our day do not realize failure to obey God's Sabbath command is what caused that new baby church to divide up into a megaamount of different churches. So they do not know they need to change in order to obey God. God's Word teaches us the mother church will refuse to be converted, and that she will never go back to being God's true, pure church, again. She will do all she can to destroy reform. That is why God tells His people to, "Come out of her, my people, that ye be not partakers of her sins, and that ye receive not of her plagues" (Rev. 18:4).

> *The Bible clearly teaches the seventh-day Sabbath is God's only Sabbath day.*

Now, the mother church has daughters. They do not realize they are following the antichrist power when they try to keep Sunday holy. Why does the Bible call them daughters? Because they have innocently followed in the footsteps of the mother church. Mothers teach their children how to live.

God wants to reach the people in each one of these churches. He wants those churches to be His churches, but their members do not realize they are disobeying God and are in real danger. They do not know they are being fed a lie, just as the members in that new baby church. Thus, innocently, they refuse to adopt the command that is paramount in worshiping God. Innocently, they are desecrating God's holy day. Oh, how wonderful it would be if the pastors of those churches would bring their whole congregations back into a complete relationship with God, but unfortunately, the devil has placed his hand over the eyes of their pastors too. God bless them as their eyes are opened.

This pertains to all of the new churches the earlier reformers gave birth to. I hope we will be surprised and see many of them accept the Sabbath of the Lord our God and keep it holy today. Isn't it sad that the mother church refuses to do that! As we know, many are beginning to come out of her. Oh, how I wish all of them would. We are all brothers and sisters. God's children! God patiently waits for the day when we will all keep the seventh-day Sabbath holy with Him in heaven and then in the earth made new. He gives us this much-needed advice. "Enter ye in at the strait gate: for wide is the gate, and *broad is the way, that leadeth to destruction*, and *many there be which go in thereat*" (Matt. 7:13). Why don't they find that narrow gate? It's not God's fault; it's the fault of the false teachers, and unfortunately, many of them do not know they are false teachers. And it is their own fault if they refuse to come out because they like where they are. I've had friends say to me, "Certainly, most people won't be deceived. How could so many people be wrong and just a few saved?" So, that is why I wrote this book. I love all of my brothers and sisters in Christ, and am praying that each of you will believe what Jesus says, "few there be who find it" (Matt. 7:14).

James talks about the great temptation that causes people to be blinded to the truth. He makes it very clear! It all goes back to choice! As I have said before, God will not try to force us to love Him. He will not mess with our freedom of choice. The first step away from God is done very innocently many times or was taught us by our parents when we were children. They did not know they were teaching their children untruth.

James begins with a beautiful promise we can tuck into our hearts. Satan will be whispering in our other ear and telling us what James says is foolishness. But who is Satan accusing of being foolish? It is God Himself! God is the one who makes this very vital truth known to us. So here is that beautiful promise. It's a good one to memorize. He says, "Blessed is the man that endureth temptation: for when he is tried, he shall receive the crown of life, which the Lord has promised to them that love him"

(James 1:12). James agrees with what I just told you. He says God does not lead us where we will be tempted. He does not set us up for a fall. Satan or we ourselves do this. "Let no man say when he is tempted, I am tempted of God: for *God* cannot be tempted with evil, neither tempteth He any man: But every man is tempted, when he is drawn away of his own lust, and enticed" (James 1:13–14).

Aha! So what really tempts me are my own selfish desires. That's what gets me into trouble. And sometimes, I take myself to places where it is easier to be tempted because my desires lead me to those places. I chose not to ask God for help when my desires enticed me to go those places. So, do you see who chose to sin? No one but ourselves! James also tells us what happens because of lust. What is lust? It is our own selfish desires. He says when our desires get out of control, we need to fall on our knees and beg God to give us victory over what we are contemplating to do. He tells us there are dire consequences for hanging around places where we can be more easily tempted to disobey God. "Then when lust hath conceived, it bringeth forth sin: and sin, when it is finished, bringeth forth death" (James 1:15). That's mighty serious!

Many times I have had people say to me, certainly, all of those churches couldn't be making a wrong choice. Certainly, most people make the right choice! That's their heart. Remember what God says our heart is like? Deceitful! It tempts us to please ourselves and take the easy route. Our heart won't tell us that route isn't easy. And often they make light of it and say, "I don't agree with you! There just wouldn't be that many people who would be so wrong." But just look at the numbers, concerning this very thing from the past! For instance! How many were saved in the days of the flood?

Out of the whole population of the world at that time, only eight people were saved. That shows a drastic number of people being lost. Truly an unbelievable number! But we know this strange statistic is true because God is the one who has shared this number with us. He wants us to know! If we truly love Him and love our fellowmen, we can't just turn our heads and stand idly by while so many people go the way of destruction without anyone even trying to warn them.

Look at Sodom! The same thing happened there. And it happened all because they believed the lies of the people around them and disbelieved the words of God's messenger. Only three were saved out of that whole city, and that was a big city for that day and age. And Lot lost most of his loved ones. The statistic of huge numbers being lost will be repeated in the time of trouble that is coming upon the earth. Today could be your last day on earth. For many, an accident happens, and people are killed. You can't come to God after you are dead.

Again, God is very clear in this Bible verse in the book of Matthew also. God doesn't just repeat His message; He strengthens it! He says there won't be many who find the straight, narrow way that leads to eternal life. "Because strait is the gate, and narrow is the way, which leadeth unto life, and few there be that find it" (Matt. 7:14). What is the major reason? The answer comes to us from the parable Jesus told about sowing seed. He said, "Those by the way side are they that hear; then cometh the devil, and taketh away the word out of their hearts, lest they should believe and be saved" (Luke 8:12).

Yes! Satan is the main culprit. That is why we need to be so careful to not believe anything that disagrees with what God says. Never forget! God is stronger than Satan. With our hand in God's, we can win the battle with sin. "They on the rock are they, which, when they hear, receive the word with joy; and these have no root, which for a while believe, and in time of temptation fall away" (Luke 8:13).

These can remedy their problem by studying God's Word for themselves, not depending on someone else to tell them what God says. And by searching out a good teacher who teaches the truth of God. Every statement a teacher makes should be tested by the Word of God. Unfortunately, one of the other reasons is because they don't want to believe the truth. How sad!

Another reason is if we follow Jesus, we will not be following the crowd. It is much easier to follow the majority. It is the popular thing to do. But one can't follow the crowd and follow Jesus at the same time. He says that His people must decide not to continue to take part in the sins which the crowd, a majority of the people, are committing. When someone is saying these things to us, we need to tell them what Jesus told Satan when He was tempting Him in the wilderness. Satan was trying to get Jesus to kneel down and worship him, and isn't that what Satan is doing to us when he tempts someone to say, how could so many be wrong? Yes, Satan is enticing us to question God. Jesus said to the tempter, Satan, "Get thee hence, Satan:" Notice what Jesus said next. He was quoting the same Scripture Satan had used. Yes, Jesus guides us to read our Bibles, and what did it say? "Thou shalt worship the Lord thy God, and him ONLY shalt thou serve" (Matt. 4:10, emphasis supplied).

Jesus also cited another reason. He was talking to the Jewish religious leaders. To be saved, they needed His sharp words. He used tough love on them, and they still didn't repent. He wanted to save them. So He said, "He that is of God heareth God's words: ye therefore hear them not, because you are not of God" (John 8:47). They were choosing to not follow God. They chose to follow the antichrist of their time. Jesus says, "While ye have light, believe in the light, that ye may be the children of light. These things spake Jesus, and departed, and did hide himself from them" (John 12:36). It is dangerous to put off obeying something you know is true, for that is Satan trying to get you to follow him.

It is very important to accept the light when it is presented to us. When we don't, we are venturing into Satan's territory. He will tempt us and snatch the truth from us every chance he gets. That is what happened to the people in Jesus' parable. It is happening every day right now as people learn the truth. I pray that you will not let it happen to you. "Nevertheless among the chief rulers also many believed on him; but because of the Pharisees they did not confess him, lest they should be put out of the synagogue: For they loved the praise of men more than the praise of God" (John 12:42). And what happens to the laypeople is they do not want to give up the fellowship of the church members and the offices they hold at their church. Can you see and hear the grief this caused Jesus? He loved them!

You hold in your hand a Bible. You have taken this trip through it with me. Now you do not have to trust any human being to tell you who the antichrist is in our day, God's Word tells you. If you so choose, go to God right now in prayer and ask Him to lead you to the truth, as we take a closer look at antichrist. John says, "Let no man deceive you by any means: for that day shall not come" (the day of Jesus' second coming), "except there be a falling away first." People will stop attending the church where antichrist is.

A falling away of what? It can be none other than people falling away from worshiping God the way He asks them to. Spirituality will decrease. People will leave the false church. That is a sign that church is false. But the Holy Spirit will speak to each heart individually. We just need to read our Bibles, pray, and listen to the Spirit's leadings, and follow no matter what happens to us. The Holy Spirit will always agree with God's Word because the Holy Spirit is God. He will reveal the false church and the antichrist, "and that man of sin be revealed, the son of perdition" (2 Thess. 2:3).

That's right! The falling away will happen because the man of sin is in the Christian church. Remember! God is not secretive. He wants us to be wise unto salvation. He says antichrist will be revealed before Jesus comes. He is telling us in this verse about the end-time antichrist. Then it continues to share some of the characteristics of antichrist. Remember, the disciples experienced antichrist in the new baby church. He says people will become unhappy with their spiritual leaders. Church attendance will suffer. Antichrist will not be some evil person outside the Christian church. He is still in a Christian church! The antichrist's evil practices will still be taking place. Just before Jesus comes, many will leave the church the antichrist is in. Just look at the characteristics Paul gives us. He tells us just what antichrist will be doing at that time.

"Who opposeth and exalteth himself above all that is called God, or that is worshipped; so that he as God sitteth in the temple of God, [The writer of this verse is talking about a temple here on earth.] shewing himself that he is God." (2 Thess. 2:4). (This is a true antichrist characteristic.) Then Paul said, "Remember ye not, that, when I was yet with you, I told you these things? And now ye know what withholdeth that he might be revealed in his time" (2 Thess. 2:5–6). He will be allowing people to worship him as if he were God. Remember! God alone is holy. The antichrist will be accepting worship as if he were holy.

Also, remember that anyone who is accepting untruth is accepting the lies of antichrist. These verses are talking about the final phase of the antichrist. Not the great antichrist, Satan, but the follower of that great antichrist Satan. Paul says, "For the mystery of iniquity doth already work: only He who now letteth will let, until he is taken out of the way" (2 Thess. 2:7).

This verse says antichrist will be destroyed, taken out of the way by Jesus' coming. It also lets us know that antichrist was alive and well back when Paul wrote these verses. Antichrist has continued to be around ever since Satan chose to become an antichrist, and he is still around as antichrist, but so are other antichrists. Yes, antichrists were around in the new baby church and others are still around in our day, only it is a different person. That's because they are men and die just like we do. They are people. (A different person all along but the same antichrist practices) There has been a continuous procession of them. They all have the same characteristics of Satan, the original antichrist.

God will still be giving mankind freedom of choice until all have made their final choice to either obey God or disobey Him. What a precious God He is. Never forcing! Always gently wooing. This next verse tells us what will happen when Jesus comes to all of us who will still be here at His glorious appearing. It will be the most welcome sight ever for God's people. And each of us can be in that group watching and waiting for His coming. Isn't that exciting! "And then shall that Wicked be revealed, whom the Lord shall consume with the spirit of his mouth, and shall destroy with the brightness of his coming" (2 Thess. 2:8).

Who will be destroyed by Jesus' coming? It is all of the wicked people. That includes anyone who is refusing to turn from any of their wicked ways, who are disobeying any command of God. God's people will love each other. Also, notice that all the wicked will be killed at the second coming of Christ, not before He comes. The righteousness of our God will kill them, but they will raised at the second resurrection to receive their final punishment. And look at this verse! It is specifically talking about the antichrist in our day. Each antichrist, in succeeding generations, will accept being deceived by Satan. "Even him, [the final antichrist] whose coming is after the working of Satan with all power and signs and lying wonders" (2 Thess. 2:9). "And with all deceivableness of unrighteousness in them that perish;" Why will they be deceived? "because they received not the love of the truth, that they might be saved" (2 Thess. 2:10). That's very important; we must first receive the truth; we can't be saved without it) "And for this cause God shall send them strong delusion, that they should believe a lie" (2 Thess. 2:11).

God does not want to send delusions to anyone. And God does not send strong delusions to anyone who wants to believe the truth, those who believe so strongly that they are willing to do as God asks them no matter what their obedience brings their way. But for those who refuse to believe God, He does this, so "That they all might be damned who believe not the truth, but had pleasure in unrighteousness" (2 Thess. 2:12). If God did not destroy sinners, we would have this whole mess all over again. It's too bad, but that's the unvarnished truth.

God honors the freedom of choice of the wicked to the very end. The Bible does not teach that antichrist comes after people go to heaven. That's too late! That's what Satan would like us to think. Jesus comes to get us at the same time all of God's predictions concerning the second coming take place. Jesus and His Father come and rescue us from the antichrist and every other wicked being. Isn't it wonderful that God gives us all of this information in His Word? And isn't that just like our God of love? Loving through thick and through thin! Read your Bible—not some fictional story!

"For the Lord himself shall descend from heaven with a shout, with the voice of the archangel, and with the trump of God: and the dead in Christ shall rise first" (1 Thess. 4:16). Do you realize it is not going to be silent when Jesus comes to whisk His children away from this earth? In fact, it's going to be very noisy! And notice all of us go home together—at the same time. First, the righteous dead are raised and are caught up to God in the

clouds. We watch this taking place. *"Then we which are alive and remain shall be caught up together with them in the clouds, to meet the Lord in the air: and so shall we ever be with the Lord" (1 Thess. 4:17).* They linger there in the air until we join them. Isn't that exciting!

It all happens at the same time! Isn't that glorious! All of the righteous will go to heaven together at the same time—both those who have died throughout the years of Satan's occupation and those who are living when the Lord comes.

What a glorious trip that will be. Jesus promises to give us the strength to go through the time of trouble. God will be with His people when they go through that time. It is like the time of Jacob's trouble. We must walk Jesus' walk. Jesus walked that path ahead of us, so He could leave us an example, and so we could walk as He walked. Now I would like to run these verses by you. It is extremely important that we know the sequence of Jesus' return. Jesus lets us know how it will all happen—even the sequence. He doesn't wants to worry about when it will happen. "Now we beseech you, brethren, by the coming of our Lord Jesus Christ, and by our gathering together unto him, That ye be not soon shaken in mind, or be troubled, neither by spirit, nor by word, nor by letter as from us, as that the day of Christ is at hand" (2 Thess. 2:1–2).

Paul warned the people of his day, and he is warning us not to think Jesus is coming is sooner than He has said. Jesus told them they needed to look for the falling away first. Yes, that is what we need to look for! Down through the ages, people have been deceived as to when Jesus will come. Many thought Jesus was coming in 1844. It was after this that a group of people from many denominations got together and studied to find out why Jesus hadn't come yet. We must still be on the alert and not allow Satan to confuse us on this issue. Our concern should be: Are we ready? Are we forsaking our sins, asking Him to forgive us? And obeying His ten-commandment law?

We have the same help from God as Jesus did. Satan is still persecuting all who obey God, just as he always has. All who follow God with their whole heart will experience the result of Satan's wrath. Satan will see to that! We must hang onto God's promises. Those promises will help us through the hard times just as Job's knowledge of God did for him. That knowledge will bless us by letting us know what to expect. At the same time, Satan will be screaming in our ear, "God doesn't love you. If He did, He wouldn't be letting all these bad things happen to you." I am so glad God tells us, so we will know it is the devil causing these things, not God. God is fair. He allows Satan to choose to be as wicked as he wants to be. But there is a glorious future very soon when all sin will be no more. Salvation always has been and always will be about choice. And God's promises are still sure for us, just as they have been for all mankind down through the ages.

Yes, God's beautiful promises will give us strength just when we need it most. God will do what He has said He will do. Plus, He will either see us through our trouble, or He will give us a way out of it. He knows each of us personally. He knows just how much persecution we can take. Even Jesus, while here in human flesh, cringed under the load of pain and grief Satan heaped on Him. When He was dying on the cross, He cried out to His heavenly Father, saying, "My God, my God, why hast thou forsaken me?" (Mark 15:34).

And also remember, Jesus was tempted on every point we will ever be tempted on. He carried the load of sin of each one of us. What a load it was! No one but God could carry that heavy load and make it safely through! Only a perfect Being could win that battle. How blessed we are that Jesus was willing to fight our battle for us. Jesus trod that path ahead of us and assures us that we can make it because He made it. I'm so glad the Father was willing to allow Jesus to do that for us. I believe God placed the above words of confirmation in the Bible, so we, in the last days of earth's history, would have these love notes to hang onto. How blessed we are that God the Father and His Son were willing to do this for us. And now, They top it off by sending the Spirit to guide us.

Often, when I am feeling down and persecuted, I go to the piano and ding out the words of some beautiful song. It is good to tuck them in our hearts and memory, so we will have them when we are being harassed by Satan and his wicked followers. They will help us now too. I find they cheer me up when I am feeling down.

The truth is that God's holy Sabbath commandment is the thread of love that is going to be the biggie in the last days just before Jesus comes to take us home to heaven with Him. It will be God's last call to His people! That thread of love, the Sabbath command, is the one Satan has attacked the most severely throughout the whole history of planet Earth.

Isn't it beautiful how Jesus showed us, even in His death, by letting us know He is still honoring the seventh day of the week in heaven right now? He is going to bring it to the forefront just before He comes to get us. And I believe that time is right now! He wants to get the good news of the gospel out to every single person alive today. He won't come until all have been warned, and know the truth about His holy day loud and clear. Yes, the telling of that truth will bring trouble for the Sabbath-keepers, but God will be by their side. It will come about when people are forced to keep Sunday instead of God's holy day. Jesus and His Father tell us that those who choose to suffer affliction for a season will win the battle over their own selfish desires and over Satan. Moses is a good example of this. Look at this great example of his faith.

"By faith Moses, when he was come to years, refused to be called the son of Pharaoh's daughter; Choosing rather to suffer affliction with the people of God, than to enjoy the pleasures of sin for a season; Esteeming the reproach of Christ greater riches than the treasures in Egypt: for he had respect unto the recompence of the reward" (Heb. 11:24–26). And just look at these encouraging words from Paul. "But if our gospel be hid, it is hid to them that are lost: In whom the god of this world hath blinded the minds of them which believe not, lest the light of the glorious gospel of Christ, who is the image of God, should shine unto them" (2 Cor. 4:3–4). That's right! They did not want to believe! God never hides the truth. It is Satan who does that. But if we want to know and obey the truth, God will see that we hear and understand it. "For God, who commanded the light to shine out of darkness, hath shined in our hearts, to give the light of the knowledge of the glory of God in the face of Jesus Christ" (2 Cor. 4:6).

Look at that! He actually let Jesus come down here to die for us, and shares that knowledge with us.

Paul knew about persecution. All of them did. They died for their faith. "We are troubled on every side, yet not distressed; we are perplexed, but not in despair; Persecuted, but not forsaken; cast down, but not destroyed; Always bearing about in the body the dying of the Lord Jesus, that the life also of Jesus might be made manifest in our body. For we which live are always delivered unto death for Jesus sake, that the life also of Jesus might be made manifest in our mortal flesh" (2 Cor. 4:8–11). "For which cause we faint not; but though our outward man perish, yet the inward man is renewed day by day. For our light affliction, which is but for a moment, worketh for us a far more exceeding and eternal weight of glory; While we look not at the things which are seen, but at the things which are not seen: for the things which are seen are temporal; but the things which are not seen are eternal" (2 Cor. 4:16–18). "For he hath made him to be sin for us, who knew no sin; that we might be made the righteousness of God in him" (2 Cor. 5:21).

We must remember! As the song says—without Him, I can do nothing! But with God's help, if we purpose as Job did to obey God no matter what, God will see each of us through those last trying times. He promises that our love for Him will be well worth all of the pain we go through. Doing what is right is always satisfying in the end. Look at John the Baptist—he thought it was, or he wouldn't have died for his Lord. These thoughts bring that beautiful promise to my mind which reads thus: "For I reckon that the sufferings of this present time are not worthy to be compared with the glory which shall be revealed in us" (Rom. 8:18).

We must carefully plant our feet in Jesus' footsteps and follow Him. He is our only safe example. If we follow Him, we will be safe in the end. It won't be easy. Most worthwhile things are not easy. They all take work. But honoring God by being true to Him is the most worthwhile thing we can do in this life. Look at what Peter said about our sufferings in these last days. What a beautiful promise it is too.

"Blessed be the God and Father of our Lord Jesus Christ, which according to His abundant mercy hath begotten us again to a lively hope by the resurrection of Jesus Christ from the dead, to an inheritance incorruptible, and undefiled, and that fadeth not away, reserved in heaven for you, Who are kept by the power of God through faith unto salvation ready to be revealed at the last time. Wherein ye greatly rejoice, though now for a season, if need be, ye are in heaviness through manifold temptations: that the trial of your faith, being much more precious than of gold that perisheth, though it be tried with fire, might be found unto praise and honor and glory at the appearing of Jesus Christ: whom having not seen, ye love; in whom, though now ye see Him not, yet believing, ye rejoice with joy unspeakable and full of glory: Receiving the end of your faith, even the salvation of your souls" (1 Peter 1:3–9).

The Sabbath command in the last days on earth will be the command that will form the main dividing line between those who love and worship God and those who choose not to worship Him. Remember, Jesus said, "If ye keep my commandments, ye shall abide in my love; even as I have kept my Father's commandments, and abide in his love" (John 15:10). *"Not everyone who says to Me, 'Lord, Lord,' shall enter the kingdom of heaven, but he who does the will of My Father in heaven" (Matt. 7:21, NKJV).* This is the acid test.

We must continue to pray for ourselves and them. Only God knows when a person has crossed the line and will choose to not turn back. God will help us be kind to them. We must always be gentle like Jesus to everyone and show them that God still loves them. He will love them to the end, but He will abhor their evil ways.

It's hard to obey someone you think is lying to you. Remember? Unbelief was really the problem Eve had. She chose to be deceived. This happened to her because of her failure to believe that God was being honest with her. That's bad! It made it easy for Satan to deceive her. Sometimes we, too, fall into that trap and kneel to the idea that God is lying to us. We, too, have to fight off the devil. We, too, must listen to the Holy Spirit and believe that God does not lie. Otherwise, we, too, will be deceived by our common enemy, the devil.

I pray that I, and all of you, will continue to love God supremely rather than love the temptations Satan will send our way. He is screaming out the lie, saying we don't need to keep God's Sabbath holy any more. When he tries to deceive us, we need to put our fingers in our ears and run in the other direction as fast as our legs will go. Here is God's advice: "Submit to God. Resist the devil and he will flee from you. Draw near to God and He will draw near to you.... Humble yourselves in the sight of the Lord, and He will lift you up" (James 4:7–8, 10, NKJV).

Isn't that a beautiful promise? We all know who the liar is. Satan! Because of his lies, Jesus recognized him in the wilderness after His baptism. One other thing we must remember is that his lie is a counterfeit—counterfeits always resemble the true so closely that it is almost impossible to detect that they are a counterfeit. That's where knowing our Bibles and listening to the Holy Spirit become imperative. God's Word definitely is true. So, if we read it, we will know the truth, and that truth will set us free.

Below is another of God's solutions. God not only pleads with us to listen to the Holy Spirit, who is our God-given guide, the one who helps us recall the words of scriptures that we have placed in our memory bank. But He also gives us this valuable guidance through Paul, that great man God counseled and admonished with for the Hebrew people. Now God is using that same counsel for us: "Beware, brethren, lest there be in any of you an evil heart of unbelief in departing from the living God; but exhort one another daily, while it is called "Today," lest any of you be hardened through the deceitfulness of sin" (Heb. 3:12, NKJV).

Then Paul also left this counsel for those in our day. He said, "Therefore, since a promise remains of entering His rest, let us fear lest any of you seem to have come short of it. For indeed the gospel was preached to us as well as them; but the word which they heard did not profit them, not being mixed with faith in those who heard it. For we who have believed do enter that rest, as He has said: 'So I swore in My wrath, "They shall not enter My rest,"'' although the works were finished from the foundation of the world. For He has spoken in a certain place of the seventh day in this way: 'And God rested on the seventh day from all His works'; and again in this place: 'They shall not enter My rest.' Since therefore it remains that some must enter it, and those to whom it was first preached did not enter in because of disobedience, again, He designates a certain day, saying in David, 'Today,' after such a long time, as it has been said, 'Today, if you will hear His voice, harden not your hearts.' For if Joshua had given them rest, then He would not afterward have spoken of another day. There remains therefore a rest to the people of God" (Heb. 4:1–9, NKJV).

If Jesus no longer wanted us to keep the Sabbath holy, He wouldn't be counseling us as He is. Look at the counsel He gave His disciples just before He was taken up into heaven. He said, "pray that your flight may not be in winter or on the Sabbath." (Matt. 24:20, NKJV).

This counsel pertained to God's children who had to flee from Jerusalem when it was invaded, and the temple at Jerusalem was burned. Jesus meant this counsel to be for Jerusalem and for us in the last days, too, just before He comes back to get us. Yes, this is still His command to us today. He still wants us to honor the Sabbath. We need to pray daily and ask Him to help us when the persecution of Sabbath-keepers comes, so we won't have to flee on Sabbath. He says this so we can keep the day holy, just as Jesus kept it holy when He was lying in the tomb after His crucifixion. He also asks us to pray that it will not take place in winter so that we won't have to flee in the freezing cold. If God says, pray, it must be extremely important. We need to keep the Sabbath holy, the way Jesus kept it holy. We need to pray that we won't have to flee on the Sabbath or in the winter.

Jesus was explaining to his disciples what the destruction that would come upon Jerusalem was all about, but also, what the condition the world would be like in our day—just before His second coming. These two events were mingled together in the minds of the disciples. They were not able to sort them out. Jerusalem was destroyed in A.D. 70—forty years after Jesus rose from the dead and ascended into heaven. Yes! Jesus, through the Holy Spirit, was still having His followers tell people to keep the Sabbath day holy.

It is important! One of the ways He shows us its importance is via this promise through the prophet Isaiah. So let's look at it again. God told the prophet:

"If you turn away your foot from the Sabbath, From doing your pleasure on My holy day, and call the Sabbath a delight, the holy of the LORD honorable, and shall honor Him, not doing your own ways, nor finding your own pleasure, nor speaking your own words, Then you shall delight yourself in the LORD; and I will cause you to ride on the high hills of the earth, and feed you with the heritage of Jacob your father. The mouth of the Lord has spoken" (Isa. 58:13–14).

Consider this too: Jesus also said to the unbelieving Jews in His day, "Well did Isaiah prophesy of you hypocrites, as it is written: 'This people honors Me with their lips, But their heart is far from Me And in vain they worship Me, Teaching as doctrines the commandments of men.'" Then Jesus cited what these Jewish religious leaders were teaching the people. Jesus continued by saying, "For laying aside the commandments of God, you hold the tradition of men—the washing of pitchers and cups, and many other such things you do. He said to them, 'All too well you reject the commandment of God, that you may keep your tradition'" (Mark 7:6–9).

Sunday-keeping is one of the traditions of men. God never changed the day. He will be keeping His Sabbath holy—the seventh day of the week with us throughout eternity. God says so. "And it shall come to pass, that from one new moon to another, and from one sabbath to another, shall all flesh come to worship before Me, saith the Lord" (Isa. 66:22–23).

Yes, Jesus says we will be worshiping Him from month to month, and from Sabbath to Sabbath in the earth made new. As we said before, God tells us to come out of the churches who are not teaching people to honor His holy Sabbath day. I pray that your whole church will understand and follow Jesus all the way. I believe this verse bears repeating. "Come out of her, my people, lest you share in her sins, and lest you receive of her plagues" (Rev.18:4). This tells me that God knows most of the people will not change when they hear the truth. But our faithful God will tell them anyway. Just as He did in Noah's day and in Sodom's day. Then John wrote these words concerning the holy city that will be in the earth made new: "Blessed are those who do His commandments, that they may have the right to the tree of life, and may enter through the gates into the city" (Rev. 22:14).

God wouldn't tell us that, either, if He wasn't planning on keeping the Sabbath holy with us in the earth made new. Yes! God still expects us to keep the seventh day of the week, holy. It is His holy day. It is the Sabbath of the Lord our God. Yes, right now! This very week! He wants you to keep the seventh day of the week, holy! The seventh-day is the Sabbath of the Lord your God—the Lord's day.

Won't you consider it? Pray about it! All of these words in God's Holy Bible tell us that the seventh day of the week is God's holy day. Sunday has always been the day the pagans worshiped the sun on. We are to keep God's special day holy because we love Him, not just to get what He has promised to give to those who obey Him. It's the day He wants to meet with us for a very special date. It really is God's holy day.

I pray that each of you will decide to keep it holy and honor the Lord. He would like to spend eternity with you and me, and I would like to spend it with Him and you, too. By God's grace, we will make it! Listen to this call—and beautiful promise!

"Come unto me, all ye that labor and are heavy laden, and I will give you rest. Take my yoke upon you, and learn of me; for I am meek and lowly in heart: and ye shall find rest unto your souls. For my yoke is easy, and My burden is light" (Matt. 11:28–30). And always remember, never forget. "I can of Myself do nothing." (John 5:30, NKJV) but that "with God all things are possible" (Matt. 19:26, NKJV).

CHAPTER TWENTY-SEVEN

The Test and Positive Proof to Tell Whether You Are Obeying God or Antichrist

---

What are the leaders of your church telling you? Are they teaching you to have faith in God and believe His Word instead of the word of your pastor or priest? I believe this question bears answering with Bible answers, even though I have used many of these verses before. Repetition cements the Word in our minds.

We need that repetition to help us go through the times ahead of us. We can never hear God's words too much. And the Bible is chock full of affirmation and instruction. God says, *"If they speak not according to this word, it is because there is no light in them"* (Isa. 8:20). The Bible we use should be an authorized version of the Bible, not a version documented by a specific denomination, or a paraphrase of some church, committee, or person. If what you are being told is truly what God said, *it will always agree with the Bible.*

This verse tells us how we can test what people say. Remember! If it comes from the Bible, it is God saying it. God is always right. He is God. He is the rule-maker. God alone is the only One we can really believe and trust. You may be thinking, but there are so many versions. How do we know which one is right? Well! Even true versions have some mistakes in them. After all, those who translated them from one language to another were mere men—not God. Now, I want to be sure you know what I am talking about. I am not talking about the holy men of God who wrote them via the inspiration of God No! I am only talking about the men who translated the Bible from Hebrew and Greek to the languages of different countries.

The truth is, no ancient document on which we base human history has anywhere near the documentation of the Bible. The Jewish people very carefully preserved the Old Testament. And there is very little discrepancy. The New Testament has tens of thousands of documents going all back within a hundred years of the apostles. Some scholars are now saying that some may actually be from the time of the apostles. We know now that we have 99% of the New Testament as it was given to the early church from the apostles. What few discrepancies which remain do not hurt the teachings or the message of the Bible.

If we don't believe the Bible, then there is nothing we can trust, and we are in a deplorable condition. I ask, what other book has been written by people, covering so many generations, coming from so many walks of life, and presenting so many prophecies that have come true? The answer is, "None!" No, none of them can substantiate their claims like the Bible does. Many of the prophecies tell us of events that are still future. Praise God, we have His Word, and it has shown itself to be reliable time and time again. We need to accept the parts we understand and pray for understanding for the verses we do not understand. Ask the Holy Spirit to guide your mind as you read God's Word. The Holy Spirit is more than willing to help you understand. Here is Paul's message to Timothy. "That from a child thou hast known the holy scriptures, which are able to make thee wise unto salvation through faith which is in Christ Jesus" (2 Tim. 3:15).

The Bible doesn't just contain the word of God. It is the word of God. The Bible itself makes these claims. Just listen to what Timothy says; "All scripture is given by inspiration of God, and is profitable for doctrine, for reproof, for correction, for instruction in righteousness" (2 Tim. 3:16). The Bible would not be good for the things Timothy talks about if parts of it were untrue!

CHAPTER TWENTY-EIGHT

Why Did God Make Sure The Whole Bible Is True?

―――•◆•―――

"That the man of God" Are you a God-fearing person—a man or woman of God? God says you *"may be perfect, thoroughly furnished unto ALL good works" (2 Tim. 3:17).* But only through the power of God via the Holy Spirit.

That's huge! Listen to this advice Timothy gives us. Read all of chapter two of second Timothy. One of the things he says is, "Foolish and unlearned questions avoid, knowing that they do gender strifes" (2 Tim. 2:23). He also says, "The servant of the Lord must not strive; but be gentle unto all men, apt to teach, patient, In meekness instructing those that oppose themselves; if God peradventure will give them repentance to the acknowledging of the truth; And that they may recover themselves out of the snare of the devil, who are taken captive of him at his will" (2 Tim. 2:24–26).

That sounds mighty scary! We best listen—don't you think? What a wonderful God we have to inform us of the devil's traps. Believing God's Word is our only safe choice. Here is what God says to do about it. *"Study to shew thyself approved unto God, a workman that needeth not to be ashamed, rightly dividing the word of truth" (2 Tim.2:15).*

On the other hand, if it is antichrist we are listening to, his words will not totally agree with the Bible. Remember Satan in the garden of Eden? He called God a liar. Do you think he is any different today? Certainly not! He's had years of practice! He's worse if anything! Just read about what his plans are for the final conflict. *"For there shall arise false Christs, and false prophets, and shall shew great signs and wonders*; insomuch that, *if it were* possible, they shall deceive the very elect" (Matt. 24:24). Did you notice that it was God who put "if" there? He wants us to know it will not be possible for someone to deceive the very elect. WHY? Because God tells us in His Word, what His coming will be like. Yes! That is what this verse is talking about. Read the whole chapter. He will not allow Satan to come in the clouds like Jesus will come. Jesus' feet will not touch this earth when He comes to take the righteous to heaven.

Instead, we will be caught up to meet Him in the cloud of angels. As we read before; Jesus comes with trumpet sound, and He shouts to wake up the righteous dead, the righteous watch all of this take place, then at the very same time, those who love God and are alive to see Him come, will be caught up with the righteous people He has just raised from the dead and join them in the air. From that time on, they will be with the Lord. Jesus made this very certain! Yes, it is Jesus who told His disciples what His second coming would be like. If you can believe anybody, certainly, it is Jesus!

Walking as Jesus walked and obeying God is the key to our safety. Those who truly love Him will be listening to the Holy Spirit and obeying the Bible. Through their Bible study and close connection with the Holy Spirit, they will recognize the lies of the antichrist. Neither will they depend on what some friend, pastor, or family member has to say. They will search God's Word, believing the very easy words of Jesus and what He had to say. These verses in the Bible are not prophecy—they are the very plain words of Jesus. Jesus never said anything about people being whisked from the earth secretly. Yes, He did say, "One will be taken, and another left" (Matt. 24: 40, also 41). Of course, one will be taken to heaven, and another one left here on earth. The ones who are left will be those who chose to do what they wanted rather than obey God. They are the ones who will be destroyed by the brightness of Jesus' coming (see 2 Thess. 2:8). Only the righteous will go to heaven.

God plainly tells us throughout the Bible who antichrist is. Rome is the city where paganism became rampant right after Jesus went to heaven the first time. Yes, antichrist was in the church—God's new baby church. It will be the same way when Jesus comes back to earth—antichrist will be in a church that claims to be God's church.

But it won't be God's true commandment-keeping church. Instead, it will be a church that claims to be the true church—but is not obeying all ten of the commands of God. Actually, it is the remnant of the church that Jesus erected via He and His apostles—yes, that church that began as God's new baby church. Not only will that church not be keeping the fourth commandment, the church where the antichrist abides will also be known by God's true people, and it will be apparent to them because of their superiority and disobedience to God. Antichrist will be claiming to be God just as the devil does.

God's people who are in that church will see how sinful the church is via their spiritual adultery and their sexual disobedience. It is taking place today, right now, and they are not owning up to their sins. Their leader is continuing them. When one continues to hold onto a sin, that is an act of condoning it. This is how God makes sure His people in that church know they are disobeying Him. The Protestant churches, whatever denomination they are, will know it is a sin to accept worship that only belongs to God.

Another characteristic of the man of sin is that He will be persecuting the saints. He hasn't gotten to that point yet—but it will come. God says so. Just those three characteristics by themselves are enough to identify the final, last-day antichrist. The first antichrist was Lucifer. He became the devil. God left him in His temple in heaven as long as He could. Then the man of sin, Satan, has been on earth ever since he was cast out of heaven. He housed himself in one of the new baby churches. He is still in that church. It's not the devil who is there. It is a human being who claims to be Christ on earth. He calls himself the vicar of Christ. It is just that the people of our day are confused by him the same way Eve and those new baby Christians were.

Yes, the antichrist, who is called the man of sin, is a creation of Satan—yes, he is someone else who wanted to go their own selfish way. Look at 2 Thess. 2:1–12 again. God does not want us to be deceived. He has supplied us with everything we need in order to be safe. He even gives us a list of ways we can tell who the final days' antichrist is. Remember—there hasn't been just one. Remember—anyone who puts themselves in place of or instead of God—is an antichrist. Anyone who claims to be God on earth. No one can take God's place.

Look at this information God gave Daniel. It tells us how to identify the antichrist. In Daniel chapter two, we have an easy description of the rise and fall of nations. God sent King Nebuchadnezzar a dream, and it fell Daniel's lot to interpret it. Of course, Daniel could not do that—but he prayed and asked God for help, and God showed him the dream. God told Daniel that Nebuchadnezzar was the first king to rule all of the then-known world (see Dan. 2:28). His kingdom was Babylon. Nebuchadnezzar was a chip off the old block—just as the antichrist at the tower of Babel, and he showed up in Babylon. And there were succeeding kingdoms. They are all in the second chapter of Daniel. Each of them ruled the whole world.

These kingdoms will be around until Jesus comes. Then next thing in the dream is Jesus, our Rock, coming in the clouds of heaven.

Daniel, chapter seven, covers the same time span. What is different about it is that God gave Daniel many more details in that chapter. It builds on chapter two. In chapter seven it is talking about the same thing. The only difference is God uses animals instead of image parts to designate the kingdoms. The little horn's body was given to the flames—those flames are the fire of hell. It came out of Rome. It had "eyes like the eyes of a man, and a mouth speaking pompous words" (Dan. 7:8, NKJV).

The little horn, "that horn which had eyes and a mouth which spoke pompous words, whose appearance was greater than his fellows" (Yes, he will look like he is somebody with power—look what he will do.) "I was watching; and the same horn was making war against the saints, and prevailing against them, until the Ancient of Days came, and a judgment was made in favor of the saints of the Most High, and the time came for the saints to possess the kingdom" (Dan. 7:20–22, NKJV). The next verse tells us who the horn, i.e., antichrist spoke those pompous words against. It is none other than God Himself. That's just what antichrist does. Remember! He puts himself in the place of God and claims to be God. "He shall speak pompous words against the Most High, Shall persecute the saints of the Most High, And shall intend to change times and law" (Dan. 7:25, NKJV). (Notice it says law—not Laws.) He wants to change God's holy law. That could be none other than the command that tells us what day to worship God.

Now just look at this! "Then the saints shall be given into his hand" but only "For a time and times and a half time" (Dan. 7:25, NKJV). This is antichrist's day in court, it includes all of the antichrists down through the ages, but at this point in time, he won't be physically present at this court session. God carefully goes over the books by Himself and reviews the evidence of the sins of this man of sin. God is fair and never judges someone without a court trial. And what does it say God will do? "And they shall take away his dominion, to consume and destroy it forever" (Dan. 7:26, NKJV). Praise the Lord. He won't ever be persecuting any of God's faithful people again. God has faithful people in every church—even in the denomination where antichrist resides. That's why He calls them out of her. Look at this loving instruction and beautiful promise: "Come out of her, my people." Why? "That ye be not partakers of her sins, and that ye receive not of her plagues" (Rev. 18:4).

Satan, the initial antichrist, will use every temptation he can think of on each one of us. He will use every lie he can to make us feel as if obeying God is not worth all the trouble it will bring our way. He will try to convince us that heaven will not be fun if—and now I encourage you to supply your own personal *if*—that may be keeping you from wanting to obey God and be in heaven with Him. All the impressions the devil whispers in our ears through the various antichrists are lies—they lead to disobedience to God, and to hell. That's not God's plan for us, not who we are or how we are acting right now. If we turn to Him, He will have compassion on us.

Now just look what God does for those who turn to Him! "And the kingdom and dominion, And the greatness of the kingdom under the whole heaven, shall be given to the people, and the saints of the most High" (Dan.7:27). Yes, that is the end of antichrist. Then Jesus will come and take those who love Him to heaven. Ask the Holy Spirit to help you yield to God so that when Jesus comes to take His people to heaven, you will be in the group who are saved. God bless you as you read your Bible. (Read again Luke 11:9–10,13).

In Memorial...

Phyllis Arlene Gruesbeck
August 14, 1939–December 7, 2019

Phyllis was born the morning of August 14, 1939 at Battle Creek Osteopathic Hospital in Battle Creek, Michigan. Her Mother, Bertha Van Allen Skinner, held her and named her before she died the same day at the age of 40 years and 16 days.

Phyllis suffered a stroke Nov. 27, 2019, and died peacefully and strong in faith on Dec. 7, 2019, in the Neurology Intensive Care Unit at Sparrow Health in Lansing, MI. She was looking forward to seeing her Lord and Savior "Face to Face" at His Second Coming along with family, friends, miscarried infant, and the mother she had never knowingly seen.

Phyllis was raised on a farm near Hudsonville, MI, by her devout grandparents, Charles Van Allen and Iva (Wilson) Van Allen. They attended the Bauer Seventh-day Adventist Church.

When she was 7 or 8 years old her father, Clifford Skinner, married Odessa Cable in Battle Creek, MI. She then lived with them until she was married August 25, 1957, to Ronald M. Gruesbeck at the Urbandale Seventh-day Adventist Church, Battle Creek, MI.

At 10 she became seriously ill with measles followed by rheumatic fever. This resulted in permanent heart damage which she suffered with as it progressed throughout her life.

She attended Battle Creek Public Schools, including Battle Creek Central High School, until she transferred to Battle Creek Academy where she met her husband and received her high school diploma.

In her 40s she attended Lansing Community College, maintaining a high GPA until she abandoned the program for health reasons just short of her 2 year degree. She studied journalism, art, and psychology.

She worked as a legal secretary for two different lawyers. She was the secretary for the Director of Nursing at St. Anthony's Hospital in Florida where she typed the Nursing Procedures Manual and drew all of the illustrations (before the internet and computers). She worked as a hospital ward clerk and as a CNA in hospitals and nursing homes as well as a home health aide. In doing so she was trained for and operated oxygen units and ventilators.

She enjoyed painting pictures and sold many to professional people for office and home use. She did free-lance work for newspapers as well as religious and secular magazines. She considered it a privilege to be a lay Bible worker for a few years. She loved gardening with her husband and children, but the last few years was limited in what she could do without ending in the hospital because of multiple heart conditions. Phyllis spent many hours in deep Bible study and prayer.

She was never happier then when traveling with Ronald domestically or overseas to the seashore, mountains, waterfalls, National Parks, bird sanctuaries, whale watching, or gardens. She especially enjoyed trips with family and friends. Forty-six states were visited, many with a fifth-wheel trailer and diesel truck. She even took her turn at driving with trailer in tow! The gospel was shared with campers who joined in evening worship and gospel papers shared at gas stations and restaurants. At times she felt impressed at sundown at the beach to sing a familiar song and, to her husband's initial surprise, others would soon join in.

She was proceeded in death by her parents and beloved big brother Ivan Richard (Dick) Skinner. She had one miscarriage.

She is survived by her husband Ronald of over 62 years; three sons, Ronald V. Gruesbeck (Wife Paulina), Richard Gruesbeck, and Brent Gruesbeck; three grandsons, Ronald S. Gruesbeck, Michael Gruesbeck, Melvin Gruesbeck, and two nieces, Ginger Skinner Mielke (Husband Larry) and Dixie Skinner and several cousins.

TEACH Services, Inc.
P U B L I S H I N G
www.TEACHServices.com • (800) 367-1844

We invite you to view the complete
selection of titles we publish at:
www.TEACHServices.com

We encourage you to write us
with your thoughts about this,
or any other book we publish at:
info@TEACHServices.com

TEACH Services' titles may be purchased in
bulk quantities for educational, fund-raising,
business, or promotional use.
bulksales@TEACHServices.com

Finally, if you are interested in seeing
your own book in print, please contact us at:
publishing@TEACHServices.com
We are happy to review your manuscript at no charge.

www.ingramcontent.com/pod-product-compliance
Lightning Source LLC
Chambersburg PA
CBHW071148160426
43196CB00011B/2042